Pittsburgh Series in Bibliography

(Pittsburgh Series in Bibliography)

HART CRANE: A DESCRIPTIVE BIBLIOGRAPHY
Joseph Schwartz and Robert C. Schweik

F. SCOTT FITZGERALD: A DESCRIPTIVE BIBLIOGRAPHY
Matthew J. Bruccoli

WALLACE STEVENS: A DESCRIPTIVE BIBLIOGRAPHY
J. M. Edelstein

EUGENE O'NEILL: A DESCRIPTIVE BIBLIOGRAPHY
Jennifer McCabe Atkinson

JOHN BERRYMAN: A DESCRIPTIVE BIBLIOGRAPHY
Ernest C. Stefanik, Jr.

EDITORIAL BOARD

Matthew J. Bruccoli, General Editor

Fredson Bowers
William R. Cagle
Charles W. Mann

JOHN BERRYMAN

John Berryman

A DESCRIPTIVE BIBLIOGRAPHY

Ernest C. Stefanik, Jr.

UNIVERSITY OF
PITTSBURGH PRESS
1974

Grateful acknowledgment is made to the following for permission to use material that appears in this book:

Michael Chikiris, for supplying the photograph of John Berryman on pages iv and viii.

Robert Giroux, of Farrar, Straus & Giroux, Inc.; Ralph Ross, of Scripps College; Wallace Stegner, of Stanford University; and Margaret Wente, of Doubleday Canada Limited, for excerpts from their letters to the author.

Board of Student Publications, University of Minnesota, for a quotation from Jonathan Sisson, "My Whiskers Fly: An Interview with John Berryman," *Ivory Tower*, XIV (October 3, 1966).

Copyright © 1974, University of Pittsburgh Press
All rights reserved
Manufactured in the United States of America

Library of Congress Cataloging in Publication Data

> Stefanik, Ernest C
>   John Berryman, a descriptive bibliography.
>
>   (Pittsburgh series in bibliography)
>   1. Berryman, John, 1914-1972—Bibliography.
> I. Title. II. Series.
> Z8091.43.S732   1974   016.811'5'4   74-4093
> ISBN 0-8229-3281-4

To Cis
and Kerri and John

One for John Berryman:
Honouring the Burnt Cork

Maskt by candle footlights, footsore John
In swallow tails and tall hat
Made a crack or two, shuffled as he
Hummed a few short blues, and was done.

Master of the baffled house at last,
He gave a final wave to his shockt audience
Of one, without so much as a bow,
His lost mind off in the frosted window.

Then the singer of dreams and death,
Leaving nothing to chance but the encore,
Slipt through the trap door,
Clicking the lock behind, secure.

Beneath the shaky joists and warped floors,
In the chambers of the end, endman John
Half-hugged his smiling selves
And leaned against the looking glass.

A grief or so ago that dancing man's musick
Brought us to our feet.
But now all that is left is the memory
And dream of the night he leapt the footlights.

Contents

Acknowledgments		XIII
Introduction		XVII
A.	Separate Publications	1
B.	First-Appearance Contributions to Books	155
	BB. Supplement: Borderline Items	169
C.	Contributions to Periodicals	173
D.	Collected Materials Reprinted in Anthologies	217
E.	Interviews	227
F.	Phonorecordings	233
G.	Dust-Jacket Blurbs	239
H.	Poetry Selections	245
Appendix 1. A Chronology of the Publication of Works by Berryman		251
Appendix 2. Periodicals in Which Material by Berryman First Appeared		260
Index		263

Acknowledgments

THIS bibliography could not have been written without the generous assistance of the many people who answered inquiries, searched for information, and supplied copies of books and journals. But no dedication or mention in the acknowledgments can adequately express my first, and profoundest, debt: to my wife, Cis. Cis not only let me steal my time from her and our children, Kerri and John, to complete this project but also helped in checking nearly every entry.

I thank the members of the Editorial Board of the Pittsburgh Series in Bibliography: Matthew J. Bruccoli, Fredson Bowers, William R. Cagle, and Charles W. Mann. Their criticisms and suggestions have saved me many errors and made this a better work. But I am most grateful to Professor Bruccoli for his sound advice, encouragement, and example: he has been an invaluable source of information on bibliography, and his *F. Scott Fitzgerald* has served as my model.

I thank the following libraries and librarians: Mary Haines, Adams Memorial Library; Department of Printed Books, The British Museum; Buffalo and Erie County Public Library; John H. Stanley, John Hay Library, Brown University; Carnegie Library of Pittsburgh; Hunt Library, Carnegie-Mellon University; Geneva Warner and Patricia A. Gross, Lilly Library, Indiana University; Robert H. Land, General Reference and Bibliography Division, The Library of Congress; Richard

Kelly, University of Minnesota Library; Linda Simpson, Northwestern University Library; Bernard Block, Ohio State University Library; Hillman Library, University of Pittsburgh; St. Vincent College Library; Curtiss Campagna, Kathleen Abbey, Diane Taige, and especially Karl Gay, Curator of the Poetry Collection, Lockwood Memorial Library, State University of New York at Buffalo; Roger Mortimer, The George N. Meissner Rare Book Department, John M. Olin Library, Washington University.

I thank the following archivists and librarians who searched university and local publications for material by Berryman: Edna L. Dobler, Brandeis University Library; Evelyn Sandberg, Brown University Libraries; Allan Covici, General Library, University of California at Berkeley; Curtis Bochanyin, Joseph Regenstern Library, University of Chicago; Carol Kromminga, Cowles Library, Drake University; Clark A. Elliott, Harvard University Archives; Ada M. Stoflet, University of Iowa Libraries; E. Rosenfeld, Abernathy Library, University of Notre Dame; Carol W. Hazer, Princeton University Library; Bernadette Gualiteri, University of Washington Libraries; Patricia Bartkowski, Wayne State University Archives.

I thank the following publishers: Adam and Charles Black Ltd.; William F. Bernhardt, Columbia University Press; Arlene Reisberg, Thomas Y. Crowell Company; Anne Barrett, The Dolmen Press Ltd.; Elizabeth Bartelme and Jeanne Lavern, Doubleday & Company, Inc.; Margaret Wente, Doubleday Canada Ltd.; Robert Giroux, Farrar, Straus and Giroux; Claude Fredericks; Alice Rosengard, Harper & Row, Publishers; Intext Press; Catherine Jones, Eyre Methuen Ltd.; Adele Rose, New American Library, Inc.; Griselda Ohan-

Acknowledgments

nessian and Elenora Sassani, New Directions; and William Sloane.

I thank the following editors and assistants: Mike Finley, *Academy*; William Cookson, *Agenda*; Daniele Dubas, *The American Scholar*; Ben Bova, *Analog*; Daniel Halpern, *Antaeus*; Tim Hill, *Audience*; Glenna Luschei, *Café Solo*; Grace Schulman, *The Nation*; Elizabeth Ogilvie, *The Observer*; Stanley Lindberg, *The Ohio Review*; Ellen Nemeth, *Partisan Review*; Cindy Cummings, *Poetry*; Mary Lucia S. Cornelius, *The Sewanee Review*; Helen Schuyler, *Shenandoah*; Georgene Gordon, *The Southern Review*; Edward Brunner, *Stand*; Arthur Crook, *The Times Literary Supplement*; Suzanne Kurman, *TriQuarterly*; Jonathan Sisson, *The Twin Cities Express*; Bernice C. Maddox, *The Virginia Quarterly Review*; and John Palmer, *The Yale Review*.

I thank the following booksellers: John Bell, Covent Gardens Bookshop; B. H. Blackwell Ltd.; Mrs. Louis Henry Cohn, The House of Books Ltd.; Melvin McCosh; R. F. Perotti; The Phoenix Book Shop; and Anthony Rota, Bertram Rota Ltd.

I thank the following individuals who helped in various ways: R. Maynard Banks and Bernie Revicky, who searched for Berryman's student publications; Patricia A. Brenner and Claude Fredericks, who shared their copies of scarce publications; Dorothy Foster of the Minneapolis Symphony Orchestra; Samuel Hazo, Director of the International Poetry Forum, who read an early version of the bibliography and suggested that it be submitted to the University of Pittsburgh Press; Karleen Jacobson, who proofread the final typescript; Ralph Ross, who clarified Berryman's contributions to *The Arts of Reading*; and Regina Stefanik, my sister, who made a hundred trips to libraries to verify information or to borrow books for me, and who always had time to listen. I owe a special debt of gratitude to Ernest and Rose Stefanik, my parents, who helped in countless ways during the writing of this book, often without their knowing it. And I thank Louise Craft, Associate Editor of the University of Pittsburgh Press, who has contributed significantly to the work's accuracy through her careful readings.

Introduction

THIS bibliography describes separate publications by John Berryman and lists first appearances and reprintings of individual poems and prose pieces. It is, inevitably, incomplete – materials remain in private circulation; indexes are, unfortunately, inadequate; information in publishers' and printers' records is not always made available; posthumous volumes of previously unpublished materials will be printed. These difficulties, of course, are merely suggestive and are by no means considered to be peculiar to this compilation. A descriptive bibliography, as a standard of reference, is subject to revision as new information surfaces; it is through this process of accretion and correction that balance and accuracy are established.

FORMAT

In the matter of format, I have followed closely Professor Bruccoli's recommendations for bibliographies in the series.[1] No writings about Berryman are listed.

Section A. Separate Publications. Books, pamphlets, and keepsakes by Berryman published in the United States and in Great Britain are ar-

---

1. See Matthew J. Bruccoli, *F. Scott Fitzgerald: A Descriptive Bibliography* (Pittsburgh: University of Pittsburgh Press, 1972).

ranged chronologically by date of publication and by printings within editions. Although *Homage to Mistress Bradstreet and Other Poems, Short Poems, The Dream Songs,* and *Selected Poems 1938–1968* (A 9, A 15, A 18, A 23) contain no first-book material, these four titles are included in this section since they are not posthumous collections but books published with the author's approval and under his supervision.

No Canadian editions, issues, or reprintings have been located.[2] Seven proof copies are described (A 9.1.a†, A 13.1.b†, A 16.1.a†, A 16.1.c†, A 20.1.a†, A 22.1.c†, A 24.1.a†), but this list is not to be construed as complete. Undoubtedly proof copies exist for more of Berryman's books, but there is no way of being certain since locating them is a matter of chance. Proof copies are of interest to the collector, but they also have textual and critical significance because they may preserve earlier forms of the text, thus providing evidence of the author's intentions through his revisions.

Section B. First-Appearance Contributions to Books. Titles in which material by Berryman constitutes first publication or first book appearance are arranged chronologically by date of publication. In all applicable cases, publication of a book both in America and in England is indicated

---

2. In a letter of February 15, 1974, Margaret Wente of Doubleday Canada Ltd. wrote: "All Berryman titles originally published by Farrar, Straus and Giroux are distributed in Canada by Doubleday Canada Limited. There may well be other editions available in Canada from U.S. or U.K. publishers other than Farrar, Straus and Giroux. However, to the best of my knowledge there are no special Canadian editions of Berryman's works. Thus a list of Berryman's book available here would include whatever other foreign editions are available through other Canadian distributors." Letters of inquiry sent to other Canadian publishers cited on the copyright pages of the books in Section A are unanswered.

in the title-page transcriptions. All books are clothbound unless specified otherwise, but when a book has been published, say, in both cloth and paper wrappers, this is stipulated. A supplemental BB section includes several borderline items, such as biographical entries prepared from letters by Berryman.

Section C. Contributions to Periodicals. Materials by Berryman first published in periodicals are arranged chronologically by date of publication within two subdivisions, *Poetry* and *Prose*. Reprintings are regularly noted in this section. When an item has been published both in America and in England, the second appearance is included with the reprintings.

Section D. Collected Materials Reprinted in Anthologies. Materials first published in the books listed in Sections A and B that have been reprinted in anthologies are arranged alphabetically within two subdivisions, *Poetry* and *Prose*. In a few cases reprintings in periodicals are noted. Only the first edition of an anthology in which reprinted matter has been included is cited. Poems quoted in essays or critical articles about Berryman are not listed. Of course, no first-book material appears in this section.

Section E. Interviews. Interviews with Berryman and articles based on interviews first appearing in periodicals are arranged chronologically.

Section F. Phonorecordings. Recordings of Berryman's poetry are arranged chronologically under two headings, *Tapes* and *Discs*. No material held in private collections is listed.

Section G. Dust-Jacket Blurbs. Dust jackets of books by other authors on which quotations from comments by Berryman appear are described. The arrangement is chronological.

Section H. Poetry Selections. Selections by Berryman of the work of other poets are arranged chronologically.

Appendix 1. A Chronology of the Publication of Works by Berryman. Because the logical arrangement of a bibliography precludes a strict chronological list of the author's published material, this chronology lists books and individual items by Berryman according to their dates of publication. When dates of publication were not available from copyright applications or publishers' records, those given in the publications themselves are provided. Individual items first published in separate publications by Berryman are not listed here.

Appendix 2. Periodicals in Which Material by Berryman First Appeared. Periodicals containing first-publication material by Berryman are listed alphabetically with the pertinent facts of publication for each issue.

METHODS AND TERMS

Edition, printing, and *issue.*[3] An edition consists of all the copies of a book printed from one setting of type. This includes all printings, issues, and states from that setting. Thus the photolithographic version of *Berryman's Sonnets* (A 13.1.b) published in England from the book printed in America is considered as part of the first edition rather than as the first English edition.

A printing is part of an edition and consists of all the copies of a book printed at any one time without removing the type or plates from the press.

Issues are included within a printing; they are

---

3. See Fredson Bowers, *Principles of Bibliographical Description* (Princeton: Princeton University Press, 1949; reprinted, New York: Russell & Russell, 1962), chap. 11.

the result of the publisher's intent to make some alteration in copies of a printing, usually after some copies have been published. The only clear case of issue in this bibliography is the result of alterations on both a title page and copyright page (A 6.1.a*). For special cases see A 8.1.a* and A 20.1.a*.

Proof copy. A proof copy is a set of galley or page proofs which has been stitched, glued, or stapled—frequently in paper wrappers but not case-bound. Proof copies are sometimes a part of the prepublication stage of contemporary books in America and England—they are ordered by the publisher for use in the office or in the promotion of the book; however, they are not offered for sale by the publisher.

Numbering. The numbering system indicates the arrangement of the title within the chronological sequence of the separate publications and within the editions and printings of the specific titles. Thus A 11.1.a signifies that 77 *Dream Songs* is the eleventh separate publication (A 11), the first edition (1), the first printing (a). When no designation of edition and printing is made, it is to be assumed that there is a single edition and printing of the title. An issue is indicated by an asterisk; thus A 6.1.a* signifies the English issue on American sheets of *Stephen Crane*. A special problem is indicated by a dagger; thus A 9.1.a† is the proof copy of *Homage to Mistress Bradstreet and Other Poems*.

Title pages. In Section A title pages are facsimiled. The lettering is black (Centroid 267 — see "Color designations" below in this section) unless specified otherwise in the caption under the facsimile, which always indicates leaf measurement. If the title page does not carry the year of publication, the date appears in brackets after the edition and printing designation; otherwise, the date is in parentheses. In Section B all title pages are transcribed in quasi-facsimile.

Copyright pages. Facsimiles of copyright pages are provided for works in Section A. A wavy line on the facsimile indicates that the page has been shortened to eliminate white space.

Collation. The collational formula and the statement of pagination are given on separate lines. Inferential information is enclosed within brackets. The total number of leaves is given in the case of a perfect binding (that is, a binding in which the leaves are glued to a cloth or paper backing after the folds have been cut off) or of a plastic binding (that is, a binding in which the leaves are held together by curved prongs extending from a plastic center strip that are inserted in holes punched in the leaves).

Contents. Enclosing inferential information in brackets in the statement of pagination obviates their use in the contents note. The major parts of the book are transcribed in quasi-facsimile form. Single quotation marks have been used for these transcriptions, but there are occasional deviations from this practice when single quotation marks are part of the matter being transcribed. The contents notes for reprintings and issues are condensed—only those differences from the original text are transcribed in quasi-facsimile form. As a general rule, literary contents are listed separately, as are illustrations. For untitled poems the first line is given in double quotation marks.

Typography. The typography is described by indicating the number of lines on a typical page of text, type-page measurements, and typeface style and size. Because books of poetry do not always provide a full page of type, the number of lines is

Introduction XXIII

occasionally an inference based on measurements. Similarly, type-page measurements have required special treatment. It is important to note that typeface size is not the same as type size: the former is a measurement in American points of the impression on the page; the physical size of the type can only be inferred from this measurement. Further, because visual evidence cannot distinguish between the use of leading and the use of a larger bodied type, the term *leading* has been preferred in designating the space between lines of text. Only typeface styles appearing in the text have been identified and measured.

Paper. The note on paper deals with the sheets of the book. Paper is described by its color, whether it is wove or laid, and its watermarks. If the paper is of the laid variety, the direction of the chain lines and the space between them are stated. Paper is assumed to be unwatermarked unless specified otherwise; it is also assumed to be smooth unless specified as rough or glossy. Watermarks are transcribed in quasi-facsimile form. Leaf thickness and the bulk of the sheets are not indicated since these measurements are not required to identify printings of Berryman's books.

Binding. Binding cloth is described by color, pattern, and whether it is sized or unsized. Wrappers and endpapers are treated in the same way as the sheets of the book. Book edges are described by the terms *cut* and *trimmed,* the former indicating an edge that has been cut smooth by plough or guillotine and the latter indicating an edge that is uneven or lightly trimmed. In the transcriptions the lettering on spines when reading vertically is treated as a single line.

Dust jacket. Since dust jackets constitute part of the publication effort, they have been described in some detail. The paper is described in the same manner as the sheets of the book; measurements are provided for the height and overall width of the dust jacket.

Text. First-publication material and first-book-appearance material are identified.

Publication. The number of copies printed, the date of publication (the date a book became available to the public), and the price at which the work sold when it was first published are given. The phrase "unknown number of copies" indicates that the number of copies printed could not be determined because the publisher would not disclose the information or that the publisher no longer exists; when publishers did not respond to letters of inquiry, this fact is noted. The dates of publication were obtained from copyright applications and from publishers' records.

Printing. This note identifies the firms which were responsible for typesetting, printing, and binding. Where no typesetter is identified, it is to be assumed that the typesetting was done by the printer. This information was obtained from copyright applications and from publishers' records. *Privately printed* refers to a work (such as a keepsake) not produced to the order and expense of a commercial publisher and not offered for sale.

Copyright. The copyright registration number and the name of the copyright claimant are specified.

Locations. Location symbols are those given in the *National Union Catalogue,* with the following additions:

BM: British Museum
CF: Collection of Claude Fredericks
ECS: Collection of Ernest C. Stefanik, Jr.
Lilly: Lilly Library, Indiana University
Lockwood: Poetry Collection, Lockwood Me-

morial Library, State University of New York at Buffalo

Meissner: The George N. Meissner Rare Book Department, John M. Olin Library, Washington University

PAB: Collection of Patricia A. Brenner

Copies held by The British Museum have not been examined.

Notes. This section contains information which contributes to the understanding of a book's history or which identifies or clarifies special problems. Collations of individual poems noting revisions and textual variants are included; these notations are based on sight-collation.

Later printings. Entries in Section A for later printings of Berryman's books provide publication facts: city, publisher, and year of publication. Where the year does not appear on the title page, it is provided in brackets. Where the copyright page specifies the printing by words or a publisher's code, this information is transcribed in quasi-facsimile (for example, '*Second printing*'). The binding of a later printing is assumed to be in cloth unless specified otherwise. For first paperback printings, the serial number and the price are given. It should be noted that only those later printings seen are listed and that locating these copies is a matter of chance; thus a printing might be designated as being in printed wrappers, whereas it is possible that that printing was published both in cloth and paper wrappers.

Chronological order of entries. When a section is arranged chronologically, the order was determined by the publication dates of the entries. When these dates were unavailable from copyright applications or publishers' records, the dates given within the publications themselves were used.

Title abbreviations. Throughout the bibliography long titles of Berryman's works are abbreviated as follows:

BS: *Berryman's Sonnets*, A 13
DE: *Delusions, Etc.*, A 22
Homage: *Homage to Mistress Bradstreet*, A 7
HomageAOP: *Homage to Mistress Bradstreet and Other Poems*, A 9
L&F: *Love & Fame*, A 20
SelP: *Selected Poems 1938–1968*, A 23
77DS: *77 Dream Songs*, A 11
ShP: *Short Poems*, A 15
TD: *The Dispossessed*, A 4
TheDS: *The Dream Songs*, A 18
Thought: *His Thought Made Pockets & The Plane Buckt*, A 8
Toy: *His Toy, His Dream, His Rest*, A 16
20P: *Twenty Poems*, A 1

Color designations.[4] The ISCC-NBS system is used for designating colors of papers, book cloths, and inks. A color is specified by reference to the nomenclature and number of the sample on the *ISCC-NBS Centroid Color Charts* (Standard Sample No. 2106), for example, very light yellowish green (134). The color-matching was carried out in natural light, though not in direct sunlight; thus, a comparison of the material described in the bibliography with the charts under incandescent or fluorescent light could be misleading. Allowances were also made for differences in texture

---

4. See G. Thomas Tanselle, "A System of Color Identification for Bibliographical Description," in Fredson Bowers, ed., *Studies in Bibliography*, vol. XX (Charlottesville: Bibliographical Society of the University of Virginia, 1967), pp. 203–234.

Introduction

—the samples are glossy—and for fading. It should be noted that although this method introduces a higher level of accuracy into the description of colors in this bibliography, the color designations are approximate rather than exact—obviously the 267 color names in the ISCC-NBS system do not represent all possible colors.[5] The *Centroid Color Charts* uses abbreviations for color names and modifiers, but these abbreviations are not used in the descriptions since their use might constitute an excessive burden for the reader.[6]

Transcriptions.[7] In quasi-facsimile transcriptions each line is treated as a separate unit, with line endings indicated by a vertical rule [|]. Typeface is distinguished as roman, italic, or gothic. The use of capital and lowercase letters is followed strictly, and two sizes of type (capitals and small capitals of a font) are distinguished when they occur in the same line. The size and weight of the original letters, however, are ignored. All lettering is black (Centroid 267) and roman unless specifically noted otherwise. A typeface or color designation holds for subsequent lines until a change is designated. Thus the front cover of the dust jacket of *His Toy, His Dream, His Rest* (A 16.1.a) is transcribed in the following manner:

'[black (Centroid 267) background] [vivid greenish yellow (97)] JOHN | BERRYMAN | [strong yellow (84)] HIS TOY, [deep purplish pink (248)]

---

5. There are 267 color-name blocks on the charts, but samples are not available for 16 colors.

6. The *ISCC-NBS Centroid Color Charts* (Standard Sample No. 2106) is available from the U.S. Department of Commerce, National Bureau of Standards, Office of Standard Reference Materials, Standard Materials Unit, Washington, D.C. 20234, at $9.00.

7. See Bowers, *Principles in Bibliographical Description*, chap. 4.

HIS | DREAM, [strong greenish blue (169)] HIS | REST'.

The entire front cover is black (matching sample number 267 on the *ISCC-NBS Centroid Color Charts*); the author's name is in vivid greenish yellow lettering (matching sample number 97); the words *His Toy* are in strong yellow lettering (matching sample number 84); the words *His Dream* are in deep purplish pink lettering (matching sample number 248); and the words *His Rest* are in strong greenish blue lettering (matching sample number 169).

The spine of the same dust jacket is transcribed in the following manner:

'[black background] [reading horizontally] [vivid greenish yellow] JOHN | BERRY | MAN | [strong yellow] HIS | TOY, | [deep purplish pink] HIS | DREAM, | [strong greenish blue] HIS | REST | [vivid greenish yellow] [device] | FARRAR, | STRAUS & | GIROUX'.

Thus, the Centroid sample number is given only with the first mention of a color name in a given note, and only the color name is specified for each change.

It is desirable in bibliographical description to avoid end-of-line hyphens in transcriptions. Words should not be divided in a transcription unless they are divided in the original. Because of word length and a measured line, however, it is impossible always to achieve this optimum. End-of-line hyphens have been avoided wherever possible and always when a hyphen would create ambiguity in spelling.

Cloth patterns. Although most readers are probably accustomed to the method of designating binding cloths in Jacob Blanck, ed., *Bibliography of American Literature* (New Haven: Yale Uni-

Introduction   XXIX

versity Press, 1955-), the classification system proposed by G. Thomas Tanselle is used in this bibliography.⁸ The *BAL* method consists of an uninformative letter code keyed to an illustration, for example, B cloth; the verbal description of the cloth is arbitrary. In Tanselle's system, on the other hand, the cloth pattern is given both by a fixed verbal description and by a reference notation that indicates the group to which a pattern belongs by a three-digit number and a letter, for example, coarse linen-cloth (304b); the letter "a" indicates the norm between "coarse" and "fine" and is not attached to the number when there is no other modifier, for example, linen-cloth (304). The reference numbers and letters are, in most instances, keyed to illustrations. Tanselle gives a table of equivalences with the *BAL* scheme (as well as with those of Sadlier, Carter, and Rogers); those patterns described in this bibliography are as follows:

BAL	Tanselle
B	linen-cloth (304)
–	fine linen-cloth (304b)
H	fine diaper-cloth (124b)
V	calico-cloth (302)
–	coarse calico-cloth (302c)

My major concern in writing this bibliography has been to establish the canon of John Berryman's printed works while assuring that the facts assembled are useful to the literary scholar as well as to the librarian and the book collector. The value of this study must be determined ultimately by its accuracy and completeness. Additions and corrections are solicited.

---

8. See G. Thomas Tanselle, "The Bibliographical Description of Patterns," in Bowers, ed., *Studies in Bibliography*, vol. XXIII (Charlottesville, 1970), pp. 71-102.

A. Separate Publications

Books, pamphlets, and keepsakes by Berryman, arranged chronologically by date of publication and by printings within editions.

A 1 FIVE YOUNG AMERICAN POETS
(TWENTY POEMS)
[1940]

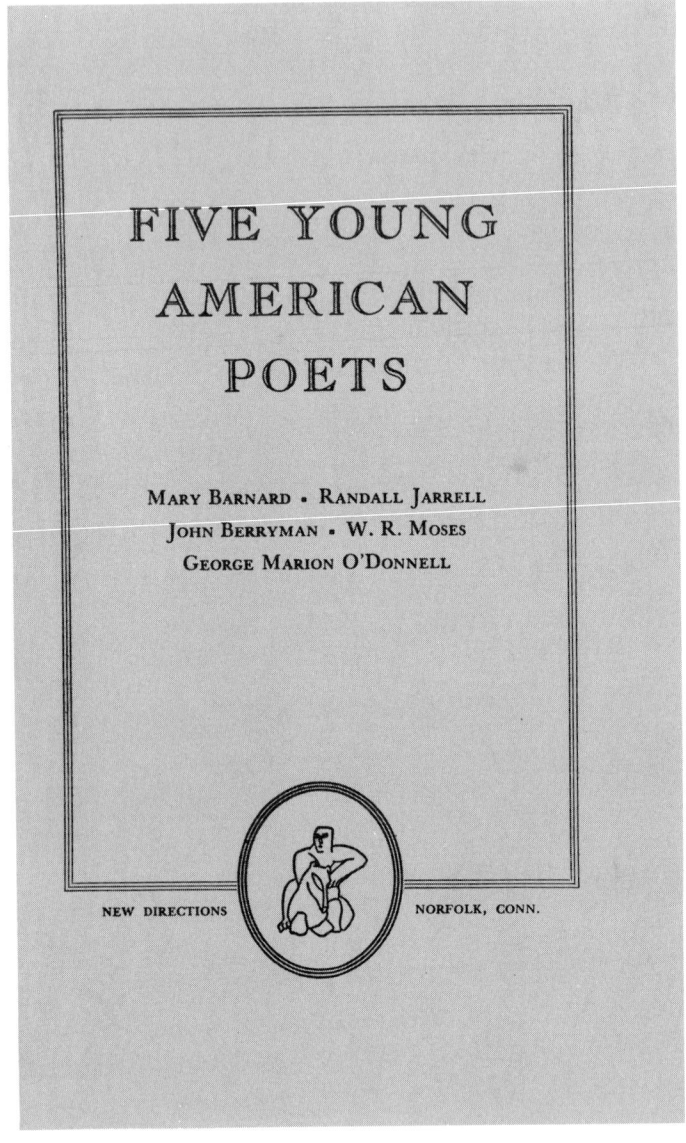

A 1: 8⅝" × 5⅜"

A 1 *Five Young American Poets*

> COPYRIGHT 1940 BY NEW DIRECTIONS
>
> *The* Five Young American Poets *anthology will be published annually and poets under thirty who have not published a book of verse are invited to compete for places in it. Manuscripts should be sent to the Editor of New Directions at Norfolk, Conn., and return postage must be enclosed.*
>
> PRINTED IN THE UNITED STATES OF AMERICA
> BY J. J. LITTLE AND IVES COMPANY, NEW YORK

[1-12]^8 [13]^{10} [14]^8

[i-vi] [1-4] 5 [6] 7-40 [41-44] 45-80 [81-84] 85-123 [124-128] 129-131 [132] 133-174 [175-178] 179-181 [182] 183-221 [222]

Contents: p. i: 'FIVE YOUNG AMERICAN POETS'. p. ii: blank. p. iii: title page. p. iv: copyright page. p. v: table of contents. p. vi: blank. pp. 1-40: 'Cool Country | *Mary Barnard*'. p. 41: 'Twenty Poems | *John Berryman*'. p. 42: blank. p. 43: 'JOHN BERRYMAN | [two unsigned paragraphs, comprising a seven-line biographical note and five lines of acknowledgments]'. p. 44: reproduction of holograph of "Parting as Descent" (untitled). pp. 45-48: 'A NOTE ON POETRY'. pp. 49-80: text. pp. 81-123: 'The Rage for the | Lost Penny | *Randall Jarrell*'. p. 124: blank. pp. 125-174: 'Arteries of Morning | *W. R. Moses*'. pp. 175-221: 'Prayer Against | the Furies | *George Marion O'Donnell*'. p. 222: blank.

Items included in Twenty Poems: A Note on Poetry; The Statue; Desires of Men and Women; On the London Train; Song from "Cleopatra"; Letter to His Brother; The Apparition; Meditation; Parting as Descent; Sanctuary; The Disciple; The Trial; Night and the City; Nineteen Thirty-Eight; The Curse; World-Telegram; Conversation; The Return; Ceremony and Vision; Winter Landscape; Caravan.

Illustrations: Single leaf of yellowish white (Centroid 92) glossy wove paper tipped in between pp. 42 and 43. Recto, blank; verso, black and white photograph of JB. Photographs of the other poets are between pp. 2 and 3, 82 and 83, 126 and 127, 176 and 177.

Typography and paper: 35 ll., $6^{5}/_{16}''$ ($6^{1}/_{2}''$) × $3^{13}/_{16}''$. Text and note in 9-pt. Linotype Baskerville with 4-pt. leading. Yellowish white (Centroid 92) laid paper (chain lines running vertically, spaced $^{31}/_{32}''$), watermarked 'WARREN'S | OLDE STYLE'.

Twenty Poems

John Berryman

A 1: p. 41, part title

A 1 *Five Young American Poets* 5

Binding: Sized coarse calico-cloth (302c), grayish blue (Centroid 186). Front cover: plain. Spine: '[reading horizontally] [goldstamped] [within double-rules frame] FIVE | YOUNG | AMERICAN | POETS | [double rule] | NEW | DIRECTIONS'. Back cover: plain. All edges cut. Yellowish white (92) wove endpapers.

Dust jacket: Yellowish white (Centroid 92) wove paper, $9^7/_8''$ × 20''. Printed in dark blue (183) ink. Front cover: '[within triple-rules frame on yellowish gray (93) background] [number the height of first two lines] 5 [script] Young American | [roman] POETS | GEORGE MARION O'DONNELL | RANDALL JARRELL | JOHN BERRYMAN | MARY BARNARD | W. R. MOSES | [below frame] [device] *NEW DIRECTIONS presents the work of five of | the most accomplished young American poets—five books of verse | in a single volume.*' Spine: '[reading vertically from top to bottom] ★ FIVE YOUNG AMERICAN POETS ★'. Back cover: '[within quadruple-rules frame, with quadruple-rules oval containing publisher's device in lower left-hand corner] [first line swash] *New Directions Books* | NOVELS | [six titles, four lines] | STORIES | [five titles, four lines] | CRITICISM | [seven titles, five lines] | POETRY | [nine titles, seven lines] | ANTHOLOGIES | [seven titles, four lines] | HISTORY | [one title] | [first two words swash] *New Directions* · NORFOLK, CONN.' Front flap: 'FIVE YOUNG | AMERICAN POETS | *An Anthology of the poetry of Mary Barnard, | John Berryman, Randall Jarrell, W. R. Moses | and George Marion O'Donnell.* | [four-paragraph unsigned comment on purpose of series and a general description of contents, thirty-six lines] | $2.50'. Back flap: 'The Poet of the Month | [two-paragraph unsigned announcement of proposed series with tentative list of authors for 1941, thirty lines] | *Subscribe now to The Poet of the Month* | NEW DIRECTIONS | Norfolk—Connecticut'.

Text: First publication of "A Note on Poetry" and "Sanctuary." First book appearance of "The Statue," "Desires of Men and Women," "On the London Train," "Song from 'Cleopatra,'" "Letter to His Brother," "The Apparition," "Meditation," "The Disciple," "The Trial," "Night and the City," "Nineteen Thirty-Eight," "World-Telegram," "Conversation," and "Winter Landscape."

Publication: 800 copies. Published November 19, 1940. $2.50.

Printing: Printed and bound by J. J. Little Ives and Company, New York, N.Y.

Copyright: Registered under A 147602 in the name of New Directions, Norfolk, Conn. Renewed under R 434648 on March 27, 1968, by New Directions, New York, N.Y., as proprietor of the work.

Locations: DLC (deposit copy not seen); Lilly (dj); Lockwood (dj).

Note: Five Young American Poets (1940), a composite work edited by James Laughlin, was the first in a series of annual volumes consisting of selections of poems by five American poets under thirty who had not published a book of poetry. Each of the five separate books of approximately forty pages each in a single volume contains a title page, a photograph of the poet, a biographical note, a reproduction of a holograph of a poem, a statement on poetry, and the text.

A 2 POEMS
[*1942*]

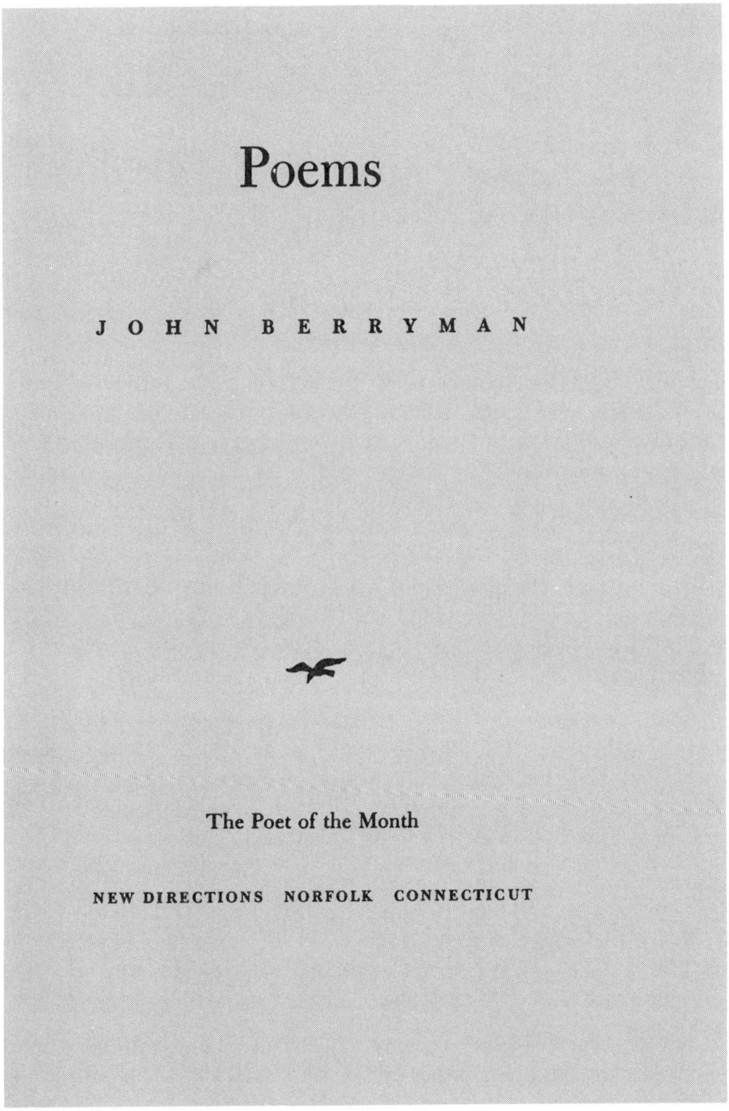
Poems

JOHN BERRYMAN

The Poet of the Month

NEW DIRECTIONS NORFOLK CONNECTICUT

A 2: Pale blue (Centroid 185) oval device containing dark grayish blue (187) silhouette of a bird in flight; $8\frac{7}{8}'' \times 5\frac{7}{8}''$. (Oval device could not be photographically reproduced.)

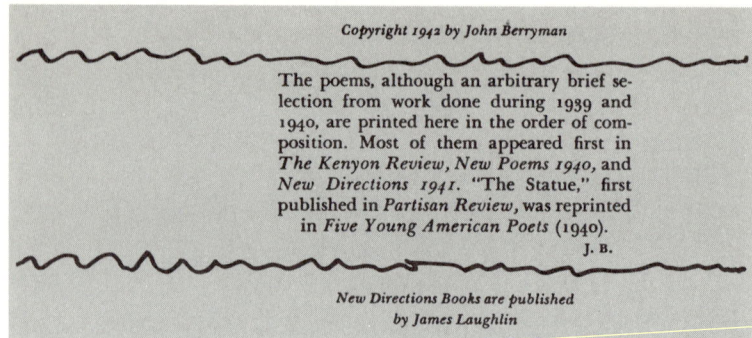

[1]¹⁶

[i–iv] [1] 2–25 [26–28]

Contents: pp. i–ii: blank. p. iii: title page. p. iv: copyright page. p. 1: "TO BHAIN CAMPBELL | 1911–1940 | I told a lie once in a verse. I said | I said I said I said 'The heart will mend, | Body will break and mend, the foam replace | For even the unconsolable his taken friend.' | This is a lie. I had not been here then." pp. 2–25: text. p. 26: '*Designed by Edmund Thompson and* | *printed from Bulmer and Linotype Baskerville types* | *in an edition of two thousand copies.* | [pale blue (Centroid 185) printer's device]'. p. 27: 'TITLES PUBLISHED IN | THE POET OF THE MONTH SERIES | 1941 | [twelve titles with names of authors, printers, and designers, twenty-nine lines]'. p. 28: blank.

Items included: The Dangerous Year; The Statue; River Rouge, 1932; At Chinese Checkers; 1 September 1939; Communist; Thanksgiving: Detroit; A Point of Age; The Moon and the Night and the Men; A Poem for Bhain; Epilogue.

Typography and paper: 30 ll., $6^{1}/_{16}$″ ($6^{3}/_{8}$″) × $3^{5}/_{8}$″. Text in 11-pt. Linotype Baskerville with 3-pt. leading. Page numbers spelled out in italics, for example, '*page two*'. Yellowish gray (Centroid 93) laid paper (chain lines running vertically, spaced $^{27}/_{32}$″), watermarked '*T & H Tru-Colour Text*'.

Binding: Light bluish green (Centroid 163) paper-covered boards. Front cover: 'Poems | JOHN BERRYMAN | [silhouette of bird in flight]'. Back cover: plain. All edges cut. Yellowish white (92) wove endpapers sewn with gathering; outer leaves pasted down, inner leaves free.

A 2 Poems

Variant binding: Yellowish white (Centroid 92) wove stiff paper wrappers. Gathering stapled. All edges cut.

Dust jacket: Light bluish green (Centroid 163) wove paper, $8^{15}/_{16}''\times 20''$. Front cover: 'Poems | JOHN BERRYMAN | [silhouette of bird in flight]'. Back cover: plain. Front flap: 'Poems | *by John Berryman* | [two unsigned paragraphs, comprising a ten-line note on *Twenty Poems* and a sixteen-line comment on JB's poetry]'. Back flap: '[seven-line advertisement for The Poet of the Month series] | [list of twelve titles with names of authors and printers for 1942 series, thirty lines] | NEW DIRECTIONS, *Norfolk, Conn.*'

Text: First publication of "A Point of Age," "A Poem for Bhain," and "Epilogue." First book appearance of "At Chinese Checkers."

Publication: 2,000 copies: 1,500 in paper wrappers; 500 bound. Published September 28, 1942.[1] Wrappers, $0.50; bound, $1.00.

Printing: Printed and bound by Hawthorn House, Windham, Conn.

Copyright: Registered under A 166237 in the name of JB. Renewed under R 467559 on August 25, 1969, by JB as author.

Locations: DLC (deposit-stamp August 13, 1942) (boards); ECS (boards) (dj); Lilly (wrappers; boards) (dj); Lockwood (boards) (dj); NBu (wrappers) (dj); PPiU (boards); PSt (wrappers; boards) (dj).

Note one: There are two variants in "The Statue" between its appearance in *20P* and in *Poems:*

   l. 3:   shop-girls [shopgirls
   l. 37: died [died,

---

1. The copyright application (A 166237) shows the date of publication as August 4, 1942, and the printer as E. L. Hildreth and Company, Brattleboro, Vt. In a letter of February 23, 1973, Griselda Ohannessian indicated that the records at New Directions show the date of publication as September 28, 1942, and the printer as Hawthorn House, Windham, Conn.; the same information also appears in "A List of the Books Published by New Directions, 1936–1963," in *A New Directions Reader,* ed. Hayden Carruth and James Laughlin (New York: New Directions, 1964). The device of Hawthorn House is printed in the colophon of *Poems.*

Note two: The Poet of the Month series, in which *Poems* is included, was begun by James Laughlin's New Directions in 1941 as a monthly series of poetry pamphlets uniform in size but diverse in typography. Although primarily devoted to publishing representative selections by contemporary American poets, the series also included translations of works by Baudelaire, Brecht, Pindar, and Rilke as well as selections from influential English poets of the past such as Donne and Herrick.

A 3 TWO POEMS
   (1942)

> # Two Poems
>
> JOHN BERRYMAN
>
> *Christmas, 1942*

A 3: 8¼" × 6¼"

> *Sixty copies printed*
> *Copyright 1942 by John & Eileen Berryman*

[1]²

[1–4]

Contents: p. 1: title page. p. 2: 'THE BALL POEM', twenty-five lines. p. 3: 'FOR HIS MARRIAGE', eighteen lines. p. 4: copyright page.

Typography and paper: $4\frac{7}{8}''$ ($5\frac{11}{16}''$) × $3\frac{5}{8}''$. Text in 12-pt. Linotype Caslon Old Face with 2-pt. leading. Pale yellow (Centroid 89) wove paper.

Binding: Unbound and single-folded folio sheet. All edges cut.

Text: First publication of "The Ball Poem" and "For His Marriage."

Publication: 60 copies. Printed ca. December 1942. Not for sale.

Printing: Privately printed. Printer not known.

Copyright: No copyright application filed.

Locations: CF; ECS; Lilly.

A 4 THE DISPOSSESSED
[1948]

JOHN BERRYMAN

THE
Dispossessed

WILLIAM SLOANE ASSOCIATES, INC.
Publishers   *New York*

A 4: 8⅜" × 5⁹⁄₁₆"

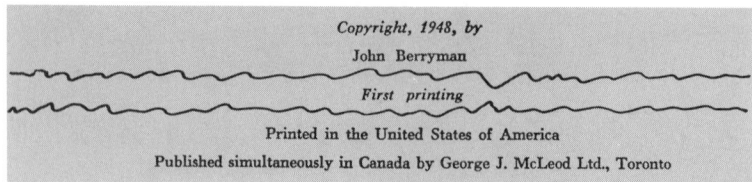

[1-6]⁸ [7]⁴ [8]⁸

[A-B] [i-vi] vii [viii] ix-x [xi-xii] [1-2] 3-15 [16-18] 19-47 [48-50] 51-68 [69-70] 71-84 [85-86] 87-103 [104-106]

Contents: pp. A-B: blank. p. i: 'THE DISPOSSESSED'. p. ii: blank. p. iii: title page. p. iv: copyright page. p. v: *'TO MY MOTHER'*. p. vi: blank. p. vii: 'NOTE | [one paragraph of acknowledgments, brief notes on eight poems, and dedications of poems to individuals, thirty-nine lines] | J.B.' p. viii: blank. pp. ix-x: table of contents. p. xi: 'THE DISPOSSESSED'. p. xii: blank. p. 1: '[ornament] I [ornament]'. p. 2: blank. pp. 3-15: text. p. 16: blank. p. 17: '[ornament] II [ornament]'. p. 18: blank. pp. 19-47: text. p. 48: blank. p. 49: '[ornament] III [ornament]'. p. 50: blank. pp. 51-68: text. p. 69: '[ornament] IV [ornament]'. p. 70: blank. pp. 71-84: text. p. 85: '[ornament] V [ornament]'. p. 86: blank. pp. 87-103: text. pp. 104-106: blank.

Items included: Note. I: Winter Landscape; The Statue; The Disciple; A Point of Age; The Traveller; The Ball Poem; Fare Well. II: The Spinning Heart; On the London Train; Caravan; The Possessed; Parting as Descent; Cloud and Flame; Letter to His Brother; Desires of Men and Women; World-Telegram; Conversation; Ancestor; World's Fair; Travelling South; At Chinese Checkers; The Animal Trainer (1); The Animal Trainer (2). III: 1 September 1939; Desire Is a World by Night; Farewell to Miles; The Moon and the Night and the Men; White Feather; The Enemies of the Angels; A Poem for Bhain; Boston Common. IV: Canto Amor; The Nervous Songs (Young Woman's Song; The Song of the Demented Priest; The Song of the Young Hawaiian; A Professor's Song; The Captain's Song; The Song of the Tortured Girl; The Song of the Bridegroom; Song of the Man Forsaken and Obsessed; The Pacifist's Song); Surviving Love; The Lightning. V: Rock-Study with Wanderer; Whether There Is Sorrow in the Demons; The Long Home; A Winter-Piece to a Friend Away; New Year's Eve; Narcissus Moving; The Dispossessed.

A 4 *The Dispossessed*

Typography and paper: 33 ll., 6⅜" (6⅝") × 3¹³⁄₁₆". Text in 10-pt. Linotype Janson with 4-pt. leading; author's note in 10-pt., set solid. Yellowish white (Centroid 92) wove paper.

Binding: Sized fine linen-cloth (304b), dark blue (Centroid 183). Front cover: '[goldstamped] THE | *Dispossessed*'. Spine: '[reading vertically from top to bottom] [goldstamped] [fleuron, horizontal] BERRYMAN · THE *Dispossessed* · *Sloane* [inverted fleuron, horizontal]'. Back cover: plain. Top edge and tail cut; fore edge trimmed. Yellowish white (92) wove endpapers of different stock than text paper.

Dust jacket: Wove paper, 8⁹⁄₁₆" × 19⅝". Front cover: '[dark red (Centroid 16) background] [on light gray (264) panel with vertical double rules at right and left sides of panel] [band of ten inverted fleurons] | [row of ornaments] | THE | D*ispossessed* | POEMS BY | *John B*erryman | [row of ornaments] | [band of ten fleurons]'. Spine: '[dark red background] [reading vertically from top to bottom] [inverted horizontal fleuron] [yellowish white (92)] *Berryman:* THE DISPOSSESSED [black (267)] [horizontal double fleuron] [yellowish white] *Sloane* [black] [horizontal fleuron]'. Back cover: '[white (263) background] RECENT VOLUMES OF POETRY | NEW POEMS by Mark Van Doren | [four-line unsigned comment] | THE QUIET CENTER by Edith Henrich | [three-line quotation from a comment in *The New York Times Book Review*] | THE IRON PASTORAL by John Frederick Nims | [five-line unsigned comment] | THE COUNTRY YEAR by Mark Van Doren, | illustrated by John O'Hara Cosgrave II | [three-line unsigned comment] | [double rule]'. Front flap: '[white background] $2.50 | THE | *Dispossessed* | by John Berryman | [two unsigned paragraphs, comprising a nine-line comment on contents and a fifteen-line note on the previous appearances of JB's poetry] | *Jacket design by Oscar Ogg* | WILLIAM SLOANE ASSOCIATES, INC. | 119 West 57th Street, New York 19, N.Y.' Back flap: '[white background] [black and white photograph of JB] | *Octave Romaine* | [two unsigned paragraphs, comprising a six-line biographical note and an eleven-line note on JB's writings] | WILLIAM SLOANE ASSOCIATES, INC. | 119 West 57th Street, New York 19, N.Y.'

Text: First publication of "Desire Is a World by Night," "The Enemies of the Angels," "A Professor's Song," "The Captain's Song," "The Song of the Tortured Girl," "The Song of the Bridegroom," "Song of the Man Forsaken and Obsessed," "The

Pacifist's Song," and "The Lightning." First book appearance of "The Traveller," "Fare Well," "Cloud and Flame," "Ancestor," "World's Fair," "Travelling South," "Farewell to Miles," "White Feather," "Canto Amor," "Young Woman's Song," "The Song of the Demented Priest," "The Song of the Young Hawaiian," "Surviving Love," "Rock-Study with Wanderer," "Whether There Is Sorrow in the Demons," "The Long Home," "A Winter-Piece to a Friend Away," "New Year's Eve," "Narcissus Moving," and "The Dispossessed."

Publication: Unknown number of copies. Published May 10, 1948. $2.50.

Printing: Printed by H. Wolff Book Manufacturing Company, New York, N.Y., from type set by The Maple Press, York, Pa. Bound by Wolff.

Copyright: Registered under A 22685 in the name of JB.

Locations: DLC (deposit-stamp May 19, 1948); ECS; Lilly (dj); Lockwood (dj); PPiU.

Note one: Variants and revisions in sixteen poems between their appearances in the collections indicated and in *TD* are noted as follows:

"Winter Landscape," *20P*
   l. 25: Descend [Descend,

"The Statue," *Poems*
   l. 28: Coriolanus, [Coriolanus
   l. 29: is [moves
   l. 30: keep [stay
   l. 35: The elder? Younger? [the elder? younger?
   l. 37: died, [died
   l. 38: due [bound
   l. 39: first born [first-born
   l. 45: Which [That
   l. 46: thighs, breasts, [thighs breasts
   l. 48: excitement [excitement,

"The Disciple," *20P*
   l. 4:   flame. [flame;
   l. 7:   a man [someone
   l. 8:   been [lain
   l. 10: intent [warm
   l. 15: gruelling [rubbing
   l. 16: that [this
   l. 19: washed [swashed
   l. 21: He [. . He

A 4 *The Dispossessed*

    l. 27:   trusted sold him to policemen,   [harboured kissed him for the coppers'
    l. 30:   stolen   [lifted
    l. 32:   with   [in
    l. 39:   disciplines,   [disciplines
    l. 40:   Those hearts, are his, and we   [Worry themselves there. We

"A Point of Age," *Poems*
    l. 11:   time – time?   [time . . time?
    l. 12:   men   [lodgers
    l. 16:   had,   [had
    l. 17:   fallen back or got   [frozen back or slipt
    l. 20:   night inherited,   [and the night falls, sad,
    l. 21:   Last year upon the lips of now is salt.   [Across the forward shadows where friends halt.
    l. 25:   been content and would be   [stood content and would stand
    l. 26:   were the look   [bore the brat
    l. 30:   sat   [reared
    l. 32:   deafen the citizen alive or dead.   [hallow the citizen deaf, half-dead.
    l. 34:   tree,   [ash,
    l. 38:   is   [sits
    l. 39:   Settle   [Sanction
    l. 43:   strange   [weird
    l. 47:   Never, in   [No longer, down
    l. 51:   Greatgrandfather, witness my simple   [Great-grandfather, attest my hopeless
    l. 52:   Among   [Amongst
    l. 57:   eye.   [eye! . .
    l. 59:   pride,   [pride
    l. 64:   Animal and Hero,   [Animal-and-Hero,
    l. 68:   Violence is   [Old friends unbolt
    l. 70:   climb,   [climb
    l. 73:   disappointed   [disillusioned
    l. 78:   man!   [man?
    l. 81:   hope   [Hope
    l. 88:   Proclaims   [Argues
    l. 91:   had   [dropt
    l. 98:   is the version   [version brightens
    l. 105:   sun is   [son flies
    l. 108:   over the   [across our
    l. 109:   a man has hoped   [someone has wished
    l. 110:   lives: [lives;
    l. 111:   face   [famine

  l. 116: a late [lagging
"The Ball Poem," *Two Poems* (1942)
  l. 11: first his [first
  l. 15: far [well
  l. 22: harbour. I [harbour . . I
"On the London Train," *20P*
  l. 9: While [Whilst
  l. 10: endless [vacant
  l. 17: been. [been . .
  l. 22: Satisfaction. And [Satisfaction, — while
  l. 29: get [twig
  l. 31: recompense, but [recompence too
"Caravan," *20P*
  l. 1: silver [silver-
  l. 2: Grey [grey
  l. 10: anxious, prone. [salt, supine.
  l. 12: is but [glitters
  l. 15: mastering [throwing off
  l. 22: steadily [tingling
  l. 23: set a place for apparition; [hang a glass for apparation . .
"The Possessed" ("The Return"), *20P*
  l. 1: afternoon innumerable [afternoon, discomfortable
  l. 2: Gather in doorways, lounge across the bridge [Drift into doorways, lounge, across the bridge,
  l. 3: edge [edge,
  l. 5: are but fatal [are, but hairy,
  l. 6: eye like the enormous tide; [eye, enlarging like a slide;
  l. 9: most unpleasant [your most awkward
  l. 10: Comfortable by [Loose-limbed before
  l. 11: terror [error
  l. 12: Look, [Look!
  l. 17: yesterday [yesterday,
  l. 18: stolen; undergraduates perhaps. [stolen, — undergraduates perhaps;
  l. 25: longer [further
  l. 29: gold [gold,
  l. 32: getting [growing
  l. 35: come through and the [lean through, and wide
  l. 40: and [&
"Parting as Descent," *20P*
  l. 1: flew. [flew;
  l. 7: move [move,

A 4 *The Dispossessed*

"Letter to His Brother," 20P
  l. 10: many [rubber
  l. 14: youth. [youth,–
  l. 15: And yet you know as well as I the [Although you know as well as I whose
  l. 16: latest [western
  l. 19: he [hé
  l. 23: chase [cry
  l. 26: comfort [bargain
  l. 31: that dignity to know the [the brazen luck to sleep with
  l. 32: gain [get

"Desires of Men and Women," 20P
  l. 6:   Eastern [eastern

"World-Telegram," 20P
  l. 23: Machine gun [Machine-gun
  l. 37: Induce [Curry
  l. 38: Paralyze [Immobilize

"Conversation," 20P
  l. 2:   gone, we said we could not tell. [slipt, we said we could not tell,
  l. 6:   see what he is [make out what he's
  l. 7:   less love, no [few love, less
  l. 12: fidelity [fidelity,
  l. 16: down at last [softly down
  l. 17: broken log fell [snapt short log pitched
  l. 20: Shrivel from the mind its [Flake from the mind its skinny
  l. 21: cool; those embers [cool, embers that
  l. 26: drank, [drank;
  l. 28: Took the alarming postures of our fear: [Assumed the alarming postures of our fear,–
  l. 30: cannot [will not
  l. 31: enemies that [subtle friends who

"At Chinese Checkers," *Poems*
  l. 13: died, [died
  l. 20: Swung [Swung,
  l. 64: That [This
  l. 68: circles [circles,

"1 September 1939," *Poems*
  l. 1:   first [first,
  l. 2:   sat [squat'
  l. 5:   resisted [resisted,
  l. 6:   fidelity, [fidelity ..
  l. 7:   waters. [waters,

l. 12:   that [this
l. 24:   shook, the Eagle soared and dropped. [ran, the Eagle soared and dropt.
"The Moon and the Night and the Men," *Poems*
l. 3:   beholder, [beholder;
l. 31: Completed [Fulfilled
l. 37: heart [moon
"A Poem for Bhain," *Poems*
l. 2:   Talk, turn, [Gossip and
l. 6:   alone [alone,
l. 10: night [summer

Note two: "A Point of Age" is not dated in *Poems* but is dated *'Detroit, 1940'* in *TD*. "Letter to His Brother" is dated *'Cornwall | 1938'* in *20P* and dated *'1938'* in *TD*. "Conversation" is not dated in *20P* but is dated *'1938'* in *TD*. "At Chinese Checkers" is dated *'Grand Marais'* in *Poems* but dated *'1939'* in *TD*. "The Moon and the Night and the Men" is dated *'June 1940'* in *Poems* but is not dated in *TD*.

Note three: In the table of contents, the title *Canto Amor* is printed as *Conto Amor*.

Note four: In all copies examined, the comma on p. 62, l. 6 ('alone,'), and the comma on p. 71, l. 11 ('woman,') are not fully impressed.

A 5 A CRITICAL SUPPLEMENT TO POETRY
(1949)

A 5: 7⅝" × 5¼"

A 5 A Critical Supplement to Poetry

> Published eight times a year, October through May, for use with *Poetry* in university classes and other study groups. Individual subscription to supplement alone (8 issues a year) $1.50; foreign, $1.75. Student rates 35c per set (magazine and supplement) in mailings of ten or more sets to one address. Desk copies free. Group orders and individual subscriptions may begin with any issue. Address *Poetry*, 232 East Erie Street, Chicago 11, Illinois.
>
> *All rights reserved*
>
> *Copyright 1949 by Modern Poetry Association*

[1]¹⁰

[i–ii] 1–17 [18]

Contents: p. i: title page. p. ii: copyright page. pp. 1–17: 'A CRITICAL SUPPLEMENT TO | POETRY | *Prepared by John Berryman* | DECEMBER 1949 | [short rule]'. p. 18: '[within single-rules frame] *announcing* | . . . for next month's POETRY, an | important group of eight new poems | by JOHN BERRYMAN | [two-paragraph unsigned note on subscription, ten lines] | [line of long dashes] | [subscription coupon]'.

Items included: Commentary on Wallace Stevens's "Things of August"; commentary on Nicholas Moore's "Unity Quitbread at Eltham"; comment and questions on Nicholas Moore's "Alteration"; comment and questions on Harvey Shapiro's "Provincetown, Mass."; comment on David Wagoner's "Finale"; commentary and questions on Vernon Watkins's "Music of Colours: The Blossom Scattered"; commentary on J. C. Crews's "A Kingdom's Utter Rail," "Concerning Less of the Sea," "Cattle the Meadows Spread," and "The Poise of Restless Wonder."

Typography and paper: 37 ll., 5⅝″ (6″) × 3½″. Text in 9-pt. Cloister Old Style with 2-pt. leading. Yellowish white (Centroid 92) wove paper.

Binding: Self-wrapper. Gathering stapled. All edges cut.

Publication: Unknown number of copies. Published November 30, 1949. $0.35.

Printing: Printed by Midway Printing Company, Chicago, Ill.

Copyright: Registered under B 220939 in the name of the Modern Poetry Association.

Location: Lockwood.

Note: The commentaries, comments, and questions are based on poems included in *Poetry*, LXXV (December 1949), 125–148.

A 6 STEPHEN CRANE

A 6.1.a
First edition, first printing [1950]

Stephen Crane

John Berryman

The American Men of Letters Series

WILLIAM SLOANE ASSOCIATES

A 6.1.a: $8\frac{5}{16}'' \times 5\frac{5}{8}''$

The author wishes to thank the publishers for their permission to reprint the numerous brief quotations from *Stephen Crane: A Study in American Letters*, by Thomas Beer, Copyright 1923 by Alfred A. Knopf, Inc., and from the twelve-volume collection, *The Work of Stephen Crane*, Copyright 1925-1926 by Alfred A. Knopf, Inc.

Copyright, *1950*, *by*
WILLIAM SLOANE ASSOCIATES, INC.

First Printing

Typography and format designed by
LEONARD W. BLIZARD

Manufactured in the United States of America

Published simultaneously in Canada
by George J. McLeod, Ltd., Toronto

$[1-10]^{16}$ $[11]^8$ $[12]^{16}$

[i-x] xi-xv [xvi-xviii] [1-2] 3-47 [48-50] 51-214 [215-216] 217-260 [261-262] 263-293 [294-296] 297-331 [332] 333-347 [348-350]

Contents: p. i: '[between tapered rules] The American Men of Letters Series'. p. ii: blank. p. iii: '[first line between tapered rules] The American Men of Letters Series | BOARD OF EDITORS | JOSEPH WOOD KRUTCH, MARGARET MARSHALL, LIONEL TRILLING, | MARK VAN DOREN | ★ | PUBLISHED | [seven titles] | ★ | IN PREPARATION | [fifteen titles]'. p. iv: blank. p. v: title page. p. vi: copyright page. p. vii: '*To* EILEEN'. p. viii: blank. p. ix: table of contents. p. x: blank. pp. xi-xv: '[between tapered rules] Preface'. p. xvi: blank. p. xvii: '[between tapered rules] Stephen Crane'. p. xviii: blank. p. 1: '*One* [wavy rule] BEGINNING'. p. 2: blank. pp. 3-26: '[between tapered rules] Very Young'. pp. 27-47: '[between tapered rules] Losses, Momentum'. p. 48: blank. p. 49: '*Two* [wavy rule] MIDDLE'. p. 50: blank. pp. 51-96: '[between tapered rules] New York'. pp. 97-120: '[between tapered rules] West'. pp. 121-149: '[between tapered rules] Fame'. pp. 150-171: '[between tapered rules] Florida'. pp. 172-184: '[between tapered rules] Greece'. pp. 185-214: '[between tapered rules] England'.

A 6.1.a *Stephen Crane* 25

p. 215: '*Three* [wavy rule] END'. p. 216: blank. pp. 217-234: '[between tapered rules] Cuba'. pp. 235-260: '[between tapered rules] Brede'. p. 261: '*Four* [wavy rule] CRANE'S ART'. p. 262: blank. pp. 263-293: '[between tapered rules] Crane's Art'. p. 294: blank. p. 295: '*Five* [wavy rule] THE COLOR OF | THIS SOUL'. p. 296: blank. pp. 297-325: '[between tapered rules] The Color of This Soul'. pp. 326-331: '[between tapered rules] A Bibliographical Note'. p. 332: blank. pp. 333-343: '[between tapered rules] General Index'. pp. 344-347: '[between tapered rules] Index of Works'. pp. 348-350: blank.

Illustration: Single leaf of white (Centroid 263) glossy wove paper tipped in between pp. iv and v. Recto, blank; verso, '[black and white photograph of Crane] | *Frances Cabané Scovel Saportas* | Stephen Crane on the *Three Friends* off Cuba, 1898'.

Typography and paper: 36 ll., $6^{9}/_{16}''$ ($7^{1}/_{16}''$) × $3^{15}/_{16}''$. Text in 11-pt. Linotype Janson with 2-pt. leading. Running heads: rectos, chapter titles in italics (for example, '*Very Young*') above a tapered rule; versos, '*Stephen Crane*' above a tapered rule. Yellowish white (Centroid 92) wove paper.

Binding: Sized fine linen-cloth (304b), moderate reddish brown (Centroid 43). Front cover: '[goldstamped] CRANE'. Spine: '[goldstamped] [reading horizontally] [double rule] | [row of ornaments] | [rule] | BERRYMAN | [reading vertically from top to bottom] CRANE | [reading horizontally] [rule] [row of ornaments] | [rule] | [script] AML | [double rule] [roman] SLOANE | [double rule] | [row of ornaments] | [rule]'. Back cover: plain. Top edge and tail cut; fore edge trimmed. Yellowish white (92) wove endpapers of different stock than text paper.

Dust jacket: Glossy wove paper, $8^{9}/_{16}''$ × 21''. Front cover: '[on dark red (Centroid 16) panel with gold rules at top and bottom edges, on yellowish white (92) panel containing a dark red single-rules frame, on gold background] [within gold frame consisting of vertical rules and horizontal rows of ornaments] [gold] [first line swash] *John Berryman* | [yellowish white] STEPHEN | Crane | [gold] [script] AML | *American Men of Letters Series*'. Spine: '[on dark red panel with gold rules at top and bottom edges, bordered by yellowish white containing dark red rules, bordered by gold at top and bottom edges] [reading horizontally] [gold] [row of ornaments] | BERRYMAN | [reading vertically from top to bottom] [yellowish white] CRANE | [reading horizontally] [gold] [script] AML | [double rule] | SLOANE | [row of ornaments]'. Back cover: '[yellowish white background] [dark red] *The American Men of Letters Series* | [tapered rule] | [two-paragraph unsigned comment on series, fourteen lines] | [photograph of editorial board in tones of red and white] | *Erich Hartmann* | *Board of Editors:* JOSEPH WOOD KRUTCH, MARGARET MARSHALL, | LIONEL TRILLING, *and* MARK VAN DOREN.' Front flap: '[white (263) background] [dark red] $3.50 | *Stephen | Crane | by* JOHN BERRYMAN | [two unsigned paragraphs, comprising a seventeen-line comment on Crane's reputation and a twelve-line biographical note on JB] | *Jacket design by Oscar Ogg* | WILLIAM SLOANE ASSOCIATES | 119 West 57th Street, New York 19, N.Y.' Back flap: '[white background] [dark red] *The American Men | of Letters Series* | [tapered rule] | PUBLISHED | [seven titles] | * | IN PREPARATION | [fifteen titles] | [tapered rule] | WILLIAM SLOANE ASSO- CIATES | 119 West 57th Street New York 19'.

Publication: Unknown number of copies. Published November 10, 1950. $3.50.

Printing: Printed and bound by H. Wolff Book Manufacturing Company, New York, N.Y.

Copyright: Registered under A 49709 in the name of William Sloane Associates, New York, N.Y.

Locations: DLC (deposit-stamp November 20, 1950); ECS (dj); Lilly (dj); Lockwood; NBuU (dj); PPiU.

Note: Stephen Crane was included in William Sloane's American Men of Letters Series. The series aimed at presenting biographical and critical appraisals of American authors who had contributed to and influenced the development and growth of a national literature. The books in the series were intended to be authoritative but not definitive in covering the subjects' lives and works; the intended audience was the general reader and the student of American literature. The subjects and writers were chosen by the Board of Editors: Joseph Wood Krutch, Margaret Marshall, Lionel Trilling, and Mark Van Doren.

A 6.1.a*
English issue of American sheets [1950]

Stephen Crane

John Berryman

METHUEN & CO. LTD. LONDON
36 Essex Street, Strand, W.C.2

A 6.1.a*: 8¼" × 5⁷⁄₁₆"

Same collation and pagination as in the first American printing.

Contents: p. i: '[between tapered rules] *The American Men of Letters Series*'. p. ii: blank. p. iii: names of editors and list of titles published and titles in preparation for the series. p. iv: blank. p. v: title page. p. vi: copyright page. p. vii: dedication. p. viii: blank. p. ix: table of contents. p. x: blank. pp. xi–xv: preface. p. xvi: blank. p. xvii: half title. p. xviii: blank. p. 1: '*One* [wavy rule] BEGINNING'. p. 2: blank. pp. 3–47: text, headed 'Very Young' and 'Losses, Momentum'. p. 48: blank. p. 49: '*Two* [wavy rule] MIDDLE'. p. 50: blank. pp. 51–214: text, headed, 'New York', 'West', 'Fame', 'Florida', 'Greece', and 'England'. p. 215: '*Three* [wavy rule] END'. p. 216: blank. pp. 217–260: text, headed 'Cuba' and 'Brede'. p. 261: '*Four* [wavy rule] CRANE'S ART'. p. 262: blank. pp. 263–293: text, p. 294: blank. p. 295: '*Five* [wavy rule] THE COLOR OF | THIS SOUL'. p. 296: blank. pp. 297–325: text. pp. 326–331: bibliographical note. p. 332: blank. pp. 333–343: general index. pp. 344–347: index of works. pp. 348–350: blank.

Illustration: Same as in the first American printing.

Typography and paper: Same as in the first American printing.

Binding: Sized calico-cloth (302), deep purplish blue (Centroid 197). Front cover: plain. Spine: '[reading horizontally] [goldstamped] [double rule] | AMERICAN | MEN OF LETTERS | SERIES | [double rule] | STEPHEN | CRANE | John | Berryman | METHUEN'. Back cover: plain. All edges cut; top edge dyed dark blue (183). Yellowish white (92) endpapers of different stock than text paper.

Dust jacket: Light bluish gray (Centroid 190) wove paper, 8½" × 20". Front cover: '[deep reddish orange (36)] Stephen | CRANE | [dark purplish blue (201)] by | John Berryman | [ornament in deep reddish orange and dark purplish blue] | [deep reddish orange] AMERICAN MEN OF LETTERS SE-

A 6.1.a* *Stephen Crane*

RIES'. Spine: '[reading horizontally] [dark purplish blue] [double rule] | AMERICAN | MEN OF LETTERS | SERIES | [double rule] | [deep reddish orange] STEPHEN | CRANE | [dark purplish blue] by | John | Berryman | METHUEN'. Back cover: '[deep reddish orange] AMERICAN MEN OF LETTERS SERIES | [dark purplish blue] [ornamental rule] [seven-line unsigned note on the series] | The following volumes have already been published: | [deep reddish orange] NATHANIEL HAWTHORNE | [dark purplish blue] *by Mark Van Doren* | [three-line quotation from a comment by Stephen Spender and two-line quotation from a comment by L. P. Hartley] | [deep reddish orange] HERMAN MELVILLE | [dark purplish blue] *by Newton Arvin* | [two-line quotation from a comment in the *Cambridge Review*] | [deep reddish orange] HENRY DAVID THOREAU | [dark purplish blue] *by Joseph Wood Krutch* | [one-line quotation from a comment in the *Spectator*] | [deep reddish orange] EDWIN ARLINGTON ROBINSON | [dark purplish blue] *by Emery Neff* | [two-line quotation from a comment in the *Manchester Guardian*] | [deep reddish orange] JAMES FENIMORE COOPER | [dark purplish blue] *by James Grossman* | [one-line quotation from a comment in *Nineteenth Century*] | [ornamental rule] | [deep reddish orange] METHUEN: LONDON | [dark purplish blue] [the letters "UBD," with the "B" within the "D" and the "D" formed by a curved line with its ends looped around the top and bottom of the right vertical stroke of the "U"]'. Front flap: '[deep reddish orange] STEPHEN | CRANE | [dark purplish blue] *by John Berryman* | [twenty-five-line unsigned comment on Crane's reputation] | [ten-line biographical note on JB, first two words, "JOHN BERRYMAN," in deep reddish orange] | [at left] CAT. NO. 5205[/]U | [lower right corner cut off]'. Back flap: '[deep reddish orange] AMERICAN MEN OF LETTERS | SERIES | [dark purplish blue] The following is a list of volumes in | preparation: | [eleven titles and authors, fourteen lines]'.

Publication: 738 copies. Published May 3, 1951. 15s.

Printing: Printed by H. Wolff Book Manufacturing Company, New York, N.Y. Binder not known.[2]

Locations: BM (deposit-stamp May 9, 1951); ECS.

---

2. In a letter of August 7, 1972, Catherine Jones of Eyre Methuen Ltd. wrote that the sheets were imported from William Sloane Associates and that the book went out of print on August 6, 1958.

A 6.1.b
Second printing: New York: William Sloane Associates, [1950].
On copyright page: *'Second printing'*.

A 6.1.c
Third printing (World Publishing Company)

STEPHEN | CRANE | [tapered rule] | JOHN BERRYMAN | [tapered rule] | Meridian Books | THE WORLD PUBLISHING COMPANY | Cleveland and New York

On copyright page: 'First Meridian printing February 1962 | MCP 262'.

Binding: Perfect binding, in printed wrappers.

Publication: Unknown number of copies. Published February 1962. $1.65.

Text: First publication of "Preface to the Meridian Edition," pp. ix-xii, and "Additional Bibliography (1962)," pp. 331-332. See B 18.

Location: ECS.

Note: Copies of the Meridian reprint were bound in cloth (with the printed wrappers removed) by Peter Smith, Gloucester, Mass., in 1967 and offered for sale at $3.75. No alterations in title and copyright pages or contents have been noted in the copies examined.

A 7 HOMAGE TO MISTRESS BRADSTREET

A 7.1.a
First edition, first printing [1956]

> Homage to
> MISTRESS
> BRADSTREET
>
> *By* John Berryman
>
> *With Pictures by* BEN SHAHN
>
> New York · FARRAR · STRAUS & CUDAHY

A 7.1.a: First three lines in strong red (Centroid 12); $9\frac{3}{8}'' \times 6\frac{1}{4}''$

A 7.1.a *Homage to Mistress Bradstreet*

> © 1956 by John Berryman
> Library of Congress
> catalog card number 56-6168
> First printing, 1956
>
> Published simultaneously in Canada
> by Ambassador Books, Ltd., Toronto.
> Manufactured in the U. S. A.

$[1]^8 \ [2]^{10} \ [3]^8$

[1-52]

Contents: p. 1: blank, p. 2: 'by the same author | [two titles]'. p. 3: title page. p. 4: copyright page. p. 5: acknowledgments, eight lines. p. 6: blank. p. 7: '[rule] | Homage to | MISTRESS | BRADSTREET | [rule] | [bracket] Born 1612 Anne Dudley, married at | 16 Simon Bradstreet, a Cambridge | man, steward to the Countess of War-|wick & protégé of her father Thomas | Dudley secretary to the Earl of Lin-|coln. Crossed in the *Arbella*, 1630, | under Governor Winthrop. [bracket] | [rule]'. p. 8: illustration. pp. 9–45: '[rule] | Homage to | MISTRESS | BRAD- STREET | [rule]'. p. 46: blank. pp. 47–49: '[rule] | Notes | [rule]'. pp. 50–52: blank.

Items included: One poem in fifty-seven numbered stanzas.

Illustrations: Ten drawings, all in black and white, occur in the text as follows: pp. 8, 15, 18 (half page), 19 (half page), 23, 28, 33, 37, 41 (half page), and 44. All drawings except that on p. 18 are signed by Ben Shahn.

Typography and paper: The typical text page consists of two eight-line stanzas, each stanza set between rules and each measuring $2^1/_{16}''$ ($3^1/_{16}''$) $\times 4^1/_2''$; notes, 34 ll., $6^3/_{16}'' \times 4''$. Text in 13-pt. Berthold Walbaum with 6-pt. leading; notes in 10-pt. with 2-pt. leading. The stanzas are numbered from 1 to 57 in arabic with each number preceded by three periods (for example, '. . . 1'). Yellowish white (Centroid 92) laid paper (chain lines running vertically, spaced $^{27}/_{32}''$).

Binding: Paper-covered boards. Front cover: on light grayish yellowish brown (Centroid 79) background, close-up of the drawing of a wooden house with bare trees in the background which appears on p. 8. Spine: '[reading vertically from top to bottom] [deep reddish orange (36) background] [light grayish yellowish brown] BERRYMAN [thick rule] Homage to Mistress Bradstreet [black (267)] FARRAR, STRAUS | & CUDAHY'. Back cover: same as front cover. All edges cut; top edge dyed

A 7.1.c *Homage to Mistress Bradstreet* 33

deep reddish orange. Yellowish white (92) laid endpapers (chain lines running vertically, spaced $^{27}/_{32}''$) of different stock than text paper.

Dust jacket: Light grayish yellowish brown (Centroid 79) laid paper (chain lines running vertically, spaced $^{15}/_{16}''$), $9^{1}/_{2}'' \times 20^{1}/_{8}''$. Front cover: same drawing as on boards; '[above house, at right edge of cover] [on deep reddish orange (36) panel with light grayish yellowish brown border at left, top, and bottom] [light grayish yellowish brown] JOHN BERRYMAN | Homage to | Mistress Bradstreet | *A poem, with pictures by* Ben Shahn'. Spine: same as on boards. Back cover: same as on boards. Front flap: 'Homage to | Mistress Bradstreet | by JOHN BERRYMAN | [six-line quotation from a comment by Conrad Aiken] | *Illustrated by* | BEN SHAHN | $3.75'. Back flap: '[fourteen-line unsigned biographical note] | FARRAR, STRAUS & CUDAHY | 101 Fifth Avenue | New York 3, N.Y.'

Text: First book appearance of *Homage to Mistress Bradstreet*. The notes to the poem had not been previously published.

Publication: Unknown number of copies. Published October 1, 1956. $3.75.

Printing: Printed and bound by Peter Pauper Press, Mt. Vernon, N.Y.

Copyright: Registered under A 259934 in the name of JB.

Locations: DLC (deposit-stamp November 5, 1956); ECS (dj); Lilly (dj); Lockwood (dj); NBuU (dj); PPi (dj); PPiU; PSt. (dj).

Note one: The text and notes of the poem are included in the collection *HomageAOP* (see A 9); the text of the poem without the notes is included in *SelP* (see A 23).

Note two: There are German and Italian translations of *Homage to Mistress Bradstreet*, but neither has been seen. They are *Huldigung für Mistress Bradstreet*, translated by Gertrude C. Schwebell (Hamburg: Hoffman u. Campe, 1967) and *Omaggio a Mistress Bradstreet*, translated by Sergio Perosa (Torino: Einaude, 1969).

A 7.1.b
Second printing: New York: Farrar, Straus and Company, [1964]. On copyright page: '*First printing, 1956* | *Second printing, 1964*'. Printed paper-covered boards.

A 7.1.c
Third printing: New York: Farrar, Straus and Giroux, [1967].

On copyright page: *'First printing, 1956 | Second printing, 1964 | Third printing, 1967'*. Printed paper-covered boards.

A 7.1.d
Fourth printing: New York: Farrar, Straus and Giroux, [1972]. On copyright page: *'Fourth printing, 1972'*. Printed paper-covered boards.

A 8 HIS THOUGHT MADE POCKETS & THE PLANE BUCKT

A 8.1.a
First edition, first printing, first issue (1958)

> Henry sats in de plane & was gay.
> Careful Henry nothing said aloud
> but where a virgin out of cloud
> to her Mountain dropt in light
> his thought made pockets & the plane buckt.
> 'Parm me, Lady.' 'Orright.'
>
> His Thought Made Pockets & The Plane Buckt
> by John Berryman
>
> to Ann
> of dxxvi copies, all on Nideggen; this is
> copyright mcmlviii by John Berryman
> Claude Fredericks / Pawlet / mcmlviii
>
> i, Venice, 182—
> ii, Scots Poem
> ii, Sonnet xxv
> iii, The Mysteries
> v, They Have
> v, The Poet's Final Instructions
> vi, from The Black Book
> ix, A Sympathy, A Welcome
> ix, Not to Live
> x, American Lights, Seen from Off Abroad
> xii, Note to Wang Wei

A 8.1.a: Line 7 in strong orange (Centroid 50); $9\frac{1}{2}'' \times 6\frac{1}{4}''$

A 8.1.a *Thought*

[1]⁸

[A–B] i–xi [xii–xiv]

Contents: p. A: title page. p. B: blank. p. i: 'Venice, 182–'. p. ii: 'scots poem' and first six lines of 'sonnet xxv'. p. iii: last eight lines of 'sonnet xxv' and first sixteen lines of 'the mysteries (a crazed man calls)'. p. iv: concluding twenty-six lines of 'the mysteries (a crazed man calls)'. p. v: 'they have' and first seven lines of 'the poet's final instructions'. p. vi: concluding seven lines of 'the poet's final instructions' and first seventeen lines of 'from The Black Book (i)'. p. vii: concluding line of 'from The Black Book (i)' and first twenty-four lines of 'from The Black Book (ii)'. p. viii: concluding sixteen lines of 'from The Black Book (ii)' and 'from The Black Book (iii). p. ix: 'a sympathy, a welcome' and 'not to live (jamestown 1957)'. pp. x–xi: 'american lights, seen from off abroad'. p. xii: concluding two lines of 'american lights, seen from off abroad', 'note to wang wei', and seven lines of acknowledgments signed 'J.B.' and within brackets. pp. xiii–xiv: blank.

Catchwords: p. iii: '[the stonechat clatters'. p. v: '[or buy'. p. xi: '[here comes'.

Typography and paper: 30 ll., 6⅜" (6⅝") × 3⅞". Text in 12-pt. ATF Garamond with 4-pt. leading; nearly all capitalized words, except initial letters of poems and some titles, set in small capitals of the font. Grayish yellow (Centroid 90) with flecks of light brown (57) laid paper (chain lines running vertically, unevenly spaced varying between 1¼" and 1½").

Numbering: The books are numbered in arabic from 1 to 500 in strong orange (Centroid 50) ink on the title page immediately after the statement 'of dxxvi copies, all on Nideggen, this is'.

Binding: White (Centroid 263) wove paper wrappers. Front cover: '[strong orange (50)] his thought made pockets & the plane buckt'. Back cover: plain. Gathering sewn into wrappers. All edges trimmed. Enclosed in manila envelope, printed at top '[strong orange] Pawlet 1 : His Thought Made Pockets &c by John Berryman'.

Text: First publication of "They Have," "The Poet's Final Instructions," and "from The Black Book (iii)." First book appearance of all other poems except "The Mysteries." The epigraph on the title page was later printed as the second stanza of Dream Song 5.

Publication: 500 copies. Published December 15, 1958. $2.00.

A 8.1.a* *Thought*

Printing: Printed in the fall of 1958 by Claude Fredericks from hand-set type at his private press in Pawlet, Vt. Hand bound by Fredericks.

Copyright: Registered under A 375541 in the name of JB.

Locations: DLC (deposit-stamp January 16, 1959); ECS; Lilly; Lockwood; NBu; PPiU; PSt.

A 8.1.a*
Second issue

Same collation and pagination as in numbered copies.

Contents: Same as in numbered copies.

Typography and paper: Same as in numbered copies.

Lettering: The books are lettered from a to z in black ink on the title page immediately after the statement 'of dxxvi copies, all on Nideggen, this is'.

Binding: Spine and $7/16''$ of boards in calfskin, deep brown (Centroid 56); remainder of boards covered with white (263) paper as used for wrappers. Front cover: plain. Spine: '[reading vertically from top to bottom] [goldstamped] HIS THOUGHT MADE POCKETS &C, BY JOHN BERRYMAN'. Back cover: plain. Binder's leaves, of the same stock as the text paper, are inserted at the front and back, each insertion consisting of one gathering of four leaves, with the outer leaves pasted down as endpapers; JB's signature in black ink over a strong orange (Centroid 50) background appears on the recto of the fourth leaf of the front gathering. Enclosed in manila envelope, printed as in numbered copies.

Publication: 26 copies. Published December 15, 1958. $10.00.

Printing: Printed in the fall of 1958 by Claude Fredericks from hand-set type at his private press in Pawlet, Vt. Hand bound by Arno Werner in Pittsfield, Mass.

Location: CF; Meissner.

Note one: The use of the term *issue* in the instance of this publication may be considered problematical and its use should be explained. During a telephone conversation on June 28, 1973, Mr. Fredericks indicated that both the numbered and lettered copies are part of a single printing. Since there is no question of the reimposition of type, the numbered and lettered copies must be considered either as states or issues since they occur within a printing. The copies can be distinguished by binding, but binding variants do not, of course, constitute states or issues. Conservatively speaking, the twenty-six lettered copies might be referred to as *states* since the copies were lettered as stop-press corrections; but no other alterations were made in the text. On the other hand, the twenty-six copies might be referred to as an *issue* since they were altered in a manner that affects the circumstances of publication; but there was no cancellation of the title page or preliminary matter. Further, states are usually created prior to publication and issues after publication. Since neither set of criteria can be applied strictly, the term *issue* has been used here to indicate that some copies of the printing were altered in a way that affected the circumstances of publication.

Note two: His Thought Made Pockets & The Plane Buckt was the first in a projected series of new writing called the Pawlet Pamphlets to be issued by Claude Fredericks. The only other pamphlet published in the series was *Poems Written in Berlin* by Barbara Gibbs.

Note three: Claude Fredericks and Milton Saul note in *A First List of Books Printed and Published by the Banyan Press* (Pawlet, Vt.: Banyan Press, 1948) that the press intended to publish "a new poem, entitled *The Black Book,* by John Berryman, with drawings by Anthony Clark" in 1949. During the June 28, 1973, telephone conversation, Mr. Fredericks said that he did not recall that the manuscript was submitted by JB. Although the poem has not been printed as a separate publication, four sections appeared in *Poetry* in 1950; two of these and a previously unpublished section were then collected in *His Thought Made Pockets & The Plane Buckt*. The "Author's Notes" in *Recovery,* p. 241, contains a reference to this work:

    I. In my old story ["The Imaginary Jew"], a confrontation as Jew is resisted, fought, failed—at last is given into *symbolically*. I identified at least with the persecution. So the 'desire' (was it?) is at least 25 years old.
   II. PLUS after that, *The Black Book*—abandoned—obsessed—perhaps now take it up again? *My position is certain.*

The publisher's footnote to JB's note states, "Three poems from *The Black Book,* a verse sequence about the Jews under Hitler, are preserved in Mr. Berryman's *Short Poems,* pages 106–9." The only other known reference by JB to the poem is in a 1966 interview:

A 8.1.a* *Thought*

I don't plan ever to do that. People ask me about it occasionally and I've never reprinted the parts of *The Black Book* that I've published, but I probably will in my next American book. The subject was—it was more than I could bear. I wrote about eight parts, I guess. It was in the form of a Mass for the Dead. It was designed to have 42 sections, and was about the Nazi murderers of the Jews. But I just found I couldn't take it. The sections published—there were eight of them in *Poetry*—are unrelievedly horrible. I wasn't able at this time—that was about twenty years ago—to find any way of making palatable the monstrosity of the thing which obsessed me. So I think what I'll do in my next book is—we're going to do a *Collected Poems* at some point—is put in those sections of *The Black Book*, but without any explanation or anything else. It was called *The Black Book* because there was a book called the *Black Book of Poland*. . . .

It's a diagnostic, an historical survey. Most of the Jews who died died in Poland or were Polish, one or the other. . . . So I think what I'll do is put those sections of *The Black Book* in the clay, just as separate sections or lyrics or whatever, but let the poem go to hell. I don't think I can do it. I don't feel I want to.[3]

---

3. Jonathan Sisson, "My Whiskers Fly: An Interview with John Berryman," *Ivory Tower*, XIV (October 3, 1966), 16.

A 9 HOMAGE TO MISTRESS BRADSTREET AND OTHER POEMS

A 9.1.a
First edition, first printing [1959]

JOHN BERRYMAN

HOMAGE TO MISTRESS BRADSTREET
And
Other Poems

FABER AND FABER LIMITED
24 Russell Square
London

A 9.1.a: $8\frac{1}{2}'' \times 5\frac{3}{8}''$

A 9.1.a *HomageAOP*

> *First published in mcmlix*
> *by Faber and Faber Limited*
> *24 Russell Square London W.C.1*
> *Printed in Great Britain by*
> *Latimer Trend & Co Ltd Plymouth*
> *All rights reserved*
>
> © *John Berryman 1959*

[A]⁸ B–F⁸ [G]⁸

[1–6] 7–8 [9–10] 11–32 [33–34] 35–60 [61–62] 63–111 [112]

Contents: p. 1: 'HOMAGE TO MISTRESS | BRADSTREET'. p. 2: blank. p. 3: title page. p. 4: copyright page. p. 5: 'To | JEFFERSON BERRYMAN'. p. 6: seven-line note on the selection of poetry for the volume, signed 'J.B.' pp. 7–8: table of contents. p. 9: 'HOMAGE TO MISTRESS | BRADSTREET | [bracket] Born 1612 Anne Dudley, married at 16 | Simon Bradstreet, a Cambridge man, | steward to the Countess of Warwick and | protégé of her father Thomas Dudley | secretary to the Earl of Lincoln. Crossed | in the *Arbella*, 1630, under Governor | Winthrop. [bracket]'. p. 10: acknowledgments for title poem, seven lines. pp. 11–29: *'Homage to Mistress Bradstreet'*. pp. 30–32: 'Notes'. p. 33: 'EARLY POEMS'. p. 34: blank. pp. 35–60: text. p. 61: 'LATER POEMS'. p. 62: blank. pp. 63–111: text. p. 112: blank.

Items included: Homage to Mistress Bradstreet; Notes. EARLY POEMS: Winter Landscape; The Statue; The Disciple; The Traveller; The Spinning Heart; Parting as Descent; Cloud and Flame; Letter to His Brother; Desires of Men and Women; World-Telegram; Ancestor; The Animal Trainer (1); The Animal Trainer (2); 1 September 1939; Desire Is a World by Night; The Moon and the Night and the Men. LATER POEMS: The Ball Poem; Canto Amor; The Enemies of the Angels; Boston Common; The Nervous Songs (Young Woman's Song; The Song of the Demented Priest; The Song of the Young Hawaiian; A Professor's Song; The Captain's Song; The Song of the Tortured Girl; The Song of the Bridegroom; Song of the Man Forsaken and Obsessed; The Pacifist's Song); Surviving Love; The Lightning; Fare Well; Rock-Study with Wanderer; Whether There Is Sorrow in the Demons; The Long Home; A Winter-Piece to a Friend Away; New Year's Eve; Narcissus Moving; The Dispossessed; Venice, 182–; Scots Poem; Sonnet 25: Not To Live; They Have; A Sympathy, A Welcome; Note to Wang Wei.

Typography and paper: 34 ll., 6⅜″ (6¹¹⁄₁₆″) × 3¾″. Text in 11-pt. Centaur with 3-pt. leading. Yellowish white (Centroid 92) wove paper.

Binding: Sized calico-cloth (302), moderate bluish green (Centroid 164). Front cover: plain. Spine: [reading vertically from top to bottom] [stamped in white (263)] [at top of spine] HOMAGE TO MISTRESS BRADSTREET | JOHN BERRYMAN | [at bottom of spine] FABER | AND FABER'. Back cover: plain. All edges cut. Yellowish white (92) wove endpapers of different stock than text paper.

Dust jacket: Light greenish blue (Centroid 172) wove paper, 8¾″ × 18⁷⁄₁₆″. Front cover: 'HOMAGE | TO | MISTRESS | BRADSTREET | [deep reddish orange (36)] [thick rule] | [black (267)] by | John | Berryman'. Spine: '[reading vertically from top to bottom] Homage to Mistress Bradstreet [deep reddish orange] · [black] Berryman | [reading horizontally] Faber'. Back cover: 'SOME FABER POETRY | Ezra Pound | [six titles, seven lines] | W. H. Auden | [nine titles] | Marianne Moore | [three titles] | Wallace Stevens | [three titles] | Randall Jarrell | [one title] | Robert Lowell | [one title] | Richard Wilbur | [two titles, three lines] | FABER AND FABER LTD 24 RUSELL SQ LONDON WCl'. Front flap: 'Homage to | Mistress Bradstreet | *and other poems* | by | JOHN BERRYMAN | [two unsigned paragraphs, comprising a fifteen-line note on JB's reputation containing quotations from comments on the title poem by Edmund Wilson and Conrad Aiken and a four-line note on the selection of poems for the book] | 18s | *net*'. Back flap: list of four anthologies with names of editors and prices (twelve-line comment from a quotation by Cyril Connolly for the first anthology listed, *The Faber Book of Modern American Verse*, ed. W. H. Auden) and four-line advertisement for catalogue.

Text: This selection of poetry made by JB himself includes the title poem and notes, thirty-nine poems from *The Dispossessed*, and seven poems from *His Thought Made Pockets & The Plane Buckt* (A 7, A 4, A 8). No first-book material.

Publication: 1,000 copies. Published April 24, 1959. 18s.

Printing: Printed by offset by Whitstable Litho, Whitstable, Kent. Bound by Nevett, Key, and Whiting Ltd., London.

Locations: BM (deposit-stamp April 1, 1959); ECS (dj).

A 9.1.a *HomageAOP* 43

Note one: Variants and revisions in thirty-three poems between their appearances in the collections indicated and in *HomageAOP* are noted as follows:

"Homage to Mistress Bradstreet," *Homage*
    l. 3:   woman.–   [woman –
    l. 24:   &   [and
    l. 135:   short.   [short,
    l. 273:   I   am   [I am
    l. 305:   faints–   [faints
"Winter Landscape," *TD*
    l. 3:   trees,   [trees
"The Statue," *TD*
    l. 32:   wreck and   [sleepless
"The Disciple," *TD*
    l. 4:   bring   [lag
    l. 8:   dead and   [dead,
    l. 11:   compassion, and   [compassion,
"The Spinning Heart," *TD*
    l. 35:   superstitions   [superstitious
    l. 47:   big as   [big
"Letter to His Brother," *TD*
    l. 4:   and of a few   [imagining
    l. 10:   rubber   [yellow
    l. 11:   the pavement   [his altar
    l. 12:   my hopeful   [or hungry
    l. 30:   its   [an
"World-Telegram," *TD*
    l. 37:   disorder   [disorders
"Ancestor," *TD*
    l. 7:   . Crossing   [. . Crossing
    l. 10:   ['Terrific & murderous' the Northern
        fire,
    l. 15:   half-forgotten   [a half-forgotten
    l. 25:   silence . .   [silence
"Desire Is a World by Night," *TD*
    l. 5:   wince   [wtnce
    l. 7:   mince   [mincn
"The Moon and the Night and the Men," *TD*
    l. 24:   'Hurt   ['. . hurt
"The Ball Poem," *TD*
    l. 18:   up   [up.
"Canto Amor," *TD*
    l. 55:   rapt   [rapt,

"The Enemies of the Angels," *TD*
  l. 30: "Sister Rough" ['Sister Rough'
  l. 60: "Jerk, what do you know?" ['Jerk, what do you know?'

"Boston Common," *TD*
  l. 65: "Accidents of history, memorials"— ['Accidents of history, memorials'—
  l. 66: "I ['I
  l. 72: live." [live.'
  l. 78: soaring Beethoven's.—Lost, lost [Beethoven's.—Lost, lost!
  l. 79: flung [hung

"Young Woman's Song," *TD*
  l. 7: fierce [free

"The Captain's Song," *TD*
  l. 12: darted [spurted

"The Song of the Tortured Girl," *TD*
  l. 7: "Nothing worse now can come to us" ['Nothing worse now can come to us'
  l. 9: broke [cracked

"Song of the Man Forsaken and Obsessed," *TD*
  l. 18: vivid [bloody

"The Pacifist's Song," *TD*
  l. 9: "Kill not .. Your ill from evil comes .. Bear all";— ['Kill not .. Your ill from evil comes .. Bear all';—

"The Lightning," *TD*
  l. 14: chocolate, [choclate,

"Rock-Study with Wanderer," *TD*
  l. 34: loose [loose,
  l. 52: And [To
  l. 57: Draw [Draw,
  l. 63: speak ... [speak ..

"Whether There Is Sorrow in the Demons," *TD*
  l. 30: rehearse ... [rehearse ..
  l. 33: breaks [cracks

"The Long Home," *TD*
  l. 49: "You ['You
  l. 54: heir." [heir.'
  l. 77: come. [come,

"A Winter-Piece to a Friend Away," *TD*
  l. 10: year: [year;
  l. 18: instruct .. Unless [instruct .. Unless

"New Year's Eve," *TD*
  l. 30: beneath : eye [beneath: eye
  l. 47: Soon soon [Soon O

A 9.1.a *HomageAOP* 45

"Narcissus Moving," *TD*
  l. 36: Une [Un
"Venice, 182–," *Thought*
  l. 3: the corners of her eyes are white. i miss, [The corners of her eyes are white. I miss.
  l. 4: she [She
  l. 6: hell [Hell
  l. 8: less [Less
  l. 11: i hear her howl now, and i [I hear her howl now, and I
  l. 12: foul [Foul
  l. 13: on [On
  l. 15: now [Now
  l. 16: pulling . . . i [pulling . . I
  l. 19: i [I
  l. 23: i [I
  l. 25: àre in love. the light hurts. 'there . . .' [are in love. The light hurts. 'There . .'
"Scots Poem," *Thought*
  l. 3: weel, [Weel,
  l. 5: peered [Peered
  l. 7: love [Love
  l. 11: braird [Braird
  l. 12: i'm [I'm
  l. 15: 'come forth, isobel mitchel, ['Come forth, Isobel Mitchel,
  l. 16: william matheson [William Matheson
"Sonnet 25," *Thought*
  l. 2: i [I
  l. 3: i [I
  l. 4: i [I
  l. 8: 'hopeless'. lockt in & humming, the captain's ['Hopeless'. Lockt in & humming, the Captain's
  l. 9: lies [Lies
  l. 11: jolly roger. wind [Jolly Roger. Wind
"Not To Live," *Thought*
  l. 2: king. i [King. I
  l. 4: i find. ghost [I find. Ghost
  l. 6: howls [Howls
  l. 7: i love the king [I love the King
  l. 10: god be with him. he & god [God be with him. He & God
  l. 11: i [I
  l. 12: thing . . . . [thing . .
  l. 13: from [From

l. 14:   God save the King.   [God save the King.
"They Have," *Thought*
   l. 1:   o   [O
   l. 6:   i   [I
   l. 8:   that   [That
   l. 9:   mâcon: i   [Macon: I
   l. 11:   now   [But
   l. 12:   i   [I
   l. 13:   but   [But
   l. 14:   i   [I
   l. 16:   the   [The
   l. 17:   they   [They
"A Sympathy, A Welcome," *Thought*
   l. 1:   i   [I
   l. 2:   paul,   [Paul,
   l. 3:   i   [I
   l. 4:   yet   [Yet
   l. 7:   not   [*not*
   l. 9:   paul,   [Paul,
"Note to Wang Wei," *Thought*
   l. 2:   disheveled,   [dishevelled,
   l. 3:   it   [It
   l. 5:   it   [It
   l. 6:   it   [It
   l. 7:   makes   [Makes
   l. 8:   (i'm reconfirming, god   [(I'm reconfirming, God
   l. 10:   i   [I
   l. 12:   be   [Be

Note two: In *TD* the stanzas of "Boston Common" are numbered from I to XVIII in roman numerals; in *HomageAOP* they are numbered from 1 to 18 in arabic numerals.

Note three: Variants in titles of poems between their previous appearances and in *HomageAOP* are noted as follows:

Desire Is a World by Night   [*Desire is a World by Night*
Rock-Study with Wanderer   [*Rock-study with Wanderer*
A Winter-Piece to a Friend Away   [*A Winter-piece to a Friend Away*
scots poem   [*Scots Poem*
sonnet xxv   [*Sonnet 25*
not to live   [*Not To Live*
they have   [*They Have*
a sympathy, a welcome   [*A Sympathy, A Welcome*
note to wang wei   [*Note to Wang Wei*

A 9.1.b *HomageAOP* 47

A 9.1.a†
Proof copy

8½" × 5⁹⁄₁₆"

[A]⁸ B–G⁸

[1–8] 9–10 [11–12] 13–34 [35–36] 37–62 [63–64] 65–112

Contents: pp. 1–2: blank. p. 3: 'HOMAGE TO MISTRESS | BRADSTREET'. p. 4: blank. p. 5: title page. p. 6: copyright page. p. 7: dedication. p. 8: six-line note on the selection of poetry for the volume, signed 'J.B.' pp. 9–10: table of contents. p. 11: 'HOMAGE TO MISTRESS | BRADSTREET | [seven-line note on the title poem, within brackets]'. p. 12: acknowledgments for title poem, seven lines. pp. 13–31: *'Homage to Mistress Bradstreet'*. pp. 32–34: *'Notes'*. p. 35: 'EARLY POEMS'. p. 36: blank. pp. 37–62: text. p. 63: 'LATER POEMS'. p. 64: blank. pp. 65–112: text.

Items included: Same as in first printing.

Typography and paper: Same typography as in first printing. Yellowish white (Centroid 92) wove paper of different stock than first printing.

Binding: Dark grayish green (Centroid 151) wove paper wrappers with strains of light green (144). Front cover: 'JOHN BERRYMAN | [rule] | HOMAGE | TO | MISTRESS | BRADSTREET | *And* | *Other Poems* | [next two words between oblique thick rules] PROOF COPY | [reading horizontally] FABER AND FABER LIMITED | 24 Russell Square | London'. Spine: '[reading vertically from bottom to top] HOMAGE TO MISTRESS BRADSTREET'. Back cover: plain. All edges cut. Cover cut flush.

Location: Lilly.

A 9.1.b
Second printing: London: Faber and Faber, [1967]. On copyright page: *'Second impression mcmlxvii'*.

A 9.1.c
First American reprint [1968]

JOHN BERRYMAN

Homage to

Mistress

Bradstreet

AND

Other Poems

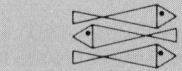

THE NOONDAY PRESS

A DIVISION OF

Farrar, Straus & Giroux

NEW YORK

A 9.1.c: 8″ × 5⁵⁄₁₆″

A 9.1.c *HomageAOP*

> Copyright © 1948, 1956, 1958, 1959,
> 1967, 1968 by John Berryman
> Library of Congress catalog card number: 68–24596
> All rights reserved
> First printing, 1968
> Published simultaneously in Canada by
> Ambassador Books, Ltd., Rexdale, Ontario
> Printed in the United States of America

56 leaves (perfect binding).

Same pagination as in the first English printing.

Contents: p. 1: '*Homage to Mistress Bradstreet* | AND OTHER POEMS'. p. 2: '*by John Berryman* | [eight titles, nine lines]'. p. 3: title page. p. 4: copyright page. p. 5: '*Note* | [ten-line note on the selection of poetry for the volume] | J.B.'. p. 6: blank. pp. 7–8: table of contents. p. 9: '*Homage to Mistress Bradstreet* | AND OTHER POEMS'. p. 10: note for title poem. pp. 11–29: '*Homage to Mistress Bradstreet*'. pp. 30–32: '*Notes*'. p. 33: 'EARLY POEMS'. p. 34: blank. pp. 35–60: text. p. 61: 'LATER POEMS'. p. 62: blank. pp. 63–111: text. p. 112: blank.

Items included: Same as in the first English printing.

Typography and paper: Same typography as in the first English printing. Yellowish white (Centroid 92) wove paper.

Binding: Perfect binding. White (Centroid 263) wove paper wrappers, outside glossy. Front cover: '*Homage to* | *Mistress Bradstreet* | *and other poems* | [deep reddish orange (36)] JOHN BERRYMAN | [black (267)] [drawing of a Jack's pulpit which appears on p. 15 of *Homage* (A 7), signed by Ben Shahn] | [deep reddish orange] NOONDAY 337 $1.95'. Spine: '[reading vertically from top to bottom] *Homage to Mistress Bradstreet* [deep reddish orange] BERRYMAN [black] [device] N 337'. Back cover: '[at left] N 337 – Poetry [at right] $1.95 | JOHN BERRYMAN | [deep reddish orange] *Homage to Mistress Bradstreet* | *and Other Poems* | [black] [six-line unsigned note on the selection of poems in the volume] | HOMAGE TO MISTRESS BRADSTREET | [one-line quotation from a comment by Robert Fitzgerald, one-line quotation from a comment in *The Times Literary Supplement*, and two-line quotation from a comment by Edmund Wilson] | SHORT POEMS | [seven-line quotation from a comment by Conrad Aiken] | COVER DRAWING BY BEN SHAHN | *Cover design by Kay Eaglin* | [deep reddish orange] THE NOONDAY PRESS | 19 Union Square West | New York 10003'. All edges cut. Cover cut flush.

Text: Includes a new note by JB on the poems in the selection.

Publication: Unknown number of copies. Published October 29, 1968. $1.95.

Printing: Printed and bound by Murray Printing Company, Forge Village, Mass.

Copyright: No copyright application filed.

Location: ECS.

A 9.1.d
Second printing: New York: Farrar, Straus and Giroux, [1969].
On copyright page: '*Second printing, 1969*'. Printed wrappers.

A 9.1.e
Third printing: New York: Farrar, Straus and Giroux, [1970].
On copyright page: '*Third printing, 1970*'. Printed wrappers.

A 9.1.f
Fourth printing: New York: Farrar, Straus and Giroux, [1973].
On copyright page: '*Fourth printing, 1973*'. Printed wrappers.

A 10 THE ARTS OF READING

A 10.1.a
First edition, first printing [1960]

> Ralph Ross, John Berryman, and Allen Tate
> UNIVERSITY OF MINNESOTA
>
> **The Arts of Reading**
>
> THOMAS Y. CROWELL COMPANY
> *New York · Established 1834*

A 10.1.a: $8\tfrac{3}{8}'' \times 5\tfrac{9}{16}''$

> Copyright © 1960 by Thomas Y. Crowell Company
> All Rights Reserved
>
> No part of this book may be reproduced in any form, by mimeograph or any other means, without permission in writing from the publisher, except by a reviewer, who may quote brief passages in a review to be published in a magazine or newspaper.
>
> Designed by Laurel Wagner
>
> Library of Congress Catalog Card Number: 60-7127
>
> Manufactured in the United States of America by Vail-Ballou Press, Inc., Binghamton, N.Y.
>
> ACKNOWLEDGMENTS
>
> Acknowledgment is gratefully made as follows (on pp. iv-vii) to reprint copyrighted material:
>
> Aristotle, *Nicomachean Ethics:* Translation by Richard McKeon in *The Basic Works of Aristotle* reprinted by permission of the Clarendon Press, Oxford.
>
> Isaak Babel, "In Odessa": Reprinted from *Benya Krik, the Gangster,* by Isaak Babel, by permission of Schocken Books, New York, copyright 1948 by Schocken Books, New York.
>
> Arnold Bennett, from *The Old Wives' Tale:* Reprinted from *The Old Wives' Tale* by Arnold Bennett, by permission of Doubleday & Company, Inc., the owner of the copyright in Arnold Bennett's *The Old Wives' Tale,* and A. P. Watt & Son.
>
> Jacob Burkhardt: From *Judgments on History and Historians* (Boston: Beacon Press, 1958) reprinted by permission of the publisher. From *Force and Freedom* (Pantheon Books, Inc.) reprinted by permission of the publisher.

[1-16][16]

[A-B] [i-iv] v-vii [viii-x] xi-xiv [xv-xvi] 1-5 [6-8] 9-193 [194-196] 197-467 [468] 469-488 [489-494]

Contents: pp. A-B: blank. p. i: '[leaf] THE ARTS OF READING'. p. ii: blank. p. iii: title page. p. iv: copyright page. pp. v-vii: acknowledgments. p. viii: blank. p. ix: ten-line unsigned note listing the sections for which each editor was responsible. p. x: blank. pp. xi-xiv: table of contents, p. xv: '[leaf] THE ARTS OF READING'. p. xvi: blank. pp. 1-5: 'Introduction'. p. 6: blank. p. 7: '[leaf] PART I | *Exposition and Argument*'. p. 8: blank. pp. 9-37: '[leaf] *Section One* | Writing, Good and Bad'. pp. 38-123: '[leaf] *Section Two* | Politics'. pp. 124-159: '[leaf] *Section Three* | Reflections'. pp. 160-182: '[leaf] *Section Four* | Literary Criticism'. pp. 183-193: '[leaf] *Final Exercises for Part I*'. p. 194: blank. p. 195: '[leaf] PART II | *Imaginative Writing*'. p. 196: blank. pp. 197-297: '[leaf] *Section One* | Fiction.' pp. 298-357: '[leaf] *Section Two* | Poetry'. pp. 358-467: '[leaf] *Section Three* | Drama'. p. 468: blank. pp. 469-480: 'Glossary of Terms | and Principles'. pp. 481-488: 'Index'. pp. 489-494: blank.

A 10.1.a *The Arts of Reading*

Items by JB included:[4] PART II: IMAGINATIVE WRITING; SECTION ONE: FICTION: commentary on Isaak Babel's "In Odessa"; definitions of twenty-four terms; commentary on Ernest Hemingway's "A Clean, Well-Lighted Place"; definitions of five terms; eleven questions on James Joyce's "Araby"; definitions of two terms; seven questions on O. Henry's "The Gift of the Magi"; definitions of three terms; six questions on Franz Kafka's "A Fratricide"; commentary on Stephen Crane's "The Open Boat"; definitions of four terms; nine questions on Franz Kafka's "An Imperial Message," "Before the Law" (selection from *The Trial*), and "Courier"; definitions of two terms. SECTION TWO: POETRY: comment and fourteen questions on Alun Lewis's "Song: (On seeing dead bodies floating off the Cape)"; definitions of four terms; comment and six questions on William Wordsworth's "Sonnet" ("Surprised by joy—impatient as the Wind"); definitions of four terms; comment and five questions on "A Handsome Young Airman"; comment and seventeen questions on "The Twa Corbies"; definitions of three terms; fourteen questions on Walter De la Mare's "The Song of the Mad Prince"; commentary on T. S. Eliot's "The Love Song of J. Alfred Prufrock"; definitions of seven terms; 'A Note' on W. B. Yeats's "Sailing to Byzantium"; comment and eight questions on Dylan Thomas's "A Refusal to Mourn the Death, by Fire, of a Child in London"; definition of one term; comment and eight questions on a speech from William Shakespeare's *Pericles, Prince of Tyre* (III.i.57–65). SECTION THREE: DRAMA: commentary on William Shakespeare's *The Tragedy of Macbeth;* definitions of thirteen terms; nine questions on Anton Chekhov's "A Marriage Proposal"; definitions of three terms.

Typography and paper: Anthology selections, 36 ll.; commentaries, 42 ll.; $6^{7}/_{16}''$ ($6^{11}/_{16}''$) × $4^{1}/_{8}''$. Text of selections in 10-pt. Times

---

4. The editors' note on p. ix reads in part: "Mr. Ross admits the original conception of the book and his primary responsibility for Part I. Mr. Berryman accepts his primary responsibility for Part II, with the exception of the analyses of the Marvell, Donne, Carew, and Ransom poems, for which Mr. Tate accepts responsibility." In a letter of June 3, 1973, Ralph Ross wrote, "The little note at the beginning of the book is correct, if not totally explicit," and on June 11, 1973, "The questions and definitions of terms after each one of the Berryman selections were done entirely by Berryman." The editors' writings in the book are not signed and are usually titled 'COMMENTARY', 'SOME QUESTIONS', or 'TERMS AND PRINCIPLES'. Any exception to the titles of contributions by JB has been indicated by enclosing the title in single quotation marks.

New Roman with 3-pt. leading; commentaries in 10-pt. with 1-pt. leading. Running heads: rectos, for selections followed by commentaries the name of the author in italics preceded by a bullet (for example, '· *Isaak Babel*') and for selections without commentaries the name of the author in italics (for example, '*James Joyce*'); versos, '*Exposition and Argument*' in Part I and '*Imaginative Writing*' in Part II. Yellowish white (Centroid 92) wove paper.

Binding: Sized calico-cloth (302), moderate greenish blue Centroid 173). Front cover: '[stamped in white (263)] [leaf] *Ross, Berryman, & Tate* | The Arts of | Reading'. Spine: '[reading vertically from top to bottom] [stamped in white] [leaf] *Ross, Berryman, & Tate* | The Arts of Reading | [reading horizontally] CROWELL'. Back cover: plain. All edges cut. Yellowish white (92) wove endpapers of different stock than text paper.

Dust jacket: Wove paper, outside glossy, $8\frac{5}{8}'' \times 21''$. Front cover: '[strong greenish blue (Centroid 169) background with light greenish blue (172) thick rules extending the width of the front cover arranged as indicated] [rule] | [white (263)] By Ralph Ross · John | [rule] | Berryman · Allen Tate | [rule] | [white background] [strong greenish blue] THE ARTS OF | READING | [rule] | [strong greenish blue background] [white] An anthology | [rule] | of the finest literature of all time, with | [rule] | critical comments about each selection by | [rule] | three of the most discriminating literary | [rule] | minds in America today. | [at right edge, reading vertically from bottom to top] [script] Dale | [reading horizontally] [rule]'. Spine: '[strong greenish blue background with light greenish blue thick rules extending the width of the spine arranged as indicated] [reading horizontally] [white] Ross | [rule] | Berryman | [rule] | Tate | [rule] | [white background] [reading vertically from top to bottom] [strong greenish blue] THE ARTS OF | READING | [reading horizontally] [rule] | [strong greenish blue background] [white] Crowell | [rule] | [rule]'. Back cover: '[white background] [strong greenish blue] *About the Authors* | [thirteen-line unsigned biographical note on Ralph Ross, nine-line unsigned biographical note on JB, and ten-line unsigned biographical note on Allen Tate]'. Front flap: '[white background] [strong greenish blue] $7.50 | THE ARTS OF READING | Ralph Ross | John Berryman | Allen Tate | [beginning of four-paragraph unsigned descriptive comment on contents, twenty-five lines] | (*Continued on back flap*) | Jacket design by NANCY DALE'. Back flap: '[white background] [strong greenish blue] (*Con-*

A 10.1.b *The Arts of Reading*

tinued from front flap) | [conclusion of descriptive comment, twenty-nine lines] | THOMAS Y. CROWELL COMPANY | *Established 1834* | New York 16'.

Text: First publication of all material by JB.

Publication: Unknown number of copies. Published April 8, 1960. $7.50.

Printing: Printed and bound by Vail-Ballou Press, Inc., Binghampton, N.Y.

Copyright: Registered under A 465697 in the name of Thomas Y. Crowell Company, New York, N.Y.

Locations: DLC (deposit-stamp August 22, 1960); ECS (dj); NBu (dj); NBuU; PPiU.

A 10.1.b
Second printing: New York: Thomas Y. Crowell Company, [1966]. On copyright page: 'Apollo Edition 1966'. A-135. Printed wrappers. $2.75.

A 11 77 DREAM SONGS

A 11.1.a
First edition, first printing [1964]

John Berryman

77 DREAM SONGS

Farrar, Straus and Company / NEW YORK

A 11.1.a: $8\frac{1}{4}'' \times 6\frac{1}{16}''$

A 11.1.a *77 Dream Songs* 57

> Copyright © 1959, 1962, 1963, 1964
> by John Berryman
> Library of Congress catalog card number 64-14107
> First printing, 1964
> Published simultaneously in Canada by
> Ambassador Books, Ltd., Toronto
> Manufactured in the U.S.A. by
> American Book-Stratford Press, Inc.
> Designed by Guy Fleming

[1–6]⁸

[i–viii] ix–xi [xii] [1–2] 3–28 [29–30] 31–55 [56–58] 59–84

Contents: p. i: '77 DREAM SONGS'. p. ii: *'Books by John Berryman* | [five titles, six lines]'. p. iii: title page. p. iv: copyright page. p. v: *"To Kate, and to Saul* | 'THOU DREWEST NEAR IN THE DAY'". p. vi: blank. p. vii: "'GO IN, BRACK MAN, DE DAY'S YO' OWN.' | . . . I AM THEIR MUSICK. | *Lam. 3:63* | BUT THERE IS ANOTHER METHOD. | *Olive Schreiner*". p. viii: *'Note:'*, one paragraph comprising brief comments on the poem, dedications of poems to individuals, and acknowledgments, nineteen lines, signed 'J.B.' pp. ix–xi: table of contents. p. xii: blank. p. 1: 'I'. p. 2: blank. pp. 3–28: text. p. 29: 'II'. p. 30: blank. pp. 31–55: text. p. 56: blank. p. 57: 'III'. p. 58: blank. pp. 59–84: text.

Items included: Note. I: 1 "Huffy Henry hid the day,"; 2 Big Buttons, Cornets: the advance; 3 A Stimulant for an Old Beast; 4 "Filling her compact & delicious body"; 5 "Henry sats in de bar & was odd,"; 6 A Capital at Wells; 7 'The Prisoner of Shark Island' with Paul Muni; 8 "The weather was fine. They took away his teeth,"; 9 "Deprived of his enemy, shrugged to a standstill"; 10 "There were strange gatherings. A vote would come"; 11 "His mother goes. The mother comes & goes."; 12 Sabbath; 13 "God bless Henry. He lived like a rat,"; 14 "Life, friends, is boring. We must not say so."; 15 "Let us suppose, valleys & such ago,"; 16 "Henry's pelt was put on sundry walls"; 17 "Muttered Henry: – Lord of matter, thus:"; 18 A Strut for Roethke; 19 "Here, whence"; 20 The Secret of the Wisdom; 21 "Some good people, daring & subtle voices"; 22 Of 1826; 23 The Lay of Ike; 24 "Oh servant Henry lectured till"; 25 "Henry, edged, decidedly, made up stories"; 26 "The glories of the world struck me, made me aria, once."

II: 27 "The greens of the Ganges delta foliate."; 28 Snow Line; 29 "There sat down, once, a thing on Henry's heart"; 30 "Collating bones: I would have liked to do."; 31 "Henry Hankovitch, con guitar,"; 32 "And where, friend Quo, lay you hiding"; 33 "An apple arc'd toward Kleitos; whose great King"; 34 "My mother has your shotgun. One man, wide"; 35 MLA; 36 "The high ones die, die. They die. You look up and who's there?"; 37 Three around the Old Gentleman; 38 "The Russian grin bellows his condolence"; 39 "Goodbye, sir, & fare well. You're in the clear."; 40 "I'm scared a lonely. Never see my son,"; 41 "If we sang in the wood (and Death is a German expert)"; 42 "O journeyer, deaf in the mould, insane"; 43 "'Oyez, oyez!' The Man Who Did Not Deliver"; 44 "Tell it to the forest fire, tell it to the moon,"; 45 "He stared at ruin. Ruin stared straight back."; 46 "I am, outside. Incredible panic rules."; 47 April Fool's Day, or, St Mary of Egypt; 48 "He yelled at me in Greek,"; 49 Blind; 50 "In a motion of night they massed nearer my post."; 51 "Our wounds to time, from all the other times,".

III: 52 Silent Song; 53 "He lay in the middle of the world, and twitcht."; 54 "'NO VISITORS' I thumb the roller to"; 55 "Peter's not friendly. He gives me sideways looks."; 56 "Hell is empty. O that has come to pass"; 57 "In a state of chortle sin – once he reflected,"; 58 "Industrious, affable, having brain on fire,"; 59 Henry's Meditation in the Kremlin; 60 "Afters eight years, be less dan eight percent,"; 61 "Full moon. Our Narragansett gales subside"; 62 "That dark brown rabbit, lightness in his ears"; 63 "Bats have no bankers and they do not drink"; 64 "Supreme my holdings, greater yet my need,"; 65 "A freaking ankle crabbed his blissful trips,"; 66 "'All virtues enter into this world:')"; 67 "I don't operate often. When I do,"; 68 "I heard, could be, a Hey there from the wing,"; 69 "Love her he doesn't but the thought he puts"; 70 "Disengaged, bloody, Henry rose from the shell"; 71 "Spellbound held subtle Henry all his four"; 72 The Elder Presences; 73 Karesansui, Ryoan-ji; 74 "Henry hates the world. What the world to Henry"; 75 "Turning it over, considering, like a madman"; 76 Henry's Confession; 77 "Seedy Henry rose up shy in de world."

Typography and paper: 20 ll., $4\frac{1}{8}''$ ($6\frac{1}{16}''$) × $4\frac{3}{16}''$. Text in 11-pt. Linotype Janson with 4-pt. leading; note in 11-pt. with 2-pt. leading. Yellowish white (Centroid 92) laid paper (chain lines running vertically, spaced $\frac{27}{32}''$).

Binding: Unsized calico-cloth (302), dark blue (Centroid 183). Front cover: plain. Spine: '[reading vertically from top to bottom] [goldstamped] *John Berryman* 77 DREAM SONGS FARRAR, STRAUS'. Back cover: plain. All edges cut; top edge

A 11.1.a *77 Dream Songs* 59

dyed moderate pink (5). Pale yellowish pink (31) wove endpapers.

Dust jacket: White (Centroid 263) wove glossy paper, $8^{7}/_{16}''$ × $20^{7}/_{8}''$. Front cover: 'John Berryman | [script] 77 Dream Songs | [ornamented shadowed roman letters] [strong purplish pink (247)] DREAM [so arranged that the *D, E,* and *M* are in a slightly descending order with the *R* positioned midway over the *E* and to the right of the *D* and the *A* positioned midway over the *M* and to the right of the *E*] | [light yellowish brown (76) except *O* in black (267)] SONG [so arranged that the first *S* and *N* are on the same line, the *O* is positioned midway below them, and the *G* and final *S* are in descending order] | [signed below first *S*] M. Lee'. Spine: '[reading vertically from top to bottom] John Berryman [first digit strong purplish pink, second digit light yellowish brown] 77 [black] Dream Songs FARRAR. STRAUS AND CO.' Back cover: *'Now in second edition* | [script] Homage to Mistress Bradstreet | [roman] by John Berryman | [quotations from comments by Conrad Aiken, two lines; Robert Fitzgerald, one line; *The Times Literary Supplement,* one line; and Edmund Wilson, two lines] | *Farrar, Straus and Company* | *19 Union Square West New York City 3'.* Front flap: '$3.95 | [reading vertically from bottom to top] John Berryman 77 Dream Songs'. Back flap: '[black and white photograph of JB] | *Daniel A. Lindley* | John Berryman | *Jacket design by Marshall Lee* | Farrar, Straus and Company | 19 Union Square West | New York City 3'.

Text: First publication of Dream Songs 2, 10, 15, 19, 23–26, 30, 32, 33, 35, 42, 43, 47, 49, 59–63, 65, 70, 72, 73, and 76. First book appearance of all other Dream Songs. The author's note had not been previously published.

Publication: Unknown number of copies. Published April 27, 1964. $3.95.

Printing: Printed and bound by American Book–Stratford Press, New York, N.Y.

Copyright: Registered under A 691662 in the name of JB.

Locations: DLC (deposit-stamp May 6, 1964); ECS (dj); Lilly (dj); PPiU (dj).

Note one: In the table of contents, untitled Dream Songs are indicated by their first lines or by part of their first lines. There are some twenty-two instances in which commas as end-of-line punctuation are omitted. Other variants in first lines as they appear in the table of contents and in the text are noted as follows:

CONTENTS

ix. 10   gatherings [gatherings.
ix. 17   Henry [Henry:
x. 4   bones [bones:
x. 15   lonely [lonely.
x. 20   ruin [ruin.
xi. 6   sin [sin–
xi. 11   dark-brown [dark brown
xi. 23   world [world.

A 11.1.b
First English reprint [1964]

John Berryman

77 DREAM SONGS

Faber and Faber, 24 Russell Square, London

A 11.1.b: 8⅜" × 6"

A 11.1.b 77 *Dream Songs*

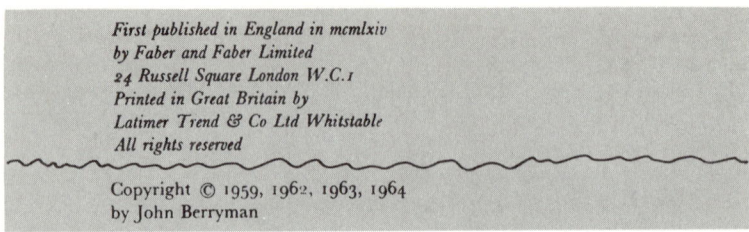

Same collation and pagination as in the first American printing.

Contents: p. i: half title. p. ii: '*by John Berryman* | [one title]'. p. iii: title page. p. iv: copyright page. p. v: dedication. p. vi: blank. p. vii: epigraphs. p. viii: author's note. pp. ix–xi: table of contents. p. xii: blank. p. 1: 'I'. p. 2: blank. pp. 3–28: text. p. 29: 'II'. p. 30: blank. pp. 31–55: text. p. 56: blank. p. 57: 'III'. p. 58: blank. pp. 59–84: text.

Items included: Same as in the first American printing.

Typography and paper: Same typography as in the first American printing. White (Centroid 263) wove paper.

Binding: Unsized calico-cloth (302), moderate yellow (Centroid 87) or light yellowish brown (76). Front cover: plain. Spine: '[reading vertically from top to bottom] [stamped in very dark green (147)] SEVENTY-SEVEN DREAM SONGS by John Berryman Faber'. Back cover: plain. All edges cut. White (263) wove endpapers of different stock than text paper.

Dust jacket: Wove paper, outside glossy, $8^{7}/_{16}''\times 19^{9}/_{16}''$. Front cover: '[yellowish white (Centroid 92) background] 77 | DREAM | SONGS | [vivid reddish orange (34)] *John* | *Berryman*'. Spine: '[yellowish white background] [reading vertically from top to bottom] 77 *Dream Songs* [vivid reddish orange] · [black (267)] *John Berryman* [vivid reddish orange] *Faber*'. Back cover: '[white (263) background] BY ROBERT LOWELL | [three titles and prices, six lines] | BY WALLACE STEVENS | [three titles and prices, seven lines] | BY MARRIANNE MOORE | [three titles and prices, six lines] | BY RICHARD WILBUR | [two titles and prices, four lines] | EDITED BY W. H. AUDEN | [one title and price, three lines] | EDITED BY THOM GUNN AND TED HUGHES | [one title and price, two lines]'. Front flap: '[white background] 77 Dream Songs | *John Berryman* | [three-line introductory statement and fifteen-line quotation from a comment by A. Alvarez, four-line quotation from a comment by Robert Lowell, eight-line quotation from a comment by Allen Tate, and five-line quotation from a comment by Conrad Aiken]

A 11.1.j *77 Dream Songs* 63

| 18s *net*'. Back flap: '[white background] also by | JOHN BERRYMAN | Homage to | Mistress Bradstreet | *and other poems* | [fifteen-line unsigned comment on JB's reputation with quotations from comments by Edmund Wilson and Conrad Aiken on the title poem and a ten-line quotation from a comment by A. Alvarez] | 18s *net* | [five-line advertisement for catalogue]'.

Publication: 1,500 copies. Published November 12, 1964. 18s.

Printing: Printed by offset by Whitstable Litho, Whitstable, Kent. Bound by A. W. Bain and Company Ltd., London.

Locations: BM (deposit-stamp October 15, 1964); ECS (dj); Lilly (dj).

A 11.1.c
Second printing: New York: Farrar, Straus and Giroux, [1965]. On copyright page: 'Second printing, 1965'.

A 11.1.d
Third printing: New York: Farrar, Straus and Giroux, [1965]. On copyright page: 'Third printing, 1965'.

A 11.1.e
Fourth printing: No copy located.

A 11.1.f
Fifth printing: New York: Farrar, Straus and Giroux, [1969]. On copyright page: 'Fifth printing, 1969'.

A 11.1.g
Second printing of English reprint: London: Faber and Faber, [1969]. On copyright page: '*Reprinted 1969*'.

A 11.1.h
Sixth printing: New York: Farrar, Straus and Giroux, [1970]. On copyright page: 'Sixth printing, 1970'. Noonday 387. Printed wrappers. $1.95.

A 11.1.i
Seventh printing: New York: Farrar, Straus and Giroux, [1970]. On copyright page: 'Seventh printing, 1970'. Cloth and printed wrappers.

A 11.1.j
Eighth printing: New York: Farrar, Straus and Giroux, [1971]. On copyright page: 'Eighth printing, 1971'. Printed wrappers.

A 12 TWO DREAM SONGS
  (1965)

Two Dream Songs

*Season's Greetings, 1965
Kate and John Berryman*

A 12: $8\frac{1}{2}'' \times 5\frac{7}{8}''$

A 12 *Two Dream Songs*

> One-hundred fifty copies printed
> Copyright 1965 by John Berryman

[1]²

[1-4]

Contents: p. 1: title page. p. 2: 'Christ-Song: Carpenter's Son | (*from Book VII*)', nineteen lines. p. 3: 'The Last Dream Song: 161', eighteen lines. p. 4: copyright page.

Typography and paper: $4\tfrac{5}{16}''$ ($5\tfrac{3}{16}''$) $\times$ $3\tfrac{5}{8}''$. Text in 10-pt. Linotype Baskerville with 4-pt. leading. White (Centroid 263) laid paper (chain lines running horizontally, spaced $\tfrac{15}{16}''$).

Binding: Unbound and single-folded folio sheet. All edges cut.

Text: First publication of "Christ-Song: Carpenter's Son"; collected in *Toy* and *TheDS* as Dream Song 234: "The Carpenter's Son." First appearance in a separate publication of "The Last Dream Song: 161." See C 137.

Publication: 150 copies. Printed ca. December 1965. Not for sale.

Printing: Privately printed. Printer not known.

Copyright: No copyright application filed.

Location: ECS.

A 13 BERRYMAN'S SONNETS

A 13.1.a
First edition, first printing [1967]

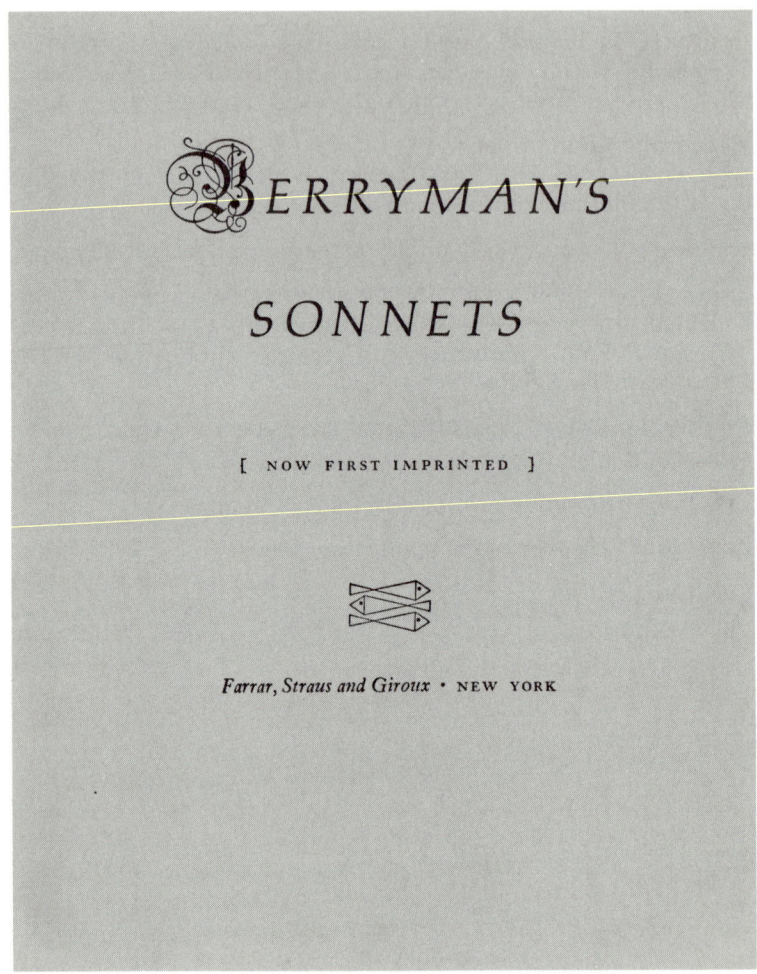

A 13.1.a: 8" × 6¼"

A 13.1.a *Berryman's Sonnets*   67

> Copyright © 1952, 1967 by John Berryman
> Library of Congress catalog card number: 67-15007
> First printing, 1967
> All rights reserved
> Published simultaneously in Canada by
> Ambassador Books, Ltd., Rexdale, Ontario
> Printed in the United States of America

[1–8]⁸

[i–viii] ix [x–xii] 1–115 [116]

Contents: p. i: *'Berryman's Sonnets'*. p. ii: *'Books by John Berryman* | [seven titles, nine lines]'. p. iii: title page. p. iv: copyright page. p. v: *'To Robert Giroux'*. p. vi: blank. p. vii: *'Note* | [comment and acknowledgments, five lines] | J.B. | Ballsbridge, Dublin | October 8th, 1966'. p. viii: blank. p. ix: introductory poem. p. x: blank. p. xi: *'Berryman's Sonnets'*. p. xii: blank. pp. 1–115: text. p. 116: blank.

Items included: Note; "He made, a thousand years ago, a-many songs"; 1 "I wished, all the mild days of middle March"; 2 "Your shining—where?—rays my wide room with gold;"; 3 "Who for those ages ever without some blood"; 4 "Ah when you drift hover before you kiss"; 5 "The poet hunched, so, whom the worlds admire,"; 6 "Rackman and victim grind: sounds all these weeks"; 7 "I've found out why, that day, that suicide"; 8 "College of flunkeys, and a few gentleman,"; 9 "Great citadels whereon the gold sun falls"; 10 "You in your stone home where the sycamore"; 11 "I expect you from the North. The path winds in"; 12 "Mutinous armed & suicidal grind"; 13 "I lift—lift you five States away your glass,"; 14 "Moths white as ghosts among these hundreds cling"; 15 "What was Ashore, then? . . Cargoed with Forget,"; 16 "Thrice, or I moved to sack, I saw you: how"; 17 "The Old Boys' blazers like a Mardi-Gras"; 18 "You, Lise, *contrite* I never thought to see,"; 19 "You sailed in sky-high, with your speech askew"; 20 "Presidential flags! and the General is here,"; 21 "Whom undone David into the dire van sent"; 22 "If not white shorts —then in a princess gown"; 23 "They may suppose, because I would not cloy your ear—"; 24 "Still it pleads and rankles: 'Why do you love *me?*'"; 25 "Sometimes the night echoes to prideless wailing"; 26 "Crouched on a low ridge sloping to where you pour"; 27 "In a poem made by Cummings, long since, his"; 28 "A wasp skims nearby up the bright warm air,"; 29 "The cold rewards trail in, when the man is blind"; 30 "Of all that weeks-long day, though call it back"; 31 "Troubling are masks . . the faces of friends, my face"; 32 "How can I sing, western & dry & thin,"; 33 "Audacities and fêtes of the drunken weeks!"; 34 "'I *couldn't leave* you' you confessed next day."; 35 "Nothing there? nothing up the sky alive,"; 36 "Keep your eyes open when you kiss: do: when"; 37 "Sigh as it ends . . . I keep an eye on your"; 38 "Musculatures and skulls. Later some throng"; 39 "And does the old wound shudder open? Shall"; 40 "Marble nor monuments whereof then we spoke"; 41 "And Plough-month peters out . . its thermal power"; 42 "The clots of age, grovel and palsy, crave"; 43 "You should be gone in winter, that Nature mourn"; 44 "Bell to sore knees vestigial crowds, let crush"; 45 "Boy twenty-one, in Donne, shied like a blow,–"; 46 *"Are we?* You murmur 'not'. What of the night"; 47 "How far upon these songs with my strict wrist"; 48 "I've met your friend at last, your violent friend,"; 49 "One note, a daisy, and a photograph,"; 50 "They come too thick, hail-hard, and all beside"; 51 "A tongue there is wags, down in the dark wood O:"; 52 "A sullen brook hardly would satisfy"; 53 "Some sketch sweat' out, unwilling swift & crude,"; 54 "It was the sky all day I grew to and saw."; 55 "When I recall I could believe you'd go"; 56 "Sunderings and luxations, *luxe,* and grief-"; 57 "Our love conducted as in heavy rain"; 58 "Sensible, coarse, and moral; in decent brown;"; 59 "Loves are the summer's. Summer like a bee"; 60 "Today is it? Is it today? I shudder"; 61 "Languid the songs I wish I willed . . I try . ."; 62 "Tyranny of your car–so much resembles"; 63 "Here too you came and sat a time once, drinking."; 64 "The dew is drying fast, a last drop glistens"; 65 "Once when they found me, some refrain *'Quoi faire?'";* 66 "Astronomies and slangs to find you, dear,"; 67 "Faith like the warrior ant swarming, enslaving"; 68 "Where the lane from the highway swerves the first drops fell"; 69 "For you am I collared O to quit my dear"; 70 "Under Scorpion both, back in the Sooner State"; 71 "Our Sunday morning when dawn-priests were applying"; 72 "A Cambridge friend put in,–one whom I used"; 73 "Demand me again what Kafka's riddles mean,"; 74 "All I did wrong, all the Grand Guignol years,"; 75 "Swarthy when young; who took the tonsure; sign,"; 76 "The two plantations Greatgrandmother brought"; 77 "Fall and rise of her midriff bells. I watch."; 78 "On the wheat-sacks, sullen with the ceaseless damp,"; 79 "I dreamt he drove me back to the asylum"; 80 "Infallible symbolist!–Tanker driven ashore,"; 81 "Four oval shadows, paired, ringed each by sun,"; 82 "Why can't, Lise, why shouldn't *they* fall in love?"; 83 "Impossible to speak to her, and worse"; 84 "How shall I do, to pass the weary time"; 85 "Spendthrift Urethra-Sphincter, frugal one-"; 86 "Our lives before bitterly our mistake!-"; 87 "Is it possible, poor kids, you must not come out?"; 88 "Anomalous I linger, and ignore"; 89 "'If long enough I sit here, she, she'll pass.'"; 90 "For you an idyl, was it not, so far,"; 91 "Itself a lightning-flash ripping the 'dark"; 92 "What can to you this music wakes my years"; 93 "The man who made her let me climb the derrick"; 94 "Most strange, my change, this nervous interim.-"; 95 "'Old Smoky' when you sing with Peter, Lise,"; 96 "It will seem strange, no more this range on range"; 97 "I say *I laid siege—you enchanted me . .*"; 98 "Mallarmé siren upside down,-rootedly!"; 99 "A murmuration of the shallow, Crane"; 100 "I am interested alone in making ready,"; 101 "Because I'd seen you not believe your lover,"; 102 "A penny, pity, for the runaway ass!"; 103 "A 'broken heart' . . but *can* a heart break, now?"; 104 "A spot of poontang on a five-foot piece,"; 105 "Three, almost, now into the ass's years,"; 106 "Began with swirling, blind, unstilled oh still,-"; 107 "Darling I wait O in my upstairs box"; 108 "I owe you, do I not, a roofer: though"; 109 "Ménage à trois, like Tristan's,-difficult! . ."; 110 "'Ring us up when you want to see us . .'-'Sure,'"; 111 "Christian to Try: 'I am so coxed in it,"; 112 "I break my pace now for a sonic boom,"; 113 "'I didn't see anyone else, I just saw Lise'"; 114 "You come blonde visiting through the black air"; 115 "All we were going strong last night this time,".

Typography and paper: 15 ll., $3^{11}/_{16}''$ ($4^{11}/_{16}''$) × $4^{5}/_{16}''$. Text in 11-pt. Linotype Janson with 7-pt. leading. Yellowish white (Centroid 92) laid paper (chain lines running vertically, spaced $^{29}/_{32}''$).

Binding: Unsized calico cloth (302), black (Centroid 267). Front cover: plain. Spine: '[reading vertically from top to bottom] [goldstamped] BERRYMAN'S SONNETS *Farrar, Straus and Giroux*'. Back cover: plain. Top edge and tail cut; fore edge trimmed; top edge dyed light yellow (86). Deep yellow (85) wove endpapers.

Dust jacket: Wove paper, $8^{3}/_{16}''$ × 21". Front cover: '[on yellowish white (Centroid 92) panel bordered by black (267) thick rules at top and bottom of panel, on moderate yellowish brown (77) background with fourteen rows of light yellowish brown (76) fleurons so arranged that the fleurons of each row are positioned midway between those in the rows above and below, with solid black borders at top and bottom edges of cover] BERRYMAN'S SONNETS'. Spine: '[moderate yellowish brown background with solid black borders at top and bottom of spine] [reading horizontally] [yellowish white] FARRAR, | STRAUS & | GIROUX | [on yellowish white panel bordered by black thick rules at top and bottom of panel] [moderate yellowish brown] [fleuron] | [on moderate yellowish background] [reading vertically from top to bottom] [yellowish white] *BERRYMAN'S SONNETS*'. Back cover: '[yellowish white background] [sepia-tone photograph of JB] | [at bottom right] [reading vertically from bottom to top] *Photo by Rohn Engh* | [below photograph] [reading horizontally] John Berryman'. Front flap: '[yellowish white background] $4.95 | JOHN BERRYMAN | [moderate yellowish brown] Berryman's Sonnet | [black] [beginning of three-paragraph unsigned descriptive comment on contents with quotations from the poems, twenty lines] | *(continued on back flap)*'. Back flap: '[yellowish white background] *(continued on front flap)* | [conclusion of comment, eleven lines including six lines from Sonnet 42] | *Jacket design by Herb Johnson* | FARRAR, STRAUS AND GIROUX | 19 UNION SQUARE WEST | NEW YORK 10003'.

Text: First publication of Sonnets 1–22, 24, 26–70, 72–102, 104–115. First book appearance of Sonnets 23, 71, and 103.

Publication: Unknown number of copies. Published April 24, 1967. $4.95.

Printing: Printed and bound by H. Wolff Book Manufacturing Company, New York, N.Y.

Copyright: Registered under A 908268 in the name of JB.

Locations: DLC (deposit-stamp May 1, 1967), ECS (dj); Lilly (dj); Lockwood (dj); NBuU; PPi (dj); PPiCI (dj); PPiU.

Note: Variants in Sonnet 25 between its appearances in *Thought* and in *BS* are noted as follows:

l. 2: low as I hunch home late & fever-tired [Low as I hunch home late and fever-tired,
l. 3: near you not, nearing the sharer I desired [Near you not, nearing the sharer I desired,
l. 4: toward whom till now I sailed back, [Toward whom till now I sailed back;
l. 5: yaws, [Yaws,
l. 6: dribble, the stores disordered & [Dribble, the stores disordered and
l. 7: skid [Skid

l. 8:   'Hopeless'. Lockt in & humming, the captain's   [Hopeless: locked in, and humming, the Captain's
l. 9:   a false log to the lurching table. Lies   [A false log to the lurching table. Lies
l. 10: &   [And
l. 11: the burgee should fly Jolly Roger. wind   [The burgee should fly Jolly Roger: wind
l. 12: madness like the tackle of a crane – outcries   [Madness like the tackle of a crane (outcries
l. 13: ascend –   [Ascend)
l. 14: irresponsible,   [Irresponsible,

A 13.1.b
First English reprint [1968]

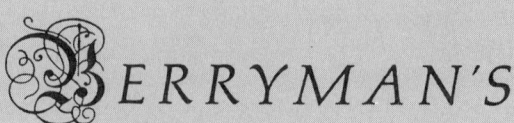

BERRYMAN'S

SONNETS

Faber and Faber · LONDON

A 13.1.b: 8½" × 5⁷⁄₁₆"

A 13.1.b *Berryman's Sonnets*

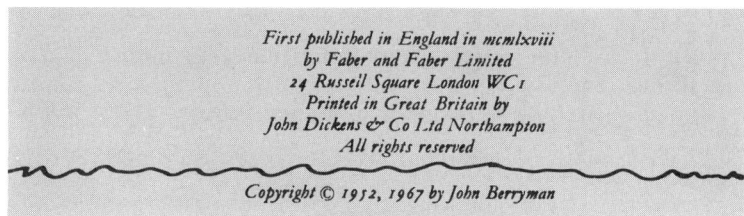

[A]⁸ B–H⁸

Same pagination as in the first American printing.

Contents: p. i: half title. p. ii: '*Books by John Berryman* | [two titles]'. p. iii: title page. p. iv: copyright page. p. v: dedication. p. vi: blank. p. vii: author's note. p. viii: blank. p. ix: introductory poem. p. x: blank. pp. 1–115: text. p. 116: blank.

Items included: Same as in the first American printing.

Typography and paper: 15 ll., $3^{11}/_{16}''$ ($4^{11}/_{16}''$) × $2^{7}/_{8}''$. Yellowish white (Centroid 92) wove paper.

Binding: Sized calico-cloth (302), light brown (Centroid 57). Front cover: plain. Spine: '[reading vertically from top to bottom] [goldstamped] BERRYMAN'S SONNETS · John Berryman | [reading horizontally] Faber'. Back cover: plain. All edges cut. White (263) wove endpapers.

Dust jacket: Wove paper, $8^{3}/_{4}''$ × $18^{1}/_{2}''$. Front cover: '[grayish blue (Centroid 186) background] [white (263)] JOHN BERRYMAN | *Berryman's* | *SONNETS* | FABER'. Spine: '[reading vertically from top to bottom] [grayish blue background] [white] *Berryman's Sonnets* | [reading horizontally] John | Berry-|man | Faber'. Back cover: '[white background] [grayish blue] BY ROBERT LOWELL | [nine titles, thirteen lines] | BY WALLACE STEVENS | [four titles] | BY MARIANNE MOORE | [four titles] | BY RICHARD WILBUR | [two titles] | EDITED BY THOM GUNN & TED HUGHES | [one title]'. Front flap: '[white background] [grayish blue] *Berryman's Sonnets* | JOHN BERRYMAN | [ten-line unsigned note on publication of the sonnets] | 21s | net'. Back flap: '[white background] [grayish blue] *also by John Berryman* | HOMAGE TO | MISTRESS BRADSTREET | *and other poems* | [three-line quotation from a comment by Conrad Aiken and six-line quotation from a comment by A. Alvarez] | 77 DREAM SONGS | [four-line quotation from a comment by Robert Lowell and six-line quotation from a comment in *The Times* (London)] | [three-line advertisement for catalogue]'.

Publication: 1,500 copies. Published April 22, 1968. 21s.

Printing: Printed from lithographic plates by John Dickens and Company, Ltd., Northampton, Northamptonshire. Bound by James Burn and Company Ltd., Esher, Surrey.

Locations: BM (deposit-stamp March 21, 1968); ECS (dj); Lilly (dj).

A 13.1.b†
Proof copy

Same leaf size, pagination, and collation as in the first English printing.

Contents: Same as in the first English printing.

Items included: Same as in the first English printing.

Typography and paper: Same as in the first English printing.

Binding: Light bluish gray (Centroid 190) wove paper wrappers. Front cover: 'BERRYMAN'S | SONNETS | FABER AND FABER LTD'. Spine: '[reading vertically from top to bottom] BERRYMAN'S SONNETS FABER'. Back cover: plain. All edges cut. Cover cut flush.

Location: ECS; Meissner.

A 13.1.c
Second printing: New York: Farrar, Straus and Giroux, [1968]. On copyright page: *'Second Printing, 1968'*.

A 13.1.d
Third printing: New York: Farrar, Straus and Giroux, [1969]. On copyright page: *'Third Printing, 1969'*. Noonday 374. Printed wrappers. $1.95.

A 13.1.e
Fourth printing: New York: Farrar, Straus and Giroux, [1969]. On copyright page: *'Fourth Printing, 1969'*. Cloth and printed wrappers.

A 13.1.f
Fifth printing: No copy located.

A 13.1.g
Sixth printing: New York: Farrar, Straus and Giroux, [1973]. On copyright page: *'Sixth Printing, 1973'*. Printed wrappers.

A 14 POETRY SEASON 1967
(1967)

POETRY SEASON 1967

SECOND PROGRAMME · 19 JUNE

JOHN
BERRYMAN

Presented by Poetry Ireland and the Lantern Theatre
with the co-operation of Bord Failte Eireann

THE GRADUATES CLUB   DUBLIN

A 14: 9″ × 5³⁄₁₆″

[1]²

[1-4]

Contents: p. 1: title page. p. 2: 'JOHN BERRYMAN | [rule] | [twelve-line unsigned biographical note]'. p. 3: '[untitled poem ("I have moved to Dublin to have it out with you,"), eighteen lines] | JOHN BERRYMAN'. p. 4: 'POETRY SEASON 1967 | [ten-line unsigned note on the Poetry Season] | FOR THE POETRY SEASON | [names of directors and editor, three lines] | [rule] | [six-line unsigned note on future productions] | *The Dolmen Press Limited Dublin.*'

Typography and paper: $4\frac{7}{16}'' \times 3\frac{5}{8}''$. Text in 14-pt. Pilgrim with 2-pt. leading. Yellowish white (Centroid 92) wove paper.

Binding: Unbound and single-folded folio sheet. All edges cut.

Text: First publication of "I have moved to Dublin ... ,"; collected in *Toy*, *TheDS*, and *SelP* as Dream Song 312.

Publication: Unknown number of copies. Distributed June 19, 1967. Not for sale.

Printing: Printed by The Dolmen Press Ltd., Dublin, on June 18, 1967.

Location: ECS.

Note one: In the biographical note, the word *Dispossessed* and the date *1964* are printed as *Dispossesed* and *1946*.

Note two: Copies were distributed for JB's poetry reading in the Second Programme of the 1967 Poetry Season at the Lantern Theatre, Dublin, on June 19, 1967.

A 15 SHORT POEMS
[1967]

JOHN BERRYMAN

Short Poems

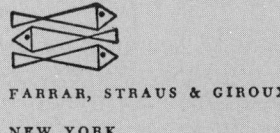

FARRAR, STRAUS & GIROUX

NEW YORK

A 15: 8″ × 5⁷⁄₁₆″

> *The Dispossessed*, copyright 1948 by John Berryman
> *His Thought Made Pockets & The Plane Buckt*, copyright © 1958
> by John Berryman
> *Formal Elegy*, copyright © 1964 by John Berryman
> Acknowledgment is made to Basic Books, Inc., in whose volume *Of Poetry and Power: Poems Occasioned by the Presidency and by the Death of John F. Kennedy*, edited by Erwin A. Glikes and Paul Schwaber, *Formal Elegy* first appeared
>
> Library of Congress catalog card number: 67-28940
> All rights reserved
> First printing, 1967
> Published simultaneously in Canada by Ambassador Books, Ltd., Rexdale Ontario
> Printed in the United States of America
> Design: Marshall Lee

$[1-8]^8$

[i-viii] [1-3] 4-15 [16-17] 18-45 [46-47] 48-64 [65] 66-78 [79] 80-95 [96-98] 99-114 [115-116] 117-120

Contents: p. i: 'JB'. p. ii: '*by John Berryman* | [seven titles]. p. iii: title page. p. iv: copyright page. pp. v-vii: table of contents. p. viii: blank. p. 1: '*THE DISPOSSESSED* | TO MY MOTHER'. p. 2: blank. pp. 3-15: 'I' and text. p. 16: blank. pp. 17-45: 'II' and text. p. 46: blank. pp. 47-64: 'III' and text. pp. 65-78: 'IV' and text. pp. 79-95: 'V' and text. p. 96: blank. p. 97: '*HIS THOUGHT MADE POCKETS* | *& THE PLANE BUCKT* | TO ANN | Henry sats in de plane & was gay. | Careful Henry nothing said aloud | but where a virgin out of cloud | to her Mountain dropt in light | his thought made pockets & the plane buckt. | "Parm me, Lady." "Orright."' p. 98: blank. pp. 99-114: text. p. 115: '*FORMAL ELEGY*'. p. 116: blank. pp. 117-120: text.

Items included: Combines the texts of *The Dispossessed*, *His Thought Made Pockets & The Plane Buckt*, and "Formal Elegy."

Typography and paper: 32 ll., $6^{7}/_{16}''$ ($6^{3}/_{4}''$) × 4''. Text in 10-pt. Linotype Caledonia with 4-pt. leading. Yellowish white (Centroid 92) laid paper (chain lines running vertically, spaced $^{27}/_{32}''$).

Binding: Spine and one half inch of boards in unsized calico-cloth (302), moderate brown (Centroid 58); remainder of boards covered with light yellowish green (101) paper with strains of dark yellow (88). Front cover: plain. Spine: '[reading vertically from top to bottom] [stamped in strong orange yellow (68)] short POEMS [goldstamped] *JOHN BERRYMAN* [device] FARRAR, | STRAUS & | GIROUX'. Back cover: plain. All edges cut; top edge dyed grayish brown (61). Deep reddish orange (36) wove endpapers.

Dust jacket: White (Centroid 263) wove paper, outside glossy, $8^{1}/_{4}''$ × 19''. Front cover: '[strong greenish blue (169)] John |

A 15 *Short Poems* 79

Berryman | [strong orange yellow (68)] SHORT | POEMS | [dark brown (59)] INCLUDING | THE DISPOSSESSED, | HIS THOUGHT MADE POCKETS & THE PLANE BUCKT | AND | FORMAL ELEGY'. Spine: '[reading vertically from top to bottom] [strong greenish blue] John Berryman [strong orange yellow] SHORT POEMS | [dark brown] Farrar, Straus & Giroux'. Back cover: '[strong greenish blue] *BERRYMAN'S SONNETS* | [dark brown] [four-line quotation from a comment by William Meredith, four-line quotation from a comment by Dudley Fitts, and two-line quotations from comment by Robert Penn Warren] | [strong greenish blue] *HOMAGE TO MISTRESS BRAD-STREET* | [dark brown] [one-line quotation from a comment by Robert Fitzgerald and two-line quotation from a comment by Edmund Wilson] | [strong greenish blue] 77 *DREAM SONGS* | [dark brown] [five-line quotation from a comment by Allen Tate and three-line quotation from a comment by Robert Lowell] | FARRAR, STRAUS & GIROUX'. Front flap: '[dark brown] $4.50 | John Berryman | [strong greenish blue] *SHORT POEMS* | [dark brown] [two-paragraph unsigned comments on contents and title of the volume, twenty-one lines] | FARRAR, STRAUS AND GIROUX | 19 UNION SQUARE WEST | NEW YORK 10003'. Back flap: '[sepia tone photograph of JB] | [at left, reading vertically from bottom to top] [dark brown] *Terence Spencer, Life Magazine © Time, Inc.* | [below photograph] [reading horizontally] [strong greenish blue] John Berryman | [dark brown] *Jacket design by Ronald Clyne* | FARRAR, STRAUS AND GIROUX | 19 UNION SQUARE WEST | NEW YORK 10003'.

Text: No first book material. *Short Poems* comprises the texts of *The Dispossessed, His Thought Made Pockets & The Plane Buckt,* and "Formal Elegy." See A 4, A 8.1.a, and B 21 for main entries.

Publication: Unknown number of copies. Published December 1, 1967. $4.50.

Printing: Printed and bound by H. Wolff Book Manufacturing Company, New York, N.Y.

Copyright: No copyright application filed.

Locations: DLC (not deposit copy); ECS (dj); Lilly (dj); Lockwood (dj); NBuU; PPi (dj); PPiCI (dj); PPiU.

Note one: Variants in twenty-one poems between their appearances in the collections indicated and in *ShP* are noted as follows:

"The Ball Poem," *TD*
  l. 13: boy, [boy.
"Ancestor," *TD*
  l. 7: . Crossing [Crossing
  l. 16: syllables [syllables'
"At Chinese Checkers," *TD*
  l. 8: paradigms of marble [paradigms
"Boston Common," *TD*
  l. 94: tine [time
"The Long Home," *TD*
  l. 47: sea . . [sea . . .
"A Winter-Piece to a Friend Away," *TD*
  l. 18: instruct . .   Unless [instruct . . Unless
  l. 34: wood . . mould [wood . . . mould
"New Year's Eve," *TD*
  l. 30: beneath : eye [beneath: eye
"Narcissus Moving," *TD*
  l. 30: once . . [once . . .
"Venice, 182–," *Thought*
  l. 3:   the corners of her eyes are white. ı [The corners of her eyes are white. I
  l. 4:   she [She
  l. 6:   нell [Hell
  l. 8:   ʟess [Less
  l. 11: ı hear her howl now, and ı [I hear her howl now, and I
  l. 12: ғoul [Foul
  l. 13: on [On
  l. 15: ɴow [Now
  l. 16: ı [I
  l. 19: ı [I
  l. 23: ı [I
  l. 25: тhe light hurts. 'тhere . . .' [The light hurts. "There . . ."
"Scots Poem," *Thought*
  l. 3:   weel, [Weel,
  l. 5:   ᴘeered [Peered
  l. 7:   ʟove [Love
  l. 11: ʙraird [Braird
  l. 12: ı'm [I'm
  l. 15: 'come forth, ısobel мitchel, ["Come forth, Isobel Mitchel,
  l. 16: william мatheson in the sky.' [William Matheson in the sky."
"Sonnet 25," *Thought*

A 15 *Short Poems*

l. 2:   I   [I
l. 3:   I   [I
l. 4:   I   [I
l. 8:   'HOPELESS'. LOCKT in & humming, the captain's   ["Hopeless." Lockt in & humming, the Captain's
l. 9:   LIES   [Lies
l. 11: JOLLY ROGER. wind   [Jolly Roger. Wind

"The Mysteries," *Thought*

l. 2:   THINKING   [Thinking
l. 3:   I   [I
l. 4:   ERICH KAHLER   [Erich Kahler
l. 5:   where   [where
l. 6:   YOU   [you
l. 7:   AND   [and
l. 8:   AT   [At
l. 9:   I   [I
l. 10: central   [central
l. 11: swelling   [swelling
l. 12: MEN   [men
l. 13: AND   [And
l. 14: FOR   [for
l. 15: MY goddess at the CROSS-WAYS. CROWN   [my goddess at the Cross-ways. Crown
l. 16: REARS   [Rears
l. 17: THE stonechat clatters in the bracken! SONG   [The stonechat clatters in the bracken! Song
l. 18: THROUGH   [through
l. 19: AND   [and
l. 20: IN the sea-green blindness I found THETIS   [In the sea-green blindness I found Thetis
l. 21: AND you will find me with you. I   [and you will find me with you. 1
l. 22: PASSIONS   [passions
l. 23: GREAT   [great
l. 24: cymbals,   [cymbals,
l. 25: AND   [and
l. 26: UNCIRCLING,   [uncircling,
l. 27: DANCE in darkness! DRIPS   [dance in darkness! Drips
l. 28: THEY   [they
l. 29: A   [a
l. 30: LIKE   [like
l. 31: AND   [and
l. 32: while   [while
l. 33: COARSE   [coarse

l. 34:   And [and
l. 35:   where I go to pieces. I [where I go to pieces. I
l. 36:   And I [and I
l. 37:   And [and
l. 38:   So [so
l. 39:   And whether will ever either back o [and whether will ever either back O
l. 40:   Is [is
l. 41:   And [and
l. 42:   The [the

"They Have," *Thought*
l. 1:   o [O
l. 6:   I [I
l. 8:   That [That
l. 9:   Mâcon: I [Mâcon: I
l. 11:   Now [Now
l. 12:   I [I
l. 13:   But [But
l. 14:   I [I
l. 16:   The [The
l. 17:   They [They

"The Poet's Final Instructions," *Thought*
l. 2:   cedar Avenue in Minneap, [Cedar Avenue in Minneap,
l. 3:   I [I
l. 4:   Do [Do
l. 5:   I [I
l. 6:   choiring [Choiring
l. 7:   I might not lie still in the waste of st paul [I might not lie still in the waste of St Paul
l. 8:   DAD's root beer; good signs I [DAD's root beer; good signs I
l. 9:   Drop [Drop
l. 12:   Assemble [Assemble
l. 13:   Bury [Bury
l. 14:   cedar on Lake street, [Cedar on Lake Street,

"from The Black Book (i)," *Thought*
l. 2:   seldom [seldom
l. 3:   we wept. The [we wept. The
l. 4:   Later we heard. Brother had pull. In [later we heard. Brother had pull. In
l. 5:   He, [he,
l. 6:   Later [Later
l. 7:   The [The
l. 8:   Broke [broke

A 15 *Short Poems*   83

    l. 9:   Before [Before
    l. 10:   only [Only
    l. 11:   And soon he died. He [and soon he died. He
    l. 12:   our [our
    l. 13:   when he stopt. Abraham, [when he stopt. Abraham,
    l. 14:   write, I beg, in your Book. [write, I beg, in your Book.
    l. 15:   No [No
    l. 16:   call to our pall; we call or gibber; Hell's [call to our pall; we call or gibber; Hell's
    l. 17:   Irritable [irritable
    l. 18:   Despairs [despairs

"from The Black Book (ii)," *Thought*

    l. 1:   L*uftmenschen* [Luftmenschen
    l. 2:   of [of
    l. 3:   peaceful [peaceful
    l. 4:   The [the
    l. 5:   soundless [soundless
    l. 6:   No [no
    l. 7:   Hands [Hands
    l. 8:   while [while
    l. 9:   Prolong the woolen night – solomon [Prolong the woolen night – Solomon
    l. 10:   And [and
    l. 11:   But [but
    l. 12:   Ecstatic, [ecstatic,
    l. 13:   August [August
    l. 14:   In [in
    l. 15:   Blue [Blue
    l. 16:   (An Ashkenazi genius stoned Ivan; [(An Ashkenazi genius stoned Ivan;
    l. 17:   'Boleslaus brought us here, surnamed the Good, ["Boleslaus brought us here, surnamed the Good,
    l. 18:   whose [whose
    l. 19:   towards sirius: we thank that King [towards Sirius; we thank that King
    l. 20:   As [as
    l. 21:   Night [night
    l. 22:   Armbands [armbands
    l. 23:   Be glad but the black troops gather.' [be glad but the black troops gather."
    l. 24:   So [So
    l. 25:   Dawn [Dawn
    l. 26:   Alleys [alleys

  l. 27: Down [down
  l. 28: The Lazienki Gardens' [the Lazienki Gardens'
  l. 29: Monument [monument
  l. 30: who far vienna from the Turks [who far Vienna from the Turks
  l. 31: Bloodily [bloodily
  l. 32: For [For
  l. 33: one [One
  l. 34: cupshot, [cupshot,
  l. 35: Native [native
  l. 36: That [that
  l. 37: Hurts [hurts
  l. 38: Drove [drove
  l. 39: Brooding [Brooding
  l. 40: He reddens suddenly. He [he reddens suddenly. He

"from The Black Book (iii)," *Thought*
  l. 1: Lover [Lover
  l. 2: From [From
  l. 3: who [who
  l. 4: Foul [foul
  l. 5: Grows [grows
  l. 6: Away [Away
  l. 7: Disrobing, Achtung! [disrobing, *Achtung!*
  l. 8: They [they
  l. 9: Lift them an elegy, poor you and I, [Lift them an elegy, poor you and I,
  l. 10: Fair [fair
  l. 11: Under [under

"A Sympathy, A Welcome," *Thought*
  l. 1: i [I
  l. 2: paul, [Paul,
  l. 3: i [I
  l. 4: yet [Yet
  l. 9: paul, [Paul,

"Not To Live," *Thought*
  l. 2: King. I [King. I
  l. 4: I find. Ghost [I find. Ghost
  l. 6: Howls [Howls
  l. 7: I love the King [I love the King
  l. 10: God be with him. He & God [God be with him. He & God
  l. 11: i [I
  l. 13: From [From
  l. 14: God save the King. [God save the King.

A 15 *Short Poems*

"American Lights, Seen From Off Abroad," *Thought*
- l. 2:   DOLLARTOWN   [Dollartown
- l. 3:   NEBUCHADNEZZAR   [Nebuchadnezzar
- l. 4:   HOLLYWOOD   [Hollywood
- l. 5:   I never think, I   [I never think, I
- l. 6:   PALM SPRINGS   [Palm Springs
- l. 7:   I   [I
- l. 8:   state   [State
- l. 9:   I have no plans, I   [I have no plans, I
- l. 10: GEORGETOWN   [Georgetown
- l. 11: I   [I
- l. 12: NIAGARA   [Niagara
- l. 13: we   [We
- l. 14: DALLAS   [Dallas
- l. 15: I   [I
- l. 16: WASHINGTON   [Washington
- l. 17: (I have a brave old so-and-so,   [(I have a brave old So-and-So,
- l. 18: INDEPENDENCE, MO.)   [Independence, Mo.)
- l. 19: I cast a shadow, what I   [I cast a shadow, what I
- l. 20: ABILENE   [Abilene
- l. 21: BOTH   [Both
- l. 23: HE   [He
- l. 25: 'BASKETBALL IN OUTER SPACE'   ["Basketball in outer space"
- l. 26: WHITE NEW HAMPSHIRE HOUSE   [White New Hampshire House
- l. 27: I'll have a smaller one, later, MAC,   [I'll have a smaller one, later, Mac,
- l. 28: CAL TECH   [Cal Tech
- l. 29: I   [I
- l. 30: LITTLE ROCK   [Little Rock
- l. 31: I   [I
- l. 32: LAS VEGAS   [Las Vegas
- l. 33: I   [I
- l. 34: BEVERLY HILLS   [Beverly Hills
- l. 35: PROUD   [Proud
- l. 36: SAN FRANCISCO   [San Francisco
- l. 37: I   [I
- l. 38: NEW YORK   [New York
- l. 39: I   [I
- l. 40: BOSTON   [Boston
- l. 41: HERE   [Here
- l. 42: HERE comes a cropper.' THAT'S what I   [Here comes a cropper.' That's what I

"Note to Wang Wei," *Thought*
l. 3:   ɪt   [It
l. 5:   ɪt   [It
l. 6:   ɪt   [It
l. 7:   ᴍakes   [Makes
l. 8:   (ɪ'm reconfirming, ɢod   [(I'm reconfirming, God
l. 10:   ɪ   [I
l. 11:   'freedom from ten thousand matters'.   ["freedom from ten thousand matters."
l. 12:   ʙe   [Be

Note two: In "A Winter-Piece to a Friend Away," on p. 87 of *ShP*, the second and third stanzas (ll. 9–16 and 17–24) are not divided. In "from The Black Book (ii)" in *Thought* the third and fourth stanzas (ll. 17–24 and 25–32) are divided by a series of seven spaced periods, but these are omitted in *ShP*, page 107.

Note three: Variants in titles of poems between their appearances in *Thought* and in *ShP* are noted as follows:

Venice, 182–   [*Venice, 182–*
sᴄots ᴘoem   [*Scots Poem*
sonnet xxv   [*Sonnet XXV*
ᴛhe ᴍysteries   [*The Mysteries*
ᴛhey ʜave   [*They Have*
ᴛhe ᴘoet's ғinal ɪnstructions   [*The Poet's Final Instructions*
from The Black Book (i)   [from *The Black Book (i)*
from The Black Book (ii)   [from *The Black Book (ii)*
from The Black Book (iii)   [from *The Black Book (iii)*
ᴀ sympathy, ᴀ welcome   [*A Sympathy, A Welcome*
ɴot ᴛo ʟive   [*Not to Live*
ᴀmerican ʟights, seen ғrom off ᴀbroad   [*American Lights, Seen from Off Abroad*
ɴote to wang wei   [*Note to Wang Wei*

Note four: In all copies examined, the following letters and mark of punctuation are not fully impressed: the *T* in the word *To*, the *l* in the word *place*, and the *W* in the word *Were* on p. 13, l. 8; the *L* in the word *Light* on p. 23, l. 9; the colon following the word *Heart* and the *s* in the word *animals* on p. 44, l. 22; and the *T* and *h* in the word *The* on p. 77, l. 1.

A 16 HIS TOY, HIS DREAM, HIS REST

A 16.1.a
First edition, first printing [1968]

John Berryman

HIS TOY, HIS DREAM, HIS REST

308 Dream Songs

Farrar, Straus and Giroux / NEW YORK

A 16.1.a: $8^{3}/_{16}'' \times 6^{1}/_{8}''$

> Copyright © 1964, 1965, 1966, 1967, 1968
> by John Berryman
> Library of Congress catalog card number: 67-21526
> First printing, 1968
> All rights reserved
> Published simultaneously in Canada
> Printed in the United States of America
> by American Book-Stratford Press, Inc.
> Designed by Guy Fleming

[1-18]⁸ [19]⁴ [20-22]⁸

[A-B] [i-x] xi-xxi [xxii] [1-2] 3-16 [17-18] 19-72 [73-74] 75-173 [174] 175-207 [208-210] 211-317 [318-320]

Contents: pp. A-B: blank. p. i: 'HIS TOY, | HIS DREAM, | HIS REST'. p. ii: *'Books by John Berryman* | [six titles, eight lines]'. p. iii: title page. p. iv: copyright page. p. v: 'To Mark Van Doren, and to | the sacred memory of Delmore Schwartz'. p. vi: blank. p. vii: 'NO INTERESTING PROJECT CAN BE EMBARKED ON WITHOUT | FEAR. I SHALL BE SCARED TO DEATH HALF THE TIME. | *Sir Francis Chichester in Sydney* | FOR MY PART I AM ALWAYS FRIGHTENED, AND VERY MUCH | SO. I FEAR THE FUTURE OF ALL ENGAGEMENTS. | *Gordon in Khartoum* | I AM PICKT UP AND SORTED TO A PIP. MY IMAGINATION IS | A MONASTERY AND I AM ITS MONK. | *Keats to Shelley* | HE WENT AWAY AND NEVER SAID GOODBYE. | I COULD READ HIS LETTERS BUT I SURE CAN'T READ HIS MIND. | I THOUGHT HE'S LOVIN ME BUT HE WAS LEAVIN ALL THE TIME. | NOW I KNOW THAT MY TRUE LOVE WAS BLIND. | *Victoria Spivey?'.* p. viii: blank. p. ix: *'Note:',* four paragraphs comprising four-line note on contents, eleven lines of acknowledgments, five lines of dedications of songs to individuals, and eleven-line comment on the poem, signed 'J.B.' p. x: blank. pp. xi-xxi: table of contents. p. xxii: blank. p. 1: 'IV'. p. 2: blank. pp. 3-16: text. p. 17: 'V'. p. 18: blank. pp. 19-72: text. p. 73: 'VI'. p. 74: blank. pp. 75-207: text. p. 208: blank. p. 209: 'VII'. p. 210: blank. pp. 211-317: text. pp. 318-320: blank.

Items included: Note. IV: 78 Op. posth. no. 1; 79 Op. posth. no. 2; 80 Op. posth. no. 3; 81 Op. posth. no. 4; 82 Op. posth. no. 5; 83 Op. posth. no. 6; 84 Op. posth. no. 7; 85 Op. posth. no. 8; 86 Op. posth. no. 9; 87 Op. posth. no. 10; 88 Op. posth. no. 11; 89 Op. posth. no. 12; 90 Op. posth. no. 13; 91 Op. posth. no. 14.

V: 92 Room 231: the forth week; 93 "General Fatigue stalked in, & a Major-General,"; 94 "Ill lay he long, upon this last return,"; 95 "The surly cop lookt out at me in sleep"; 96

A 16.1.a *His Toy, His Dream, His Rest*

"Under the table, no. That last was stunning,"; 97 "Henry of Donnybrook bred like a pig,"; 98 "I met a junior – not so junior – and"; 99 Temples; 100 "How this woman came by the courage, how she got"; 101 "A shallow lake, with many waterbirds,"; 102 "The sunburnt terraces which swans make home"; 103 "I consider a song will be as humming-bird"; 104 "Welcome, grinned Henry, welcome, fifty-one!"; 105 "As a kid I believed in democracy: I"; 106 28 July; 107 "Three 'coons come at his garbage. He be cross,"; 108 "Sixteen below. Our cars like stranded hulls"; 109 "She mentioned 'worthless' & he took it in,"; 110 "It was the blue & plain ones. I forget all that."; 111 "I miss him. When I get back to camp"; 112 "My framework is broken, I am coming to an end,"; 113 or Amy Vladeck or Riva Freifeld; 114 "Henry in trouble whirped out lonely whines."; 115 "Her properties, like her of course & frisky & new:"; 116 "Through the forest, followed, Henry made his silky way."; 117 "Disturbed, when Henry's love returned with a hubby, – "; 118 "He wondered: Do I love? all this applause,"; 119 "Fresh-shaven, past months & a picture in New York"; 120 "Foes I sniff, when I have less to shout"; 121 "Grief is fatiguing. He is out of it,"; 122 "He published his girl's bottom in staid pages"; 123 "Dapples my floor the eastern sun, my house faces north,"; 124 "Behold I bring you tidings of great joy – "; 125 "Bards freezing, naked, up to the neck in water,"; 126 A Thurn; 127 "Again, his friend's death made the man sit still"; 128 "A hemorrhage of his left ear of Good Friday – "; 129 "Thin as a sheet his mother came to him"; 130 "When I saw my friend covered with blood, I thought"; 131 "Come touch me baby in his waking dream"; 132 A Small Dream; 133 "As he frew famous – ah, but what is fame? – "; 134 "Sick at 6 & sick again at 9"; 135 "I heard said 'Cats that walk by their wild lone'"; 136 "While his wife earned the living, Rabbi Henry"; 137 "Many's the dawn sad Henry has seen in,"; 138 Combat Assignment; 139 "Green grieves the Prince over his girl forgone"; 140 "Henry is vanishing. In the first of dawn"; 141 "One was down on the Mass. One on the masses."; 142 "The animal moment, when he sorted out her tail"; 143 " – That's enough of that, Mr Bones. *Some* lady you make."; 144 "My orderly tender having too a gentle face"; 145 "Also I love him: me he's done no wrong".

VI: 146 "These lovely motions of the air, the breeze,"; 147 "Henry's mind grew blacker the more he thought."; 148 Glimmerings; 149 "This world is gradually becoming a place"; 150 "He had followers but they could not find him;"; 151 "Bitter & bleary over Delmore's dying:"; 152 "I bid you then a raggeder farewell"; 153 "I'm cross with god who has wrecked this generation."; 154 "Flagrant his young male beauty, thick his mind"; 155 "I can't get him out of my mind, out of my mind,"; 156 "I give in. I must not leave the scene of this same death"; 157 "Ten Songs, one solid block of agony,"; 158 "Being almost ready now to say Goodbye,"; 159 "Panic & shock, together. They are all going away."; 160 "Halfway to death, from his young years, he failed"; 161 "Draw on your resources. Draw on your resources."; 162 Vietnam; 163 "Stomach & arm, stomach & arm"; 164 "Three limbs, three seasons smashed; well, one to go."; 165 "An orange moon upon a placid sea"; 166 "I have strained everything except my ears,"; 167 Henry's Mail; 168 The Old Poor; 169 "Books drugs razor whisky shirts"; 170 "—I can't read any more of this Rich Critical Prose,"; 171 "Go, ill-sped book, and whisper to her or"; 172 "Your face broods from my table, Suicide."; 173 In Mem: R. P. Blackmur; 174 Kyrie Eleison; 175 "Old King Cole was a merry old soul and a merry old soul was Henry"; 176 "All that hair flashing over the Atlantic,"; 177 "Am tame now. You may touch me, who had thrilled"; 178 "Above the lindens tops of poplars waved"; 179 "A terrible applause pulls Henry's ear,"; 180 The Translator—I; 181 The Translator—II; 182 "Buoyant, chockful of stories, Henry lingered"; 183 News of God; 184 "Failed as a makar, nailed as scholar, failed"; 185 "The drill was after or is into him."; 186 "There is a swivelly grace that's up from grace"; 187 "Them lady poets must not marry, pal."; 188 "There is a kind of undetermined hair,"; 189 "The soft small snow gangs over my heavy house."; 190 "The doomed young envy the old, the doomed old the dead young."; 191 "The autumn breeze was light & bright. A small bird"; 192 "Love me love me love me love me love me"; 193 "Henry's friend's throat hurt. (Yvor Winters' dead.)"; 194 "If all must hurt at once, let yet more hurt now,"; 195 "I stalk my mirror down this corridor"; 196 "I see now all these deaths are to one end—"; 197 "(I saw in my dream"; 198 "—I held all solid, then I let some jangle,"; 199 "I dangle on the rungs, an open target."; 200 "I am interested & amazed: on the building across the way"; 201 "Hung by a thread more moments instant Henry's mind"; 202 "With shining strides hear his redeemer come,"; 203 "Nothing!—These young men come to interview me"; 204 "Henry, weak at keyboard music, leanèd on"; 205 "Come & dance, Housman's hopeless heroine"; 206 "Come again closer, Dr Swift & Professor Housman,"; 207 "—How are you? —Fine, fine. (I have tears unshed."; 208 "His mother wrote *good* news: somebody was still living."; 209 "Henry lay cold & golden in the snow";

210 "—Mr Blackmur, what are the holy cities of America?"; 211 "Forging the Andes, the sea-bottom, Angkor,"; 212 "With relief to public action, briefly stopt"; 213 "Wan shone my sun on Easter Monday,—ay,"; 214 "Which brandished goddess wide-eyed Henry's nights—"; 215 "Took Henry tea down at the Athenaeum with Yeats"; 216 "'Scads a good eats', dere own t'ree cars, the 'teens"; 217 "Some remember ('Pretty well') the Korean war."; 218 "Fortune gave him to know the flaming best,"; 219 So Long? Stevens; 220 "—If we're not Jews, how can messiah come?"; 221 "I poured myself out thro' my tips. What's left?"; 222 "It *was* a difficult crime to re-enact,"; 223 "It's wonderful the way cats bound about,"; 224 Eighty; 225 Pereant qui ante nos nostra dixerunt; 226 "Phantastic thunder shook the welkin, high."; 227 "Profoundly troubled over Miss Birnbaum—"; 228 "The Father of the Mill surveyed his falls,"; 229 "They laid their hands on Henry, kindly like,"; 230 "There are voices, voices. Light's dying. Birds have quit."; 231 Ode; 232 "They work not well on all but they did for him."; 233 Cantatrice; 234 The Carpenter's Son; 235 "Tears Henry shed for poor old Hemingway"; 236 "When Henry swung, in that great open square,"; 237 "When in the flashlights' flare the adultering pair"; 238 Henry's Programme for God; 239 "Am I a bad man? Am I a good man?"; 240 "Air with thought thick, air scratched. The desks are hinged,"; 241 "Father being the loneliest word in the one language"; 242 "About that 'me.' After a lecture once"; 243 "An undead morning. I . . . shuffle my poss's."; 244 "Calamity Jane lies very still"; 245 A Wake-Song; 246 "Flaps, on winter's first day, loosely the flag"; 247 "Henry walked as if he were ashamed"; 248 "Snowy of her breasts the drifts, I do believe,"; 249 "Bushes lay low. Uneven grass even lay low."; 250 "sád sights. A crumpled, empty cigarette pack.", 251 Walking, Flying—I; 252 Walking, Flying—II; 253 Walking, Flying—III; 254 "Mrs Thomas, Mrs Harris, and Mrs Neevel"; 255 "My twin, the nameless one, wild in the woods"; 256 "Henry rested, possessed of many pills"; 257 "The thunder & the flaw of their great quarrel"; 258 "Scarlatti spurts his wit across my brain,"; 259 "Does then our rivalry extend beyond"; 260 "Tides of dreadful creation rocked lonely Henry"; 261 "Restless, as once in love, he put pen to paper—"; 262 "The tenor of the line of your retreats,"; 263 "You couldn't bear to grow old, but we grow old."; 264 "I always wanted to be old, I wanted to say"; 265 "I don't know one damned butterfly from another"; 266 "Dinch me, dark God, having smoked me out."; 267 "Can Louis die? Why, then it's time to join him"; 268

"Henry, absent on parade, hair-triggered, mourned"; 269 "Acres of spirits every single day"; 270 "This fellow keeps on sticking at his drum,"; 271 "Why then did he make, at such cost, *crazy* sounds?"; 272 "The subject was her. He was the object. Clings"; 273 "Survive—exist—who is at others' will"; 274 "It's lovely just here now in the midst of night:"; 275 July 11; 276 Henry's Farewell—I; 277 Henry's Farewell—II; 278 Henry's Farewell—III.

VII: 279 "Leaving behind the country of the dead"; 280 "Decision taken, Henry'll be back abroad,"; 281 The Following Gulls; 282 "Richard & Randall, & one who never did,"; 283 "Shrouded the great stars, the great boat moves on."; 284 "The hand I shook will operate no more"; 285 "Much petted Henry like a petal throve,"; 286 "So Henry's enemy's lost, not paranoia"; 287 "A best word across a void makes a hard blaze."; 288 "In neighbourhoods evil of noise, he deployed, Henry,"; 289 "It is, after all her! & in the late afternoon"; 290 "Why *is* Ireland the wettest place on earth"; 291 "Cold & golden lay the high heroine"; 292 "The Irish sky is raining, the Irish winds are high,"; 293 "What gall had he in him, so to begin Book VII"; 294 "I broke a mirror, in which I figured you."; 295 "You dear you, clearing up Henry's foreign affairs,"; 296 "Of grace & fear, said Lady Valerie,"; 297 "Golden his mail came at his journey's end,"; 298 "Henry in transition, transient Henry,"; 299 "The Irish have the thickest ankles in the world"; 300 Henry Comforted; 301 "Shifted his mind & was once more full of the great Dean"; 302 "Cold & golden lay the high heroine"; 303 Three in Heaven I Hope; 304 "Maris & Valerie held his grand esteem"; 305 "Like the sunburst up the white breast of a black-footed penguin"; 306 "The Danish priest has horns of solid fire"; 307 "The Irish monk with horns of solid mire"; 308 An Instructions to Critics; 309 "Fallen leaves & litter. It is September."; 310 "His gift receded. He could write no more."; 311 "Famisht Henry ate everything in sight"; 312 "I have moved to Dublin to have it out with you,"; 313 "The Irish sunshine is lovely but a Belfast man"; 314 "Penniless, ill, abroad, Henry lay skew"; 315 "Behind me twice her necessary knight"; 316 "Blow upon blow, his fire-breath hurt me sore,"; 317 "My mother threw a tantrum on a high terrace"; 318 "Happy & idle, songless Henry swung"; 319 "Having escaped, except in his dreams, many dooms"; 320 "Steps almost unfamiliar toward his door"; 321 O land of Connolly & Pearse, what have"; 322 "I gave my love a cookie, as I said,"; 323 "Churchill was ever-active & crammed with glee,"; 324 An Elegy for W.C.W., the lovely man; 325 "Control it now, it

A 16.1.a *His Toy, His Dream, His Rest*   93

can't do any good,"; 326 "My right foot being colder than my left knee,"; 327 "Freud was some wrong about dreams, or almost all;"; 328 "−I write with my stomach: Henry ruefully;"; 329 "Henry on LSD was Henry indeed"; 330 "The Twiss is a tidy bundle, chirped joyous Henry,"; 331 "This is the third. What have I more to say"; 332 "Trunks & impedimenta. My manuscript won't go"; 333 "And now I've sent, custodian of Songs,"; 334 "Thrums up from nowhere a distinguisht wail,"; 335 "In his complex investigations of death"; 336 "Henry as a landlord made his eight friends laugh"; 337 "The mind is incalculable. Greatly excited"; 338 "According to the Annals of the Four Masters"; 339 "A maze of drink said: I will help you through the world."; 340 "The secret is not praise. It's just being accepted"; 341 The Dialogue, aet. 51; 342 "Fan-mail from foreign countries, is that fame?"; 343 "Another directory form to be corrected."; 344 Herbert Park, Dublin; 345 "Anarchic Henry thought of laying hands"; 346 "Henry's *very* rich American friends"; 347 "The day was dark. The day was hardly day."; 348 "700 years? It's too soon to decide,"; 349 "The great Bosch in the Prado, castles in Spain,"; 350 "All the girls, with their vivacious littles,"; 351 "Animal Henry sat reading the *Times Literary Supplement*"; 352 "The Cabin, Congdon St, & the Old Gristmill"; 353 "These massacres of the superior peoples,"; 354 "The only happy people in the world"; 355 Slattery's, in Ballsbridge; 356 "With fried excitement he looked across at life"; 357 "Henry's pride in his house was almost fierce,"; 358 The Gripe; 359 "In sleep, of a heart attack, let Henry go."; 360 "The universe has gifted me with friends,"; 361 The Armada Song; 362 "And now I meet you in the thinky place,"; 363 "I cast as feminine Miss Shirley Jones"; 364 *"There* is one book that Henry hasn't read:"; 365 "Henry, a foreigner, lustful & old,"; 366 "Chilled in this Irish pub I wish my loves"; 367 Henry's Crisis; 368 "At a gallop through his gates came monsters, buoyant"; 369 "I threw myself out helter-skelter-whiz"; 370 "Henry saw with Tolstoyan clarity"; 371 Henry's Guilt; 372 "O yes I wish her well. Let her come on"; 373 "My eyes with which I see so easily"; 374 "Drum Henry out, called some. Others called No,"; 375 His Helplessness; 376 "Christmas again, when you're supposed to be happiest."; 377 "Father Hopkins, teaching elementary Greek"; 378 "The beating of a horse fouled Nietszche's avatar,"; 379 "To the edge of Europe, the eighteenth edge,"; 380 From the French Hospital in New York, 901; 381 "Cave-man Henry grumbled to his spouse"; 382 "At Henry's bier let some thing fall out well:"; 383 "It brightens with power, when the dawn begins."; 384 "The marker slants, flowerless, day's almost done,"; 385 "My daughter's heavier. Light leaves are flying."

Typography and paper: 20 ll., $4\frac{1}{16}''$ ($5\frac{15}{16}''$) × $4\frac{3}{16}''$. Text in 11-pt. Linotype Janson with 4-pt. leading; note in 11-pt. with 2-pt. leading. Yellowish white (Centroid 92) laid paper (chain lines running vertically, spaced $\frac{27}{32}''$).

Binding: Unsized calico cloth (302), dark blue (Centroid 183). Front cover: plain. Spine: '[reading vertically from top to bottom] [goldstamped] *John Berryman* HIS TOY, HIS DREAM, HIS REST | FARRAR, STRAUS & GIROUX'. Back cover: plain. All edges cut; top edge dyed moderate pink (5). Pale yellowish pink (31) laid endpapers (chain lines running vertically, spaced $\frac{27}{32}''$), watermarked 'TWEEDWEAVE'.

Dust jacket: Wove paper, outside glossy, $8\frac{7}{16}''$ × 21". Front cover: '[black (Centroid 267) background] [vivid greenish yellow (97)] JOHN | BERRYMAN | [strong yellow (84)] HIS TOY, [deep purplish pink (248)] HIS | DREAM, [strong greenish blue (169)] HIS | REST'. Spine: '[black background] [reading horizontally] [vivid greenish yellow] JOHN | BERRY- | ·MAN | [strong yellow] HIS | TOY, | [deep purplish pink] HIS | DREAM, | [strong greenish blue] HIS | REST | [vivid greenish yellow] [device] | FARRAR, | STRAUS & | GIROUX'. Back cover: '[white (263) background] BERRYMAN'S SONNETS | [three-line quotation from a comment by William Meredith, four-line quotation from a comment by Dudley Fitts, and two-line quotation from a comment by Robert Penn Warren] | HOMAGE TO MISTRESS BRADSTREET | [one-line quotation from a comment by Robert Fitzgerald and two-line quotation from a comment by Edmund Wilson] | 77 DREAM SONGS | [four-line quotation from a comment by Allen Tate and three-line quotation from a comment by Robert Lowell] | SHORT POEMS | [six-line quotation from a comment by Conrad Aiken] | FARRAR, STRAUS & GIROUX'. Front flap: '[white background] $6.50 | JOHN BERRYMAN | HIS TOY, HIS DREAM, | HIS REST | [two unsigned paragraphs comprising a seven-line note on *The Dream Songs* and a sixteen-line quotation from the final paragraph of the author's note] | *Jacket design by Guy Fleming* | FARRAR, STRAUS AND GIROUX | 19 UNION SQUARE WEST | NEW YORK 10003'. Back flap: '[white background] [black and white photograph of JB] | [at left, reading vertically from bottom to top] *Terence Spencer, Life Magazine* © *Time Inc.* | [below photograph] [reading horizontally] John Berryman | FARRAR,

A 16.1.a *His Toy, His Dream, His Rest*   95

STRAUS AND GIROUX | 19 UNION SQUARE WEST | NEW YORK 10003'.

Text: First publication of Dream Songs 91, 92, 94, 96, 99-104, 106-146, 149, 158-160, 162-164, 166, 169, 173-179, 182-185, 188-190, 192, 193, 195-198, 202, 203, 205-208, 211-215, 218, 220-223, 225-232, 235-257, 259-263, 266-297, 299-311, 313-383. First book appearance of all other Dream Songs except 90, 93, 97, 234, 312, 385.

Publication: Unknown number of copies. Published October 25, 1968. $6.50.

Printing: Printed and bound by the American Book-Stratford Press, New York, N.Y.

Copyright: Registered under A 29638 in the name of JB.

Locations: DLC (deposit-stamp November 14, 1968); ECS (dj); Lilly (dj); Lockwood (dj); NBuU; PPi (dj); PPiCI; PPiU.

Note one: Variants and revisions in three poems between their appearances in the separate publications indicated and in *Toy* are noted as follows:

  Dream Song 234, *Two Dream Songs* (1965)
      l. 1:   stood, [stood
      l. 2:   saning [& saned
      l. 3:   cónjoined [conjoined
      l. 4:   toward them until he stood [with them until he got
      l. 7:   Repent, [—Repent,
      l. 8:   Did [Díd
      l. 12a: Stood strength, hung gentleness. [
      l. 13:   O   some [O one
      l. 16:   us [as
      l. 17:   manlihood. [manlihood,
      l. 18:   This [this
  Dream Song 312, *Poetry Season 1967*
      l. 15:   your [Your
      l. 17:   welled [walled
  Dream Song 385, *Two Dream Songs* (1965)
      l. 3:   & [and
      l. 9:   & [and
      l. 10:   grievy— [grievy,
      l. 13:   & [and
      l. 14:   Henry. [Henry;
      l. 15:   That's [that's

l. 16: middle ground between things & [
       middle   ground between things and
l. 18: scold
            my heavy daughter. [
       scold
                my heavy daughter.

Note two: Punctuation, spelling, and usage in 77DS and *Toy* are highly idiosyncratic, and it is impossible to say whether these forms are the author's intentions or whether they are typographical errors. For example, in Dream Song 316, line 15 ends with a period and the first word in line 16 does not begin with a capital letter, and this form is preserved in *SelP;* in Dream Song 192, *Kierkegaardian* is spelled as *Kierkegardian* in line 5, but the word *Kierkegaard* appears in line 13 of Dream Song 53; in Dream Song 118, the word *theirselves* appears in line 11, but the word is replaced by *themselves* in *SelP*.

Note three: In the table of contents, untitled Dream Songs are indicated by their first lines or by part of their first lines. There are some seventy-eight instances in which commas as end-of-line punctuation are omitted. Other variants in titles and first lines as they appear in the table of contents and in the text are noted as follows:

```
            CONTENTS
xii. 3      junior [ junior—
xii. 12     garbage [ garbage.
xiii. 8     famous [ famous—
xiv. 23     mem: [ Mem:
xv. 20      amazed [ amazed:
xv. 28      news [ news:
xvi. 6      Scads a good eats [ 'Scads a good eats',
xvi. 9      long? [ Long?
xvi. 14     Lonely in his great age [ Eighty
xvii. 2     'me' [ 'me.'
xvii. 10    Sad [ sád
xix. 7      tramped [ tramped.
xix. 8      hope [ Hope
xx. 3       stomach [ stomach:
xx. 12      incalculable [ incalculable.
xx. 14      said [ said:
xx. 18      corrected [ corrected.
xx. 29      only [ only happy
xxi. 30     heavier [ heavier.
```

A 16.1.a† *His Toy, His Dream, His Rest* 97

A 16.1.a†
Proof copy

8³⁄₈" × 5⁷⁄₁₆"

173 leaves (plastic binding)

[A–B] I–VI vii VIII–X xi–xxi 22 1–317 [318–322]

Contents: p. A: 'ATTENTION, READER! | [six-paragraph unsigned note, comprising statements on the copy as an uncorrected galley proof and not a finished book, the correction of errors in the published book, the intention of the copy as "pre-publicity proof," the method of production, the uniformity of color of the type lines, and an endorsement of the work, twenty-seven lines] | CRANE DUPLICATING SERVICE, INC. | on Cape Cod | Box 487, Barnstable, Massachusetts 02630 | [telephone number]'. p. B: blank. p. I: half title. p. II: '*Books by John Berryman* | [six titles, eight lines]'. p. III: title page. p. IV: copyright page. p. V: dedication. p. VI: blank. p. vii: epigraphs. p. VIII: blank. p. IX: author's note. p. X: blank. pp. xi–xxi: table of contents. p. 22: blank. p. 1: 'I'. p. 2: blank. pp. 3–16: text. p. 17: 'V'. p. 18: blank. pp. 19–72: text. p. 73: 'VI'. p. 74: blank. pp. 75–207: text. p. 208: blank. p. 209: 'VII'. p. 210: blank. pp. 211–317: text. pp. 318–322: blank.

Items included: Same as in the first printing.

Typography and paper: Same typography as in the first printing. Yellowish white (Centroid 92) wove paper.

Binding: Plastic binding. White (Centroid 263) plastic strip. Very light greenish blue (171) wove paper covers. Front cover: '[pasted-on label] [on yellowish white (92) panel with vivid purplish blue (194) border] [vivid purplish blue] <u>A SET OF GALLEYS</u> | from | FARRAR, STRAUS & GIROUX, INC. | NOONDAY PAPERBACKS Book Publishers | 19 Union Square West, New York, New York 10003 | [rule] | TITLE [typewritten above a vivid purplish blue line] [black (267)] HIS TOY, HIS DREAM, HIS REST | [vivid purplish blue] AUTHOR [typewritten above a vivid purplish blue line] [black] JOHN BERRYMAN | [vivid purplish blue] PUBLICATION DATE [typewritten above a vivid purplish blue line] [black] OCT. 25, 1968 [vivid purplish blue] PRICE [typewritten above a vivid purplish blue line] [black] $6.50 | [below label] [black] *John Berryman* | HIS TOY, | HIS DREAM, | HIS REST | *308 Dream Songs* | *Farrar, Straus and Giroux* [slash] NEW YORK'. Spine: plain. Back cover: plain. Sheets hole-punched. All edges trimmed.

Location: Meissner.

Note: The following page numbers are written in: I–VI, VIII–X, 22 [xxii], 1–2, 17–18, 73–74, 174, 208–210.

A 16.1.b
Second printing: New York: Farrar, Straus and Giroux, [1968].
On copyright page: 'Second printing, 1968'.

A 16.1.c
First English reprint [1969]

John Berryman

HIS TOY, HIS DREAM, HIS REST

308 Dream Songs

Faber and Faber / LONDON

A 16.1.c: 8¼" × 5¹³⁄₁₆"

> First published in England in 1969
> by Faber and Faber Limited
> 24 Russell Square London W C 1
> Printed in Great Britain by
> John Dickens & Co Ltd Northampton
> All rights reserved
>
> SBN 571 09088 5
>
> © 1964, 1965, 1966, 1967, 1968
> by John Berryman

[1–20]⁸ [21]⁴ [22]⁸

Same pagination as in the first American printing.

Contents: pp. A–B: blank. p. i: half title. p. ii: '*Books by John Berryman* | [three titles]'. p. iii: title page. p. iv: copyright page. p. v: dedication. p. vi: blank. p. vii: epigraphs. p. viii: blank. p. ix: author's note. p. x: blank. pp. xi–xxi: table of contents. p. xxii: blank. p. 1: 'IV'. p. 2: blank. pp. 3–16: text. p. 17: 'V'. p. 18: blank. pp. 19–72: text. p. 73: 'VI'. p. 74: blank. pp. 75–207: text. p. 208: blank. p. 209: 'VII'. p. 210: blank. pp. 211–317: text. pp. 318–320: blank.

Items included: Same as in the first American printing.

Typography and paper: 20 ll., $4\tfrac{1}{16}''$ ($5\tfrac{15}{16}''$) × $4\tfrac{5}{16}''$. Yellowish white (Centroid 92) wove paper.

Binding: Unsized calico-cloth (302), brilliant blue (Centroid 177). Front cover: plain. Spine: '[reading horizontally] [gold-stamped] HIS TOY | HIS DREAM | HIS REST | · | John | Berryman | FABER'. Back cover: plain. All edges cut. Yellowish white (92) wove endpapers of different stock than text paper.

Dust jacket: Wove paper, $8\tfrac{1}{2}''$ × $20\tfrac{1}{2}''$. Front cover: '[deep reddish orange (Centroid 36) background] JOHN | BERRYMAN | [white (263)] [thick rule] | [grayish blue (186) background] HIS TOY | HIS DREAM | HIS REST'. Spine: '[reading horizontally] [deep reddish orange background] [thick rule] | JOHN | BERRY-|MAN | [white] [thick rule] | [grayish blue background] [black (267)] HIS | TOY, | HIS | DREAM, | HIS | REST | [thick rule] | Faber'. Back cover: '[white background] also by John Berryman | BERRYMAN'S SONNETS | [eight-line quotation from a comment by Martin Dodsworth] | HOMAGE TO MISTRESS BRADSTREET | *and other poems* | [two-line quotation from a comment by Conrad Aiken and three-line quotation from a comment by A. Alvarez] | 77 DREAM SONGS | [two-line

A 16.1.e *His Toy, His Dream, His Rest*

quotation from a comment by Robert Lowell and three-line quotation from a comment in *The Times* (London)] | [rule] | [three-line advertisement for catalogue]'. Front flap: '[white background] His Toy, His Dream, | His Rest | JOHN BERRYMAN | [two unsigned paragraphs comprising a seven-line note on *The Dream Songs* and a fifteen-line quotation from the author's note] | 50s | £2.50 |*net*'. Back flap: '[white background] [black and white photograph of JB] JOHN BERRYMAN | *author of* | HIS TOY, HIS DREAM, HIS REST | BERRYMAN'S SONNETS | HOMAGE TO | MISTRESS BRADSTREET | 77 DREAM SONGS'.

Publication: 2,000 copies. Published May 5, 1969. 50s.

Printing: Printed from lithographic plates by John Dickens and Company, Ltd., Northampton, Northamptonshire. Bound by James Burn and Company Ltd., Esher, Surrey.

Locations: BM (deposit-stamp April 18, 1969); ECS.

A 16.1.c†
Proof copy

$8^{5}/_{16}'' \times 5^{15}/_{16}''$

Same collation and pagination as in the first English printing.

Contents: Same as in the first English printing.

Items included: Same as in the first English printing.

Typography and paper: Same typography and paper as in the first English printing.

Binding: Light bluish gray (Centroid 190) wove paper wrappers. Front cover: '*John Berryman* | HIS TOY, | HIS DREAM, | HIS REST | *FABER AND FABER*'. Spine: '[reading vertically from top to bottom] HIS TOY, HIS DREAM, HIS REST *John Berryman*'. Back cover: plain. All edges cut. Cover cut flush.

Location: Meissner.

A 16.1.d
Third printing: New York: Farrar, Straus and Giroux, [1969]. On copyright page: 'Third printing, 1969'.

A 16.1.e
Fourth printing: New York: Farrar, Straus and Giroux, [1969]. On copyright page: 'Fourth printing, 1969'.

A 17 ACCEPTANCE SPEECH FOR NATIONAL BOOK AWARD
(1969)

[at top of page, at left] John Berryman | National Book Award in Poetry 1969 | Acceptance Speech 3 [slash] 12 [slash] 69

$11'' \times 8\frac{1}{2}''$

One leaf

[1-2]

Contents: p. 1: untitled five-paragraph address, thirty-six lines; below text, '[three spaced asterisks (* * *) centered on the page] | [at left] (425 words) | #N166 (3 [slash] 12 [slash] 69)'. p. 2: blank.

Typography and paper: 40 ll., $6^{11}/_{16}''$ (9") $\times$ $6\frac{1}{2}''$. Mimeographed on recto only. Typewritten, elite type. White (Centroid 263) wove paper.

Binding: Unbound single leaf.

Publication: Unknown number of copies. Distributed March 12, 1969. Not for sale.

Printing: Issued by The National Book Committee, New York, N.Y.

Locations: ECS; Lilly; Lockwood.

Note one: This speech was presumably mimeographed, but it is impossible to determine whether the copies are mimeographed or multilithed. Electrostatic copies were also distributed.

Note two: It was presumably issued for publicity purposes. Specific information was not made available by The National Book Committee.

Note three: JB delivered his acceptance speech for the National Book Award in Poetry for *His Toy, His Dream, His Rest* at Philharmonic Hall, Lincoln Center, New York, N.Y., on March 12, 1969.

Note four: A brief excerpt from the speech appeared in "The Book Industry Presents the 20th National Book Awards," *Publishers Weekly,* CXCV (March 24, 1969), 26-32 [28-29].

A 18 THE DREAM SONGS

A 18.1.a
First edition, first printing [1969]

> John Berryman
>
> # THE DREAM SONGS
>
> Farrar, Straus and Giroux / NEW YORK

A 18.1.a: 8¼" × 6¹⁄₁₆"

A 18.1.a *The Dream Songs*

> Copyright © 1959, 1962, 1963, 1964, 1965, 1966, 1967, 1968, 1969
> by John Berryman
> Library of Congress catalog card number: 74-93811
> First printing, 1969
> Published simultaneously in Canada by
> Doubleday Canada Ltd., Toronto
> Printed in the United States of America
> Designed by Guy Fleming

[1-13]¹⁶ [14]⁴ [15]¹⁶

[i-vi] vii-xx [xxi-xxvi] [1-2] 3-28 [29-30] 31-55 [56-58] 59-84 [85-92] 93-106 [107-108] 109-162 [163-164] 165-263 [264] 265-297 [298-300] 301-407 [408] 409-423 [424] 425-427 [428-430]

Contents: p. i: 'THE DREAM SONGS'. p. ii: '*Books by John Berryman* | [seven titles]'. p. iii: title page. p. iv: copyright page. pp. v-vi: '*Note:*', four paragraphs comprising a three-line note on the volume, eighteen lines of acknowledgments, thirteen lines of dedications of songs to individuals, and a thirteen-line comment on the poem, signed 'J.B.' pp. vii-xx: table of contents. p. xxi: '77 DREAM SONGS'. p. xxii: blank. p. xxiii: "*To Kate, and to Saul* | 'THOU DREWEST NEAR IN THE DAY'". p. xxiv: blank. p. xxv: "'GO IN, BRACK MAN, DE DAY'S YO' OWN.' | . . . I AM THEIR MUSICK. | *Lam. 3:63* | BUT THERE IS ANOTHER METHOD. | *Olive Schreiner*". p. xxvi: blank. p. 1: 'I'. p. 2: blank. pp. 3-28: text. p. 29: 'II'. p. 30: blank. pp. 31-55: text. p. 56: blank. p. 57: 'III'. p. 58: blank. pp. 59-84: text. p. 85: '*HIS TOY,* | *HIS DREAM,* | *HIS REST*'. p. 86: blank. p. 87: '*To Mark Van Doren,* | *and to the sacred memory* | *of Delmore Schwartz*'. p. 88: blank. p. 89: 'NO INTERESTING PROJECT CAN BE EMBARKED ON WITHOUT | FEAR. I SHALL BE SCARED TO DEATH HALF THE TIME. | *Sir Francis Chichester in Sydney* | FOR MY PART I AM ALWAYS FRIGHTENED, AND VERY MUCH | SO. I FEAR THE FUTURE OF ALL ENGAGEMENTS. | *Gordon in Khartoum* | I AM PICKT UP AND SORTED TO A PIP. MY IMAGINATION IS | A MONASTERY AND I AM ITS MONK. | *Keats to Shelley* | HE WENT AWAY AND NEVER SAID GOODBYE. | I COULD READ HIS LETTERS BUT I SURE CAN'T READ HIS MIND. | I THOUGHT HE'S LOVIN ME BUT HE WAS LEAVIN ALL THE TIME. | NOW I KNOW THAT MY TRUE LOVE WAS BLIND. | *Victoria Spivey?*'. p. 90: blank. p. 91: 'IV'. 92: blank. pp. 93-106: text. p. 107: 'V'. p. 108: blank. pp. 109-162: text. p. 163: 'VI'. p. 164: blank. pp. 165-297: text. p. 298: blank. p. 299: 'VII'. p. 300: blank. pp. 301-407: text. p. 408: blank. pp. 409-423: '*Index of First Lines*'. p. 424: blank. pp. 425-427: '*Index of Titles*'. pp. 428-430: blank.

A 18.1.a *The Dream Songs* 105

Items included: Combines the sections of 77 *Dream Songs* and *His Toy, His Dream, His Rest*, Dream Songs 1-385.

Typography and paper: 20 ll., 4⅛" (6¹/₁₆") × 4¼" for 77 *Dream Songs*; 4¹/₁₆" (5¹⁵/₁₆") × 4¼" for *His Toy, His Dream, His Rest*. Text in 11-pt. Linotype Janson with 4-pt. leading; note in 11-pt. with 2-pt. leading. Yellowish white (Centroid 92) laid paper (chain lines running vertically, spaced ²⁷/₃₂").

Binding: Unsized calico-cloth (302), dark blue (Centroid 183). Front cover: plain. Spine: '[reading vertically from top to bottom] [goldstamped] *John Berryman* THE DREAM SONGS | Farrar, Straus & Giroux'. Back cover: plain. All edges cut; top edge dyed moderate pink (5). Moderate yellow green (120) wove endpapers.

Dust jacket: Wove paper, outside glossy, 8⅜" × 21¼". Front cover: '[black (Centroid 267) background] [white (263)] John | Berryman | [brilliant yellow green (116)] The | [moderate purplish pink (250)] Dream | [brilliant yellow green] Songs | [moderate purplish pink] The only complete one-volume edition of | 77 *Dream Songs* [bracket] PULITZER PRIZE [bracket] and | *His Toy, His Dream, His Rest* [bracket] NATIONAL BOOK AWARD [bracket]'. Spine: '[black background] [reading horizontally] [white] John | Berryman | [brilliant yellow green] The | Dream | Songs | [moderate purplish pink] [device] | FARRAR | STRAUS | GIROUX'. Back cover: '[white background] HOMAGE TO MISTRESS BRADSTREET | [one-line quotation from a comment by Robert Fitzgerald and two-line quotation from a comment by Edmund Wilson] | BERRYMAN'S SONNETS | [two-line quotation from a comment by Robert Penn Warren and three-line quotation from a comment by Dudley Fitts] | SHORT POEMS | [three-line quotation from a comment by Conrad Aiken] | 77 DREAM SONGS | [four-line quotation from a comment by Allen Tate] | HIS TOY, HIS DREAM, HIS REST | [three-line quotation from a comment by Karl Shapiro and five-line quotation from a comment by Helen Vendler] | FARRAR, STRAUS & GIROUX'. Front flap: '[white background] $10.00 | John Berryman | THE DREAM SONGS | [beginning of two-paragraph unsigned note on the poem, containing quotations from comments by Denis Donoghue and A. Alvarez, twenty-five lines, and lines 7-8 of Dream Song 311] | *(continued on back flap)*'. Back flap: '[white background] *(continued from front flap)* | [lines 9-12 of Dream Song 311 and conclusion of note, containing quotation from a comment by James Schevill, five lines] | *Jacket design by Charles Skaggs* | Farrar, Straus and Giroux | 19 union square west | new york 10003'.

Text: The text comprises 385 sections (Books I–VII), combining 77 *Dream Songs* and *His Toy, His Dream, His Rest.* The author's "Note" combines the notes of the two earlier volumes. The "Index of First Lines" and the "Index of Titles" constitute new matter.

Publication: Unknown number of copies. Published December 5, 1969. $10.00.

Printing: Printed by H. Wolff Book Manufacturing Company, New York, from plates made by Book Printers, Inc., Mamaroneck, N.Y. Bound by Wolff.

Copyright: Registered under A 224130 in the name of JB.

Locations: DLC (deposit-stamp April 1, 1971); ECS (dj); Lilly (dj); Lockwood (dj); NBuU; PPi (dj); PPiCI (dj); PPiU (dj); PPT (dj).

Note one: In the table of contents, untitled Dream Songs are indicated by their first lines or by part of their first lines. There are some one hundred instances in which commas as end-of-line punctuation are omitted. Variants in titles and first lines as they appear in the table of contents and in the text are noted as follows:

	CONTENTS	
vii.10	gatherings	[gatherings.
vii.17	Henry	[Henry:
viii.4	bones	[bones:
viii.15	lonely	[lonely.
viii.20	ruin	[ruin.
ix.6	sin	[sin–
ix.11	dark-brown	[dark brown
ix.14	angle	[ankle
ix.23	world	[world.
xi.3	junior	[junior–
xi.12	garbage	[garbage.
xii.8	famous	[famous–
xiii.23	*mem:*	[*Mem:*
xiv.20	amazed	[amazed:
xiv.28	news	[news:
xv.6	Scads a good eats	['Scads a good eats',
xv.9	*long?*	[*Long?*
xv.14	Lonely in his great age	[*Eighty*

A 18.1.a *The Dream Songs*

```
xvi.2      'me'  [  'me.'
xvi.10     sad   [  sád
xviii.7    tramped  [  tramped.
xviii.8    hope  [  Hope
xix.3      stomach  [  stomach:
xix.12     incalculable  [  incalculable.
xix.14     said  [  said:
xix.18     corrected  [  corrected.
xix.29     only  [  only happy
xx.30      heavier  [  heavier.
```

Note two: Variants between the first lines of poems in the "Index of First Lines" and in the text are noted as follows:

```
           INDEX
409.6      ears,  [  ear,
410.8      fame?  [  fame? —
411.11     daily  [  daily,
413.8      beams'  [  beans'
414.17     full  [  full,
414.19     less  [  less,
415.20     jangle  [  jangle,
416.17     races,  [  graces,
416.21     was  [  was
418.1      'NO VISITORS'  [  'NO VISITORS'
418.20     shook  [  shook the
419.2      of  [  a
419.16     war  [  war.
419.17     Path  [  Path.
420.5      St  [  St,
420.25     done  [  done,
421.29     Ike  [  Ike.
422.4      Heaven  [  heaven
422.8      rocks  [  rocked
423.9      here  [  hear
```

Note three: In the "Index of First Lines," the first lines of Dream Song 52 ("Bright-eyed & bushy-tailed woke not Henry up.") and Dream Song 92 ("Something black somewhere in the vistas of his heart.") are not included. The second line of Dream Song 92 ("Tulips from Tates teazed Henry in the mood") is listed as the first line of that poem. The first line of Dream Song 319 ("Having escaped, except in his dreams, many dooms") is listed as being that of Dream Song 299.

Note four: In the "Index of Titles," the title "Eighty" (Dream Song 224) is not included; "In Mem: R. P. Blackmur" (Dream

Song 173) is misnumbered as 178; and "Sabbath" (Dream Song 12) is repeated on p. 427.

A 18.1.b
Second printing: New York: Farrar, Straus and Giroux. Not differentiated on copyright page, but probably published in 1971. Sunburst 12. Printed wrappers. $3.95.

A 18.1.c
Third printing: New York: Farrar, Straus and Giroux, [1972]. On copyright page: '*Second printing, 1972*'. Printed wrappers.

A 19 TWO DREAM SONGS
(1969)

Two Dream Songs

Seasons Greetings

Kate, Martha & John Berryman   1969

A 19: 7″ × 5″

[1]²

[1-4]

Contents: p. 1: title page. p. 2: 'Rembrandt Van Rijn Obiit 8 October 1669', eighteen lines. p. 3: 'The Handshake, The Entrance: Henry's Prayer', nineteen lines. p. 4: blank.

Typography and paper: 4½" (5") × 3½". Text in 9-pt. Linotype Baskerville Bold with 7-pt. leading. Yellowish white (Centroid 92) wove paper.

Binding: Unbound and single-folded folio sheet. Fore edge of first leaf deckled; all other edges cut.

Text: First publication of "Rembrandt Van Rijn Obiit 8 October 1669" and "The Handshake, The Entrance: Henry's Prayer" (collected in *DE* as "The Handshake, The Entrance").

Publication: Unknown number of copies. Printed ca. December 1969. Not for sale.

Printing: Privately printed. Printer not known.

Copyright: No copyright application filed.

Locations: ECS; PAB.

A 20 LOVE & FAME

A 20.1.a
First edition, first printing, first issue (1970)

LOVE & FAME
JOHN BERRYMAN

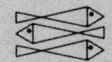 NEW YORK

FARRAR, STRAUS AND GIROUX

1970

A 20.1.a: 8½" × 6"

> Copyright © 1970 by John Berryman
> All rights reserved
> Library of Congress catalog card number: 74-137749
> SBN 374.1.9233.2
>
> FIRST EDITION, 1970
>
> Printed in the United States of America
> Published simultaneously in Canada
> by Doubleday Canada Ltd., Toronto
> DESIGNED BY HERB JOHNSON
>
> Acknowledgments are made to the editors
> of *The New Yorker*, in which "Death Ballad" was
> first published; and for other
> poems to the editors of *American Scholar, Atlantic
> Monthly, Harper's, Minneapolis Tribune, The Nation, New Republic,
> The New York Review, Saturday Review, Shenandoah,* and *The Times
> Literary Supplement*

[1]² [2-8]⁸

[i-xvi] [1-2] 3-31 [32-34] 35-52 [53-54] 55-82 [83-84] 85-96 [97-100]

Contents: pp. i-ii: blank. p. iii: 'This edition of *Love & Fame,* | signed by the author, is limited to | two hundred and fifty numbered copies, | of which this is copy number [number or letter written in] | [signed by JB]'. p. iv: blank. p. v: '*LOVE & FAME*'. p. vi: blank. p. vii: '*Other Books by John Berryman* | [nine titles]'. p. viii: blank. p. ix: title page. p. x: copyright page. p. xi: "To the memory of | the suffering lover & young Breton master | who called himself 'Tristan Corbière' | (I wish I versed with his bite) | SLEEP! IN YOUR BOAT BROUGHT INTO THE LIVING-ROOM | SUPREME ADMIRER OF THE ANCIENT SEA | YOUR MOCKERY OF THE PRETENTIOUS GREAT | YOUR SELF-REVELATIONS | CONSTITUTE STILL IN ANY SUNSET SKY | A CURSING GLORY". p. xii: blank. pp. xiii-xv: table of contents. p. xvi: blank. p. 1: '*PART ONE*'. p. 2: blank. pp. 3-31: text. p. 32: blank. p. 33: '*PART TWO*'. p. 34: blank. pp. 35-52: text. p. 53: '*PART THREE*'. p. 54: blank. pp. 55-82: text. p. 83: '*PART FOUR*'. p. 84: blank. pp. 85-96: text. pp. 97-100: blank.

Items included: PART ONE: Her & It; Cadenza on Garnette; Shirley & Auden; Freshman Blues; Images of Elspeth; My Special Fate; Drunks; Down & Back; Two Organs; Olympus; Nowhere; In & Out; The Heroes; Crisis; Recovery. PART TWO: Away; First Night at Sea; London; The Other Cambridge; Friendless; Monkhood; Views of Myself; Transit; Thank You, Christine; Meeting; Tea; A Letter; To B—— E——. PART THREE: The Search; Message; Relations; Antitheses; The

Soviet Union; The Minnesota 8 and the Letter-Writers; Regents' Professor Berryman's Crack on Race; Have a Genuine American Horror-&-Mist on the Rocks; To a Woman; A Huddle of Need; Damned; Of Suicide; Dante's Tomb; Despair; The Hell Poem; Death Ballad; 'I *Know*'; Purgatory; Heaven; The Home Ballad. PART FOUR: Eleven Addresses to the Lord: 1 "Master of beauty, craftsman of the snowflake,"; 2 "Holy, as I suppose I dare to call you"; 3 "Sole watchman of the flying stars, guard me"; 4 "If I say Thy name, art Thou there? It may be so."; 5 "Holy, & holy. The damned are said to say"; 6 "Under new management, Your Majesty:"; 7 "After a Stoic, a Peripatetic, a Pythagorean,"; A Prayer for the Self; 9 "Surprise me on some ordinary day"; 10 "Fearful I peer upon the mountain path"; 11 "Germanicus leapt upon the wild lion in Smyrna,".

Typography and paper: 36 ll., $6^9/_{16}''$ ($6^{13}/_{16}''$) × $5^5/_{16}''$. Text in 11-pt. Linotype Janson with 2-pt. leading. White (Centroid 263) laid paper (chain lines running vertically, spaced $3^1/_{32}''$).

Numbering and signing: All copies examined were numbered in arabic numerals in black ink after the statement on p. iii and signed by JB in blue ink at the bottom of the page.[5]

Binding: Spine and 1" of boards in unsized calico-cloth (302), strong reddish purple (Centroid 237); remainder of boards in sized calico-cloth (302), yellowish white (92). Front cover: plain. Spine: '[reading vertically from top to bottom] [within a black (267) rectangular compartment notched at the corners and bordered in gold] [goldstamped] JOHN BERRYMAN LOVE & FAME FSG'. Back cover: plain. All edges cut and gilt. End-papers: the visible side of the lining papers and the corresponding side of the free endpapers have swirls in brownish pink (33), moderate green (145), dark grayish purple (229), and white; the other side of the free endpapers are white (263); laid paper (chain lines running vertically, spaced 1").

---

5. Robert Giroux wrote on January 16, 1974: "The entire limited edition consisted of 250 copies, signed by the author. Most of them were numbered with arabic numerals, but I recall that some of the presentation copies were lettered by Berryman, not only from A to J, but from Alpha to Kappa, Roman numeral I to V, lower case i to v, and perhaps others. This was the author's joke. No record was kept, of course, since these were his presentation copies, but they were all included in the total of 250 copies. . . . [M]y guess (and that is what it has to be) would be 30 to 50 such copies. The remaining 200 to 220 copies were numbered." None of the presentation copies have been seen.

Slipcase: Cardboard covered with sized calico-cloth (302), black (Centroid 267).

Text: First publication of "Cadenza on Garnette," "Shirley & Auden," "Freshman Blues," "Images of Elspeth," "My Special Fate," "Two Organs," "In & Out," "Crisis," "Recovery," "Away," "London," "Views of Myself," "Thank You, Christine," "A Letter," "Message," "Relations," "Regents' Professor Berryman's Crack on Race," "Have a Genuine American Horror-&-Mist on the Rocks," "A Huddle of Need," "Damned," "Of Suicide," "Dante's Tomb," "Despair," "'I *Know*'," "Purgatory," "The Home Ballad," "Eleven Addresses to the Lord" (Sections 6, 7, 9, and 10). First book appearance of all other poems.

Publication: 250 copies. Published December 14, 1970. $25.00.

Printing: Printed and bound by H. Wolff Book Manufacturing Company, New York, N.Y.

Copyright: Registered under A 201314 in the name of JB.

Locations: ECS; Lilly; PPiCI (no slipcase).

A 20.1.a*
Second issue

$8\tfrac{7}{8}'' \times 6''$

$[1-7]^8$

[i-xii] [1-2] 3-31 [32-34] 35-52 [53-54] 55-82 [83-84] 85-96 [97-100]

Contents: p. i: half title. p. ii: blank. p. iii: list of titles by JB. p. iv: blank. p. v: title page. p. vi: copyright page. p. vii: dedication. p. viii: blank. pp. ix-xi: table of contents. p. xii: blank. p. 1: '*PART ONE*'. p. 2: blank. pp. 3-31: text. p. 32: blank. p. 33: '*PART TWO*'. p. 34: blank. pp. 35-52: text. p. 53: '*PART THREE*'. p. 54: blank. pp. 55-82: text. p. 83: '*PART FOUR*'. p. 84: blank. pp. 85-96: text. pp. 97-100: blank.

Items included: Same as in the first issue.

Typography and paper: Same typography as in the first issue. Yellowish white (Centroid 92) laid paper (chain lines running vertically, spaced $\tfrac{27}{32}''$).

Binding: Unsized calico-cloth (302), black (Centroid 267). Front cover: plain. Spine: '[reading vertically from top to bot-

A 20.1.a* *Love & Fame*

tom] [goldstamped] [first letter of first two words swash] *JOHN BERRYMAN* [slash] *LOVE & FAME* [slash] *Farrar, Straus & Giroux'*. Back cover: plain. All edges cut; top edge dyed light purple (222). Pale yellow (89) wove endpapers.

Dust jacket: Pale yellow (Centroid 89) wove paper, $8\frac{3}{4}'' \times 20''$. Front cover: 'John | Berryman | [open letters outlined in deep purple (219)] LOVE | [solid black (267)] & | [open letters outlined in deep purple] FAME'. Spine: '[reading vertically from top to bottom] John Berryman [open letters outlined in deep purple] LOVE [solid black] & [open letters outlined in deep purple] FAME | [reading horizontally] [solid black] FARRAR | STRAUS | GIROUX'. Back cover: photograph of JB in tones of black and pale yellow. Front flap: '[at left] SBN 374.1.9233.2 [at right] $6.50 | JOHN BERRYMAN | LOVE & FAME | [two unsigned paragraphs comprising an eight-line note on JB's achievements and a fourteen-line descriptive comment on contents, containing lines 9–12 of "Freshman Blues"] | FARRAR, STRAUS AND GIROUX | 19 UNION SQUARE WEST | NEW YORK 10003'. Back flap: 'by John Berryman | [nine titles, twelve lines] | *Jacket design by Charles Skaggs* | *Photo on jacket verso by Terence Spencer* | FARRAR, STRAUS AND GIROUX | 19 UNION SQUARE WEST | NEW YORK 10003'.

Publication: Unknown number of copies. Published December 14, 1970. $6.50.

Printing: Printed and bound by H. Wolff Book Manufacturing Company, New York, N.Y.

Locations: DLC (deposit-stamp December 16, 1970); ECS (dj); Lilly (dj); Lockwood (dj); NBuU; PPi (dj).

Note: In a letter of May 16, 1973, Robert Giroux wrote: "The limited signed edition of *Love & Fame* consisted of 250 copies on special paper, printed before the first regular edition went through the press on different stock. Every copy of the limited edition, signed by Mr. Berryman while he was in New York, bears the legend 'First Edition, 1970.'" In response to a request for clarification, Mr. Giroux wrote on July 9, 1973: "As you define it, the first regular edition of *Love & Fame* was an issue, not a second printing. The limited edition was run off first and the paper changed with the plates still on the press." Thus, according to the best evidence available, the plates were not removed from the press although the paper stock was changed; the copies of *Love & Fame* are distinguished as issues.

A 20.1.a†
Proof copy

11" × 5⁷⁄₁₆"

37 leaves (plastic binding)

[i–ii] [1–10] 11–29 [30–31] 32–42 [43–44] 45–69 [70–72]

Contents: p. i: 'ATTENTION, READER! | [six-paragraph unsigned note, comprising statements on the copy as an uncorrected galley proof and not a finished book, the correction of errors in the published book, the intention of the copy as "prepublicity proof," the method of production, the uniformity of color of the type lines, and an endorsement of the work, twenty-seven lines] | CRANE DUPLICATING SERVICE, INC. | on Cape Cod | Box 487, Barnstable, Massachusetts 02630 | [telephone number]'. p. ii: blank. p. 1: half title. p. 2: *'Other Books by John Berryman* | [six titles]'. p. 3: title page. p. 4: copyright page. pp. 5–6: table of contents. p. 7: dedication. p. 8: blank. p. 9: 'PART ONE'. p. 10: blank. pp. 11–29: text. p. 30: blank. p. 31: 'PART TWO'. pp. 32–42: text. p. 43: 'PART THREE'. p. 44: blank. pp. 45–69: text. pp. 70–72: blank.

Items included: PART ONE: Her & It; Cadenza on Garnette; Shirley & Auden; Freshman Blues; Images of Elspeth; My Special Fate; Drunks; Revival; Down and Back; Two Organs; Olympus; Nowhere; In & Out; The Heroes; Crisis; Recovery. PART TWO: Away; First Night at Sea; London; The Other Cambridge; Friendless; Monkhood; Views of Myself; Transit; Thank You, Christine; Meeting; Tea; A Letter; To B—— E——. PART THREE: The Search; Message; A Huddle of Need; Relations; The Soviet Union; Antitheses; Love & Honour to the Chinese; The Minnesota 8 and the Letter-Writers; Regents' Professor Berryman's Crack on Race; Damned; Of Suicide; Dante's Tomb; Despair; The Hell Poem; Death Ballad; 'I Know'; Purgatory; Heaven; The Home Ballad; Beginning Ultimate Treatment; O Jo in Shock; Eleven Addresses to the Lord: 1 "Master of beauty, craftsman of the snowflake,"; 2 "Holy, as I suppose I dare to call you"; 3 "Sole watchman of the flying stars, guard me"; 4 "If I say Thy name, art Thou there? It may be so,"; 5 "Holy, & holy. The damned are said to say"; 6 "Under new management, Your Majesty:"; 7 "After a Stoic, a Peripatetic, a Pythagorean,"; 8 "Whom am I worthless that You spent such pains"; 9 "Surprise me on some ordinary day"; 10 "Fearful I peer upon the mountain path"; 11 "Germanicus leapt upon the wild lion in Smyrna,".

A 20.1.a† *Love & Fame*

Typography and paper: 54 ll., $10^{1}/_{16}'' \times 4^{7}/_{16}''$. Same typeface and typeface size as in the first printing. White (Centroid 263) wove paper.

Binding: Plastic binding. White (Centroid 263) plastic strip. Strong red (12) wove paper covers. Front cover: '[reading diagonally] UNCORRECTED PROOF | [reading horizontally] LOVE & FAME | [first letter of next two words swash] *JOHN BERRYMAN* | [device] [next two words swash] *NEW YORK* | *FARRAR, STRAUS AND GIROUX* | 1970'. Spine: plain. Back cover: plain. Sheets hole-punched. All edges trimmed.

Text: "Revival," "Love & Honour to the Chinese," "Beginning Ultimate Treatment," and "O Jo in Shock" appear in the proof copy but are not included in the first printing. "Have a Genuine American Horror-&-Mist on the Rocks" and "To a Woman" do not appear in the proof copy but are included in the first printing. For "Revival," see C 201.

Location: Meissner.

Note one: The page numbers (pages 11–29, 32–42, 45–69) are written in.

Note two: The copyright page bears the notice '*Copyright* © *1971 by John Berryman*' and the legend 'FIRST EDITION, 1971'.

Note three: "The Minnesota 8 and the Letter-Writers" and "Regents' Professor Berryman's Crack on Race" are not included in the table of contents.

Note four: The position of "A Huddle of Need" and "The Soviet Union" in the arrangement of Part Three is changed between their appearances in the proof copy and in the first printing. "Eleven Addresses to the Lord" is included in Part Three in the proof copy, but it forms Part Four in the first printing.

Note five: Handwritten corrections in strong red (Centroid 12) ink appear on p. 15 (the word "Blues" is written immediately after the title '*Freshman*'), on p. 42 (in "A Letter," in line 1, the word 'LOVED' is deleted and "throned" written above it, and in line 3, the phrase 'seven times' is deleted and "thrice" written in the left-hand margin), and on p. 56 (in "Despair," in line 16, the letter "s" and a period following it are written immediately after the word 'Vanishing').

A 20.2.a
First English edition, first printing [1971]

JOHN BERRYMAN

Love & Fame

FABER & FABER
3 Queen Square London

A 20.2.a: 8½" × 5⁵⁄₁₆"

A 20.2.a *Love & Fame*

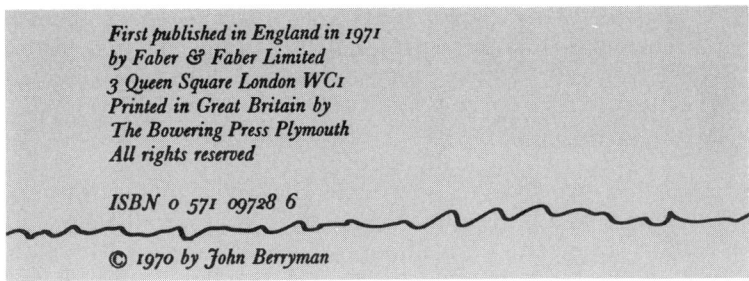

[A]⁸ B-F⁸

[1-8] 9-10 [11-12] 13-39 [40-42] 43-55 [56-58] 59-80 [81-82] 83-96

Contents: pp. 1-2: blank. p. 3: 'Love & Fame'. p. 4: '*by the same author* | [four titles]'. p. 5: title page. p. 6: copyright page. p. 7: "To the memory of | the suffering lover & young Breton master | who called himself 'Tristan Corbière' | (I wish I versed with his bite) | *Sleep! In your boat brought into the living-room | supreme admirer of the ancient sea | Your mockery of the pretentious great | your self-revelations | constitute still in any sunset sky | a cursing glory*". p. 8: acknowledgments, nine lines. pp. 9-10: table of contents. p. 11: 'Part One'. p. 12: blank. pp. 13-39: text. p. 40: blank. p. 41: 'Part Two'. p. 42: blank. pp. 43-55: text. p. 56: blank. p. 57: 'Part Three'. p. 58: blank. pp. 59-80: text. p. 81: 'Part Four'. p. 82: blank. pp. 83-94: text. pp. 95-96: '*Afterword*' signed 'J.B.' and dated 'Minneapolis | 20 June 1971'.

Items included: The same as in the American first edition except that "Afterword" was added and the following six poems were deleted from the contents: "Thank you, Christine," "A Letter," "To B—— E——," "The Soviet Union," "The Minnesota 8 and the Letter-Writers," and "Regents' Professor Berryman's Crack on Race."

Typography and paper: 40 ll., 6⅝" (6¹³⁄₁₆") × 4". Text in 10-pt. Monotype Baskerville with 2-pt. leading. Yellowish white (Centroid 92) wove paper.

Binding: Unsized calico-cloth (302), vivid red (Centroid 11). Front cover: plain. Spine: '[reading vertically from top to bottom] [goldstamped] *Love & Fame* JOHN BERRYMAN FABER'. Back cover: plain. All edges cut. Yellowish white (92) wove endpapers of different stock than text paper.

Dust jacket: Wove paper, $8^{13}/_{16}''\times 19^{1}/_{8}''$. Front cover: '[deep red (Centroid 13) background] JOHN | BERRYMAN | [white (263)] Love | and | Fame'. Spine: '[deep red background] [reading vertically from top to bottom] LOVE & FAME JOHN BERRYMAN FABER'. Back cover: '[white background] BY E. E. CUMMINGS | [two titles, three lines] | BY EMILY DICKINSON | [three titles, five lines] | BY ALAN DUGAN | [one title] | BY ROBERT LOWELL | [eight titles, nine lines] | BY MARIANNE MOORE | [three titles, four lines] | BY SYLVIA PLATH | [four titles] | BY LAURA RIDING | [one title, two lines] | BY THEODORE ROETHKE | [four titles] | BY WALLACE STEVENS | [four titles] | BY RICHARD WILBUR | [two titles] | [one-line note on prices]'. Front flap: '[white background] Love and Fame | JOHN BERRYMAN | [two unsigned paragraphs, comprising a six-line note on JB's poetry and an eleven-line descriptive comment on contents] | £1.40 | *net*'. Back flap: '[white background] *also by John Berryman* | BERRYMAN'S SONNETS | [four-line quotation from a comment by Martin Dodsworth] | 77 DREAM SONGS | [five-line quotation from a comment in *The Times* (London)] | HIS TOY, HIS DREAM, HIS REST | [six-line quotation from a comment by A. Alvarez] | HOMAGE TO | MISTRESS BRADSTREET | *and other poems* | [four-line quotation from a comment by A. Alvarez] | [four-line advertisement for catalogue]'.

Text: First publication of "Afterword."

Publication: 3,000 copies. Published November 22, 1971. £1.40.

Printing: Printed by The Bowering Press, Plymouth, Devonshire, between July 29 and August 3, 1971. Bound by C. & J. Kitkat Ltd., London, in August 1971.

Locations: BM (deposit-stamp October 20, 1971); ECS.

Note one: Variants and revisions in twenty-six poems between their appearances in the American first edition and the first English edition are noted as follows:

"Cadenza on Garnette"
 l. 20: Poets! . . Lovers   [Poets! . . . Lovers
"Shirley & Auden"
 l. 16: chauffeured   [chauffered
 l. 38: Coquet . .   [Coquet . . .
 l. 65: first   [*first*
"Drunks"

        l. 18:   young new   [young
"Olympus"
        l. 17:   15¢   [15c
        l. 34   but never so   [less
"Nowhere"
        l. 10:   blues, at the Apollo & on records.   [blues,
"In & Out"
        l. 8:   Corbière   [Corbiére
        l. 29:   ball   [bull
        l. 41:   a little   [witty &
        l. 43:   pounded   [beat
        l. 62:   & slovenly, he   [and slovenly, Zauder
        l. 68:   Mr. Creeley,   [Mr C,
"The Heroes"
        l. 9:   maneuvered in my mind their rôles   [manoeuvred
                 in my mind their roles
"Crisis"
        l. 17:   Neff   [N
        l. 26:   Neff,   [N,
        l. 58:   installment,   [instalment,
"Recovery"
        l. 10:   wheel-chair,   [wheel-chair
"First Night at Sea"
        l. 21:   ballads,   [ballads.
"London"
        l. 17:   Hotel, sir'   [Hotel sir,'
"The Other Cambridge"
        l. 18:   swear   [sweart
        l. 41:   Queens'   [Queen's
"Friendless"
        l. 21:   Frean's   [Freans
"Monkhood"
        l. 28:   pride'   [pride',
        l. 41:   One   [one
"Views of Myself"
        l. 27:   bite   [bit
"Meeting"
        l. 3:   center   [centre
"Tea"
        l. 13:   He lives   [Lives
"Relations"
        l. 4:   Peckinpah   [Pekinpah
        l. 8:   be   [resume
"Antitheses"
        l. 17:   Leonardo ..   [Leonardo ...

    l. 19:   skeptical.   [sceptical.
    l. 23:   as   [at
"Have a Genuine American Horror-&-Mist on the Rocks"
    l. 3:   'Waal . . if   ['Waal . . . if
"Damned"
    l. 7:   mustache   [moustache
"The Hell Poem"
    l. 4:   except when   [except for when
    l. 13:   she came   [coming
"Purgatory"
    l. 20:   67.   [67
    l. 25:   retired, frail,   [retired,
"Heaven"
    l. 11:   was killed in a car accident soon after she married,   [married before she died,
    l. 15:   my lust for her   [whatever yen —
    l. 16:   persuade me to forgive   [forgive
"Eleven Addresses to the Lord: 1"
    l. 21:   Peter &   [Peter and
"Eleven Addresses to the Lord: 6"
    l. 3:   suicide   [blow-it-all

Note two: The poem titled "Away" in the American first edition appears as "Anyway" in both the table of contents and the text of the first English edition. The title "I *Know*" appears as "I Know" in the table of contents of the first English edition.

A 20.3.a
American second edition, first printing [1972]

LOVE & FAME
JOHN BERRYMAN
SECOND EDITION, REVISED

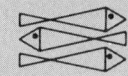 *NEW YORK*
FARRAR, STRAUS AND GIROUX

A 20.3.a: $7^{15}/_{16}'' \times 5^{3}/_{16}''$

> Copyright © 1970 by John Berryman
> Copyright © 1972 by the estate of John Berryman
> All rights reserved
> Library of Congress catalog card number: 74-137749
>
> SECOND EDITION, 1972
>
> Printed in the United States of America
> Published simultaneously in Canada
> by Doubleday Canada Ltd., Toronto
> DESIGNED BY HERB JOHNSON
>
> Acknowledgments are made to the editors
> of *The New Yorker*, in which "Death Ballad" was
> first published; and for other
> poems to the editors of *American Scholar, Atlantic
> Monthly, Harper's, Minneapolis Tribune, The Nation, New Republic,
> The New York Review, Saturday Review, Shenandoah,* and *The Times
> Literary Supplement*

56 leaves (perfect binding)

[A–B] [i–xvi] [1–2] 3–31 [32–34] 35–49 [50–52] 53–75 [76–78] 79–89 [90–94]

Contents: pp. A–B: blank. p. i: 'LOVE & FAME'. p. ii: blank. p. iii: 'Books by John Berryman | [eleven titles]'. p. iv: blank. p. v: title page. p. vi: copyright page. p. vii: *"To the memory of | the suffering lover & young Breton master | who called himself 'Tristan Corbière' | (I wish I versed with his bite)* | SLEEP! IN YOUR BOAT BROUGHT INTO THE LIVING-ROOM | SUPREME ADMIRER OF THE ANCIENT SEA | YOUR MOCKERY OF THE PRETENTIOUS GREAT | YOUR SELF-REVELATIONS | CONSTITUTE STILL IN ANY SUNSET SKY | A CURSING GLORY". p. viii: blank. pp. ix–xi: table of contents. p. xii: blank. pp. xiii–xiv: *'Scholia to Second Edition'* signed 'J.B.' and dated *'Minneapolis | 25 January 1971'*. p. xv: half title. p. xvi: blank. p. 1: 'PART ONE'. p. 2: blank. pp. 3–31: text. p. 32: blank. p. 33: 'PART TWO'. p. 34: blank. pp. 35–49: text. p. 50: blank. p. 51: 'PART THREE'. p. 52: blank. pp. 53–75: text. p. 76: blank. p. 77: 'PART FOUR'. p. 78: blank. pp. 79–90: text. pp. 91–94: blank.

Items included: The same as in the American first edition except that "Scholia to Second Edition" was added and the following six poems were deleted from the contents: "Thank You, Christine," "A Letter," "To B—— E——," "The Soviet Union," "The Minnesota 8 and the Letter-Writers," and "Regents' Professor Berryman's Crack on Race."

A 20.3.a *Love & Fame* 125

Typography and paper: 36 ll., 6¹/₁₆" (6¹/₄") × 3¹³/₁₆". Text in typeface size equivalent to 10-pt. with 2-pt. leading. Yellowish white (Centroid 92) wove paper.

Binding: Perfect binding. Wove paper wrappers: outside, pale yellow (Centroid 89) glossy; inside, white (263). Front cover: 'John | Berryman | [open letters outlined in strong violet (207)] LOVE | [solid black] & | [open letters outlined in strong violet] FAME | [solid black] REVISED EDITION | NOONDAY 437 $2.25'. Spine: '[reading vertically from top to bottom] JOHN Berryman [strong violet] LOVE [black] & [strong violet] FAME [black] [device] | [reading horizontally] N 437'. Back cover: '[at left] N437–Literature | ISBN 0-374-51031-8 [at right] $2.25 | LOVE & FAME | JOHN BERRYMAN | *Winner of the Pulitzer Prize | and the National Book Award* | [three-line quotation from a comment by William H. Pritchard, eight-line quotation from a comment by Paul Fussell, Jr., ten-line quotation from a comment by Daniel Jaffe] | OTHER NOONDAY BOOKS BY JOHN BERRYMAN | [four titles, five lines] | *Cover design by Charles Skaggs* | THE NOONDAY PRESS 19 UNION SQUARE WEST NEW YORK 10003'.

Text: First publication of portions of "Scholia to Second Edition." See note two.

Publication: Unknown number of copies. Published November 15, 1972. $2.25.

Printing: Printed and bound by Murray Printing Company, Forge Village, Mass.

Copyright: No copyright application filed.

Locations: DLC (not deposit copy; rebound); ECS.

Note one: Revisions in two poems from their appearance in the American first edition are noted as follows:

"In & Out"
  l. 68: Creeley, [C,
"Crisis"
  l. 17: Neff [N
  l. 26: Neff, [N,

Note two: The text of "Scholia to Second Edition" is the same as that of "Afterword" in the first English edition except for the deletion of a sentence in the next to last paragraph of the "Afterword" and revision of the final paragraph. Although "Scholia" is dated before "Afterword," the latter was published first.

A 20.3.b
Second printing: New York: Farrar, Straus and Giroux, [1974]. On copyright page: 'SECOND EDITION, 1972 | *Second printing, 1974*'. Printed wrappers.

A 21 TWO POEMS
(1970)

> # TWO POEMS
>
> *John Berryman*
>
> *Season's Greetings, 1970*
> *from*
> *Martha and Kate and John*
> *and Bob Giroux*

A 21: 8½" × 5½"

[1]⁴

[1-2] 3-7 [8]

Contents: p. 1: title page. p. 2: blank. pp. 3-5: '*In Memoriam (1914-1953)*'. pp. 6-7: 'ANOTHER NEW YEAR'S EVE'. p. 8: blank.

Typography and paper: $6^{11}/_{16}''$ (7") × $4^{3}/_{16}''$. Text in 11-pt. Linotype Spartan Light with 5-pt. leading (p. 4 in 11-pt. with 3-pt. leading). Pale greenish yellow (Centroid 104) wove paper.

Binding: Self-wrapper. Gathering stapled. All edges cut.

Text: First publication of "In Memoriam (1914-1953)" and "Another New Year's Eve." "Another New Year's Eve" reprinted as "Year's End, 1970." See D 1.

Publication: Unknown number of copies. Printed ca. December 1970. Not for sale.

Printing: Privately printed. Printer not known.

Copyright: No copyright application filed.

Locations: ECS; PAB.

A 22 DELUSIONS, ETC.

A 22.1.a
First edition, first printing [1972]

DELUSIONS, ETC.

of

JOHN BERRYMAN

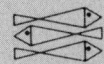 NEW YORK

FARRAR, STRAUS AND GIROUX

A 22.1.a: 8½" × 6"

A 22.1.a *Delusions, Etc.*

> Copyright © 1969, 1971 by John Berryman
> Copyright © 1972 by the Estate of John Berryman
> All rights reserved
> Library of Congress catalog card number: 76-186660
> ISBN 0-374-13798-6
>
> FIRST EDITION, 1972
>
> Printed in the United States of America
> Published simultaneously in Canada
> by Doubleday Canada Ltd., Toronto
>
> Acknowledgments are made to the editors of *The New Yorker*, in which "Ecce Homo" and "King David Dances" were first published; and for other poems to the editors of *Esquire*, *The Harvard Advocate*, and *The New York Review*.

[1]¹⁶ [2]⁸ [3]¹⁶

[i–viii] ix–x [1–2] 3–16 [17–18] 19–30 [31–32] 33–48 [49–50] 51–55 [56–58] 59–69 [70]

Contents: p. i: '*DELUSIONS, ETC.*' p. ii: '*by John Berryman* | [ten titles]'. p. iii: title page. p. iv: copyright page. p. v: 'TO MARTHA B | passion & awe'. p. vi: blank. p. vii: "We haue piped vnto you, and ye haue not danced: | wee haue mourned vnto you, and ye haue not lamented. | *On parle toujours de 'l'art réligieux'. L'art est* | *réligieux*. | And indeed if Eugène Irténev was mentally deranged | everyone is in the same case; the most mentally de-|ranged people are certainly those who see in others | indications of insanity they do not notice in themselves. | *Feu! feu! feu!* | Than longen folk to goon on pilgrimages". p. viii: blank. pp. ix–x: table of contents. p. 1: 'I   OPUS DEI | (a layman's winter mockup, wherein moreover | the Offices are not within one day said | but thro' their hours at intervals | over many weeks—such being the World) | *Lord, have mercy on my son: for he is lunatick,* | *and sore vexed: for ofttimes he falleth into* | *the fire, and oft into the water.* | *And he did evil, because he prepared not* | *his heart to seek the Lord.*' p. 2: blank. pp. 3–16: text. p. 17: '*II*'. p. 18: blank. pp. 19–30: text. p. 31: '*III*'. p. 32: blank. pp. 33–48: text. p. 49: '*IV   SCHERZO*'. p. 50: blank. pp. 51–55: text. p. 56: blank. p. 57: '*V*'. p. 58: blank. pp. 59–70: text.

Items included: I   OPUS DEI: Lauds; Matins; Prime; Interstitial Office; Tierce; Sext; Nones; Vespers; Compline. II: Washington in Love; Beethoven Triumphant; Your Birthday in Wisconsin You Are 140; Drugs Alcohol Little Sister; In Memoriam (1914–1953). III: Gislebertus' Eve; Scholars at the Orchid Pavilion; Tampa Stomp; Old Man Goes South Again Alone; The Handshake, The Entrance; Lines to Mr Frost; He Resigns; No;

A 22.1.a *Delusions, Etc.* 131

The Form; Ecce Homo; A Prayer After All; Back; *Hello.* IV SCHERZO: Navajo Setting the Record Straight; Henry by Night; Henry's Understanding; Defensio in Extremis; Damn You, Jim D., You Woke Me Up. V: Somber Prayer; Unknowable? perhaps not altogether; Minnesota Thanksgiving; A Usual Prayer; Overseas Prayer; Amos; Certainty Before Lunch; The Prayer of the Middle-Aged Man; 'How Do You Do, Dr Berryman, Sir?'; The Facts & Issues; King David Dances.

Typography and paper: 36 ll., $6^{9}/_{16}''$ ($6^{7}/_{8}''$) × $4^{5}/_{16}''$. Text in 11-pt. Linotype Janson with 2-pt. leading. Yellowish white (Centroid 92) laid paper (chain lines running vertically, spaced $^{27}/_{32}''$).

Binding: Unsized calico-cloth (302), black (Centroid 267). Front cover: plain. Spine: '[reading vertically from top to bottom] [goldstamped] [first letter of first two words swash] JOHN BERRYMAN [slash] DELUSIONS, ETC. [slash] *Farrar Straus Giroux*'. Back cover: plain. All edges cut; top edge dyed moderate reddish orange (37). Pale yellow (89) wove endpapers.

Dust jacket: Wove paper, $8^{3}/_{4}''$ × $20^{1}/_{4}''$. Front cover: '[black (Centroid 267) background] [brilliant greenish yellow (98)] JOHN BERRYMAN | [vivid reddish orange (34)] DELUSIONS, ETC. | [black and white photograph of JB]'. Spine: '[black background] [reading vertically from top to bottom] [brilliant greenish yellow] JOHN BERRYMAN [slash] [vivid reddish orange] DELUSIONS, ETC. [slash] *Farrar Straus Giroux*'. Back cover: '[white background] [vivid reddish orange] HOMAGE TO MISTRESS BRADSTREET | [black] [one-line quotation from a comment by Robert Fitzgerald and two-line quotation from a comment by Edmund Wilson] | [vivid reddish orange] BERRYMAN'S SONNETS | [black] [two-line quotation from a comment by Robert Penn Warren and three-line quotation from a comment by Dudley Fitts] | [vivid reddish orange] LOVE & FAME | [black] [two-line quotation from a comment by Carolyn Kizer] | [vivid reddish orange] SHORT POEMS | [black] [three-line quotation from a comment by Conrad Aiken] | [vivid reddish orange] THE DREAM SONGS | (I. 77 DREAM SONGS II. HIS TOY, HIS DREAM, HIS REST) | [black] [one-line quotation from a comment by Larry P. Vonalt and three-line quotation from a comment by Karl Shapiro] | [vivid reddish orange] FARRAR, STRAUS AND GIROUX'. Front flap: '[white background] [at left] ISBN 0-374-13798-6 [at right] $6.95 | JOHN BERRYMAN | [vivid reddish orange] Delusions, Etc. | [black] [lines 24–31 of "Nones" and beginning of one-paragraph unsigned descriptive comment on contents, sixteen lines, reading in part, "Mr. Berryman's posthumous book | of poems, *Delusions, Etc.*, had been | completed and was in proof before | his death on January 7, 1972...."] | *(continued on back flap)*'. Back flap: '[white background] *(continued from front flap)* | [conclusion of comment, seventeen lines] | *Cover photo by Tom Berthiaume* | *Jacket design by Guy Fleming* | [vivid reddish orange] FARRAR, STRAUS AND GIROUX | 19 UNION SQUARE WEST | NEW YORK 10003'.

Text: First publication of "Lauds," "Matins," "Prime," "Interstitial Office," "Tierce," "Sext," "Nones," "Compline," "Your Birthday in Wisconsin You Are 140," "Drugs Alcohol Little Sister," "Scholars at the Orchid Pavilion," "Old Man Goes South Again Alone," "He Resigns," "No," "A Prayer After All," "Back," "*He*llo," "Defensio in Extremis," "Damn You, Jim D., You Woke Me Up," "Somber Prayer," "Unknowable? perhaps not altogether," "A Usual Prayer," "Overseas Prayer," "Amos," "Certainty Before Lunch," "The Prayer of the Middle-Aged Man," "'How Do You Do, Dr Berryman, Sir?'," "The Facts & Issues." First book appearance of all other poems except "In Memoriam *(1914-1953)*" and "The Handshake, The Entrance."

Publication: Unknown number of copies. Published April 28, 1972. $6.95.

Printing: Printed and bound by H. Wolff Book Manufacturing Company, New York, N.Y.

Copyright: Registered under A 335398 in the name of the estate of JB.

Locations: DLC (deposit-stamp May 8, 1972); ECS (dj); Lilly (dj); Lockwood (dj); PPiU (dj).

Note one: Variants and revisions in two poems between their first appearances in separate publications and their appearances in *DE* are noted as follows:

"In Memoriam (1914-1953)," *Two Poems 1970*
l. 1: last leave [leave (last)
l. 2: & even with those [and even past these
l. 3: was standing [*was* highlone
l. 5: none else was, [no other hovered,
l. 7: when I moved near after a little [trembling nearer after some small
l. 8: found [came on
l. 9: & silence, unable to say just [and silence—O unable to say
l. 10: she had [she

A 22.1.a *Delusions, Etc.*

l. 12: & [and
l. 13: [Tubes all over, useless versus coma,
l. 14: [on the third day his principal physician
l. 15: [told me to pray he'd die, brain damage such.
l. 16: [His bare stub feet stuck out.
l. 18: started – when this fact emerged, [surfaced – when this fact emerged
l. 19: & [and
l. 20: & [and
l. 21: Berryman!! [Berryman!'
l. 22: Ah, he had that. He was [Ah he had that, – so far
l. 25: utter for all [bottomless for
l. 26: I loved Yeats & he was amused by this: [Yeats I worshipped: he was amused by this,
l. 28: have me [turn me up
l. 29: He downed me daily at shove-ha'penny, [Downing me daily at shove-ha'penny
l. 30: *English* on the thing. Caitlin would sit [with *English* on the thing. C——— would slump
l. 31: fat as a lump for hours – my god, [plump as a lump for hours, my word
l. 32: After her husband's death [Hard on her widowhood –
l. 32a: she came for me at the Slivkas' with a knife [
l. 32b: & breasts out, howling lust, Noah Greenberg [
l. 32c: that musical saint interposed his calm bulk [
l. 32d: & got me thro' the door. [
l. 33: ... Apart [Apart
l. 34: advanced [intoned
l. 35: declaiming, with his hand out, which I clasped. [putting out a fat hand. We shook hands.
l. 36: good [shook
l. 37: Liz [one
l. 39: God, [the Creator,
l. 40: heart to be [will to go
l. 42: while pot-pals yapped, [mid potpals' yapping,
l. 45: He wrote [Scribbled
l. 46: about [word of
l. 47: & [and
l. 48: & [and
l. 50: & [and

"The Handshake, The Entrance," *Two Dream Songs* (1969)
l. 3: 'Ain't [Ain't
l. 12: murmurs [Murmurs

Note two: In *Two Poems* (1970) "In Memoriam (1914-1953)" is divided into twelve sections numbered from I to XII in roman numerals; each of the first eleven sections consists of four lines and the twelfth section consists of a four-line stanza and a two-line stanza. In *DE* the poem is divided into three sections numbered from I to III in roman numerals; each of the first two sections consists of four four-line stanzas and the third section consists of four four-line stanzas and a two-line stanza.

Note three: In all copies examined, the *m* in the word *them* and the period which follows the word are not fully impressed on p. 25, l. 10.

Note four: In l. 4 of "Lauds" (p. 3), the word *parsecs* is printed as *parsees*.

Note five: In all American printings page numbers appear at the foot of the type page, at the right on both rectos and versos. (In the first English reprinting, the page numbers appear at the foot of the type page, at the right on rectos and at the left on versos.)

A 22.1.b
Second printing: New York: Farrar, Straus and Giroux, [1972]. On copyright page: 'Second printing, 1972'.

Note: The following corrections are noted: on p. 3, l. 4, of "Lauds" the word *parsees* of the first printing is corrected to read *parsecs*. In the first printing the first stanza of "The Form" (pp. 42-43) is set in roman and the remaining six stanzas in italics, but in the second printing the entire poem is set in roman. The *m* in the word *them* and the period which follows the word on p. 25, l. 10, are fully impressed.

A 22.1.c
First English reprint [1972]

DELUSIONS, ETC.

of

JOHN BERRYMAN

FABER AND FABER
3 Queen Square London

A 22.1.c: 8½" × 5⁵⁄₁₆"

> First published in Great Britain in 1972
> by Faber and Faber Limited
> 3 Queen Square London WC1
> Printed in Great Britain by
> John Dickens & Co Ltd Northampton
> All rights reserved
>
> ISBN 0 571 10197 6
>
> Acknowledgments are made to the editors of *The New Yorker*, in which "Ecce Homo" and "King David Dances" were first published; and for other poems to the editors of *Esquire*, *The Harvard Advocate*, and *The New York Review*.
>
> Copyright © 1969, 1971 by John Berryman
> Copyright © 1972 by the Estate of John Berryman

[1–5]⁸

Same pagination as in the first American printing.

Contents: p. i: half title. p. ii: 'also by John Berryman | [six titles]'. p. iii: title page. p. iv: copyright page. p. v: dedication. p. vi: blank. p. vii: epigraphs. p. viii: blank. pp. ix–x: table of contents. p. 1: 'I OPUS DEI | [epigraphs]'. p. 2: blank. pp. 3–16: text. p. 17: 'II'. p. 18: blank. pp. 19–30: text. p. 31: 'III'. p. 32: blank. pp. 33–48: text. p. 49: 'IV SCHERZO'. p. 50: blank. pp. 51–55: text. p. 56: blank. p. 57: 'V'. p. 58: blank. pp. 59–70: text.

Items included: Same as in the first American printing.

Typography and paper: 36 ll., 6½″ (6⅞″) × 4″. White (Centroid 263) wove paper.

Binding: Sized fine diaper-cloth (124b), dark bluish green (Centroid 165). Front cover: plain. Spine: '[reading vertically from top to bottom] [goldstamped] Delusions, Etc. JOHN BERRYMAN faber'. Back cover: plain. All edges cut. White (263) wove endpapers of different stock than text paper.

Dust jacket: Wove paper, outside glossy, 8¹³⁄₁₆″ × 19¼″. Front cover: '[brilliant greenish blue (Centroid 168) background] JOHN | BERRYMAN | [white (263) background] Delusions, Etc. | [title repeated eight more times, each on a new line and in diminishing typeface sizes]'. Spine: '[reading vertically from top to bottom] [brilliant greenish blue background] Delusions, Etc. [white background] JOHN BERRYMAN faber'. Back cover: '[brilliant greenish blue background] JOHN | BERRYMAN |

A 22.1.e *Delusions, Etc.* 137

[white background] [black and white photograph of JB]'. Front flap: '[white background] Delusions, Etc. | JOHN BERRYMAN | [eight-line unsigned note on publication] | £1.50 | *net*'. Back flap: '[white background] JOHN BERRYMAN | [two-paragraph unsigned biographical note, sixteen lines]'.

Publication: Unknown number of copies. Published December 4, 1972. £1.50.

Printing: Printed by John Dickens and Company Ltd., Northampton, Northamptonshire. Bound by James Burn and Company Ltd., Esher, Surrey.

Locations: BM (deposit-stamp November 20, 1972); ECS (dj).

Note: Page numbers appear at the foot of the type page, at the right on rectos and at the left on versos. (In the American printings, the page numbers are at the foot of the type page, at the right on both rectos and versos.)

A 22.1.c†
Proof copy

Same leaf size, pagination, and collation as the first English printing.

Contents: Same as in the first English printing.

Items included: Same as in the first English printing.

Typography and paper: Same as in the first English printing.

Binding: Light yellowish brown (Centroid 76) wove paper wrappers. Front cover: 'DELUSIONS, ETC. | of | JOHN BERRYMAN | *FABER AND FABER* | *3 Queen Square London*'. Spine: '[reading vertically from top to bottom] DELUSIONS, ETC. JOHN BERRYMAN'. Back cover: plain. All edges cut. Cover cut flush.

Location: ECS.

A 22.1.d
Third printing: New York: Farrar, Straus and Giroux, [1973]. On copyright page: '*First Noonday Edition, 1973*'. N 451. Printed wrappers. $2.45.

A 22.1.e
Fourth printing: New York: Farrar, Straus and Giroux, [1973]. On copyright page: '*First Noonday Edition, 1973* | *Second printing, 1973*'. Printed wrappers.

A 23 SELECTED POEMS 1938–1968
[1972]

SELECTED POEMS

1938–1968

JOHN BERRYMAN

FABER & FABER
3 QUEEN SQUARE
LONDON

A 23: $7^{5}/_{16}'' \times 4^{13}/_{16}''$

A 23 *Selected Poems 1938–1968*

> First published in 1972
> by Faber and Faber Ltd.,
> 3 Queen Square, London W.C.1
> Printed in Great Britain by
> Latimer Trend and Co. Ltd., Whitstable
> ISBN 0 571 09766 9 (paper covered edition)
>
> All rights reserved
>
> Copyright John Berryman 1952, 1959, 1962,
> 1963, 1964, 1965, 1967, 1968, 1972
>
> CONDITIONS OF SALE
> *This book is sold subject to the condition that it shall not, by way of trade or otherwise, be lent, re-sold, hired out or otherwise circulated without the publisher's prior consent in any form of binding or cover other than that in which it is published and without a similar condition including this condition being imposed on the subsequent purchaser*

[1–4]¹⁶ [5]⁸ [6]¹⁶

[1–8] 9–27 [28–30] 31–34 [35–36] 37–44 [45–46] 47–65 [66–68] 69–172 [173–176]

Contents: p. 1: 'SELECTED POEMS 1938–1968 | by | JOHN BERRYMAN'. p. 2: 'BY THE SAME AUTHOR: | [four titles]'. p. 3: title page. p. 4: copyright page. pp. 5–6: table of contents. p. 7: '*from* | THE DISPOSSESSED | (1948)'. p. 8: blank. pp. 9–27: text. p. 28: blank. p. 29: '*from* | HIS THOUGHT MADE POCKETS | (1958)'. p. 30: blank. pp. 31–34: text. p. 35: 'BERRYMAN'S SONNETS | (1952, 1967)'. p. 36: blank. pp. 37–44: text. p. 45: 'HOMAGE TO | MISTRESS BRADSTREET | (1953)'. p. 46: blank. pp. 47–65: text. p. 66: blank. p. 67: '*from* | THE DREAM SONGS (1964, 1968)'. p. 68: "TO KATE, AND TO SAUL | 'THOU DREWEST NEAR IN THE DAY' | [rule] | 'GO IN, BRACK MAN, DE DAY'S YO' OWN.' | . . . I AM THEIR MUSICK. | *Lam. 3:63* | BUT THERE IS ANOTHER METHOD. | *Olive Schreiner* | [rule]". pp. 69–101: text. p. 102: '[rule] | NO INTERESTING PROJECT CAN BE EMBARKED ON WITHOUT FEAR. I SHALL BE | SCARED TO DEATH HALF THE TIME. | *Sir Francis Chichester in Sydney* | FOR MY PART I AM ALWAYS FRIGHTENED, AND VERY MUCH SO. I FEAR THE | FUTURE OF ALL ENGAGEMENTS. | *Gordon in Khartoum* | I AM PICKT UP AND SORTED TO A PIP. MY IMAGINATION IS A MONASTERY | AND I AM ITS MONK. | *Keats to Shelley* | HE WENT AWAY AND NEVER SAID GOODBYE. | I COULD READ HIS LETTERS BUT I SURE CAN'T READ HIS MIND. | I THOUGHT HE'S LOVIN ME BUT HE WAS LEAVIN ALL THE TIME. | NOW I KNOW THAT MY TRUE LOVE WAS BLIND. | *Victoria*

Spivey? | [rule]'. pp. 103-167: text. pp. 168-172: 'INDEX OF FIRST LINES'. pp. 173-176: blank.

Items included: FROM THE DISPOSSESSED: Winter Landscape; The Traveller; The Spinning Heart; Desires of Men and Women; The Moon and the Night and the Men; The Ball Poem; Canto Amor; The Song of the Demented Priest; The Song of the Tortured Girl; The Lightning; Whether There Is Sorrow in the Demons; New Year's Eve; The Dispossessed. FROM HIS THOUGHT MADE POCKETS: Venice, 182—; from The Black Book (i); Not To Live; A Sympathy, A Welcome; Note to Wang Wei. BERRYMAN'S SONNETS: Sonnets 9, 12, 13, 21, 22, 25, 34, 37, 65, 71, 75, 79, 97, 106, 109, 112. HOMAGE TO MISTRESS BRADSTREET. FROM THE DREAM SONGS: Dream Songs 1, 4, 5, 6, 14, 16, 22, 26, 27, 29, 31, 34, 36, 37, 42, 45, 46, 47, 48, 49, 51, 52, 53, 54, 55, 66, 67, 69, 71, 74, 75, 76, 77, 78, 84, 86, 87, 88, 89, 90, 91, 92, 99, 108, 118, 132, 142, 145, 146, 147, 153, 154, 155, 156, 166, 168, 171, 172, 173, 184, 186, 195, 201, 223, 233, 239, 279, 280, 282, 283, 288, 289, 301, 302, 305, 312, 315, 316, 321, 324, 325, 332, 334, 337, 338, 342, 357, 361, 366, 367, 370, 371, 372, 379, 380, 382, 384, 385.

Typography and paper: 42 ll., $5^{13}/_{16}''$ ($6^{3}/_{16}''$) × $3^{7}/_{16}''$. Text in 10-pt. Monotype Bembo with 2-pt. leading. White (Centroid 263) wove paper.

Binding: White (Centroid 263) wove paper wrappers, outside glossy. Front cover: '[next four lines within a box formed by grayish blue (186) rules at top and bottom, a grayish blue strip angled at its top and bottom at left, and bordered by black band at right] selected | POEMS | [grayish blue rule] | 1938-1968 | [next two lines within a box formed by grayish blue rules at top and bottom, a grayish blue strip angled at its top and bottom at left, and bordered by black band at right] John | Berryman | [at right edge of cover] [on vertical black (267) band] [reading vertically from top to bottom] [white] FABER paper covered EDITIONS'. Spine: '[reading vertically from top to bottom] [grayish blue rule] John Berryman [grayish blue rule] selected POEMS [grayish blue background] [white] FABER'. Back cover: 'also by John Berryman | LOVE AND FAME | [four-line quotation from a comment by Peter Porter] | BERRYMAN'S SONNETS | [three-line quotation from a comment by Martin Dodsworth] | 77 DREAM SONGS | [four-line quotation from a comment in *The Times* (London)] | HIS TOY, HIS DREAM, HIS REST | [four-line quotation from a comment by A. Alvarez] | HOMAGE TO MISTRESS BRADSTREET | *and other poems* | [three-line quotation from a comment by A. Alvarez] | [one-line advertisement for

A 23 *Selected Poems 1938–1968*

catalogue] | Faber & Faber 3 Queen Square London WC1N 3AU | [at left edge of cover] [on vertical black band] [reading vertically from bottom to top] [white] FABER paper covered EDITIONS'. Inside front cover: 'SELECTED POEMS 1938–1968 | by | JOHN BERRYMAN | Some months before his tragic death in January 1972, John | Berryman completed this selection from the whole of his pub-|lished poetry. He designed it to provide both an introduction to | his work and a summary of his poetic career up to the publica-|tion of *Love and Fame*. It reveals clearly that Berryman was one | of the most original and important poets of the twentieth | century. | £1.20 *net* | [within black hexagram] [white] FABER | paper covered | EDITIONS'. Inside back cover: 'FABER AND FABER | *publish books by the following poets* | [alphabetical list of thirty-nine poets in two columns]'.

Text: The text comprises 133 poems, including thirteen from *The Dispossessed*, five from *His Thought Made Pockets & The Plane Buckt*, sixteen from *Berryman's Sonnets*, the text of *Homage to Mistress Bradstreet* (without the notes), and ninety-eight from *The Dream Songs*. All poems included in JB's selection of his own poetry had been previously published. No first book material.

Publication: 3,000 copies. Published May 1, 1972. £1.20.

Printing: Printed and bound by Whitstable Litho, Whitstable, Kent.

Locations: BM (deposit-stamp March 29, 1972); DLC; ECS; Lilly; Lockwood.

Note one: Variants and revisions in twenty-three poems between their appearances in the collections indicated and in *SelP* are noted as follows:

   "Winter Landscape," *TD*
     l. 3:   trees, [trees
   "The Spinning Heart," *TD*
     l. 35: superstitions [superstitious
   "The Moon and the Night and the Men," *TD*
     l. 24: 'Hurt ['. . . hurt
   "The Ball Poem," *TD*
     l. 18: up [up.
   "Canto Amor," *TD*
     l. 24: bound, [bound
     l. 55: rapt [rapt,
   "The Song of the Tortured Girl," *TD*

l. 7:   "Nothing worse now can come to us"   ['Nothing worse now can come to us'
l. 9:   broke   [cracked
"The Lightning," *TD*
  l. 14: chocolate,   [choclate,
"Whether There Is Sorrow in the Demons," *TD*
  l. 2:   screams,   [creams,
"New Year's Eve," *TD*
  l. 30: beneath : eye   [beneath: eye
  l. 47: Soon soon   [Soon O
"Venice, 182–," *Thought*
  l. 3:   the corners of her eyes are white. i miss,   [The corners of her eyes are white. I miss.
  l. 4:   she   [She
  l. 6:   hell   [Hell
  l. 8:   less   [Less
  l. 11: i hear her howl now, and i   [I hear her howl now, and I
  l. 12: foul   [Foul
  l. 13: on   [On
  l. 15: now   [Now
  l. 16: pulling . . . i   [pulling . . I
  l. 19: i   [I
  l. 23: i   [I
  l. 25: àre in love. the light hurts. 'there . . .'   [are in love. The light hurts. 'There . .'
"from The Black Book (i)," *Thought*
  l. 2:   seldom   [seldom
  l. 3:   we wept. the   [we wept. The
  l. 4:   later we heard. brother had pull. m   [later we heard. Brother had pull. In
  l. 5:   he,   [he,
  l. 6:   later   [Later
  l. 7:   the   [The
  l. 8:   broke   [broke
  l. 9:   before   [Before
  l. 10: only   [Only
  l. 11: and soon he died. he   [and soon he died. He
  l. 12: our   [our
  l. 13: when he stopt. abraham,   [when he stopt. Abraham,
  l. 14: write, i beg, in your book.   [write, I beg, in your Book.
  l. 15: no   [No

A 23 *Selected Poems 1938–1968*

    l. 16:   call to our pall; we call or gibber; Hell's [call to our pall; we call or gibber; Hell's
    l. 17:   Irritable [irritable
    l. 18:   Despairs [despairs

"Not To Live," *Thought*
    l. 2:'   King. I [King. I
    l. 4:   I find. Ghost [I find. Ghost
    l. 6:   Howls [Howls
    l. 7:   I love the King [I love the King
    l. 10:   God be with him. He & God [God be with him. He & God
    l. 11:   I [I
    l. 12:   thing . . . . [thing . .
    l. 13:   From [From
    l. 14:   God save the King. [God save the King.

"A Sympathy, A Welcome," *Thought*
    l. 1:   I [I
    l. 2:   Paul, [Paul,
    l. 3:   I [I
    l. 4:   Yet [Yet
    l. 7:   Not [*not*
    l. 9:   Paul, [Paul,

"Note to Wang Wei," *Thought*
    l. 2:   disheveled, [dishevelled,
    l. 3:   It [It
    l. 5:   It [It
    l. 6:   It [It
    l. 7:   Makes [Makes
    l. 8:   (I'm reconfirming, God [(I'm reconfirming, God
    l. 10:   I [I
    l. 12:   Be [Be

"Homage to Mistress Bradstreet," *Homage*
    l. 3:   woman. – [woman –
    l. 24:   & [and
    l. 62:   believed, [believed.
    l. 72:   wet: [wet;
    l. 135:   short. [short,
    l. 184:   takes   us [takes us
    l. 273:   I   am [I am
    l. 305:   faints – [faints

Dream Song 6, *77DS*
    l. 4:   his [his

Dream Song 46, *77DS*
    l. 6:   "Christ!" ['Christ!'

Dream Song 74, 77DS
  l. 10: "Kyoto,   ['Kyoto,
  l. 15: on . . ."   [on . . .'
Dream Song 84, *Toy*
  l. 11: hot   [hots
Dream Song 118, *Toy*
  l. 11: theirselves   [themselves
Dream Song 147, *Toy*
  l. 17: composed.   [composed
Dream Song 280, *Toy*
  l. 10: *Times,*   [*Times*
  l. 16: mostly won,   [won,
Dream Song 342, *Toy*
  l. 17: Khōve)   [Khove)

Note two: Variants of titles of poems between their appearances in *Thought* and in *SelP* are noted as follows:

  NOT TO LIVE   [Not To Live
  A SYMPATHY, A WELCOME   [A Sympathy, A Welcome
  NOTE TO WANG WEI   [Note to Wang Wei

Note three: Line 7 of Dream Song 99 as it appears on p. 112 is included in the first stanza, whereas it is set off by itself in *Toy*. The words "excited him" in Dream Song 334 as they appear on p. 152 form the last two words of line 12, whereas they form a separate line (l. 13) in *Toy*.

Note four: The last two stanzas (ll. 26–35) of "Whether There Is Sorrow in the Demons" are not printed in *SelP*.

Note five: In all copies examined, Dream Song 53 on p. 91 is not numbered.

Note six: In the table of contents, the title "from The Black Book (i)" is printed as "The Black Book (1)" and the title "Not To Live" is printed as "Not to Live." Also, the Dream Songs are listed as being in Parts 1 through 7, but no such division is used within the text.

Note seven: Variants between the first lines of poems in the text and in the index are noted as follows:

        TEXT
  168.20   mansion,   [mansion
  169.9   guitar,   [guitar,
  170.24   'NO VISITORS'   ['NO VISITORS'

Note eight: In all copies examined, the following letters are not fully impressed: the *e* in *the* (p. 18, l. 29), the *i* in *midnight* (p. 19, l. 6), the *e* in *send* (p. 50, l. 12), the *r* in *Orion* (p. 57, l. 8), the *e* in *die* (p. 62, l. 13), the *e* in *foliate* (p. 77, l. 1), the *e* in *private* (p. 82, l. 9), the *s* in *fools* (p. 85, l. 5), the *i* in *in* (p. 97, l. 18), the *p* in *Spry* (p. 98, l. 18), the second *l* in *all* (p. 114, l. 1), the *o* in *to* (p. 116, l. 10), the *a* in *America* (p. 134, l. 8), the *ct* in *instinct* (p. 134, l. 10), the *n* in *denied* (p. 137, l. 18), and *oss* in *across* (p. 156, l. 14). Commas after the following words are not fully impressed: *for* (p. 98, l. 13), *pot* (p. 104, l. 1), and *wail* (p. 152, l. 1). Periods after the following words are not fully impressed: *died* (p. 119, l. 10) and *Delmore* (p. 120, l. 2).

A 24 RECOVERY

A 24.1.a
First edition, first printing [1973]

JOHN BERRYMAN

RECOVERY

FARRAR, STRAUS AND GIROUX
NEW YORK

A 24.1.a: 8¼" × 5⁷⁄₁₆"

A 24.1.a *Recovery* 147

> Copyright © 1973 by the Estate of John Berryman
> "The Imaginary Jew" copyright © 1945 by John Berryman,
> copyright renewed 1973 by Kate Berryman
> Foreword copyright © 1973 by Saul Bellow
> All rights reserved
> Library of Congress catalog card number: 72-84779
> ISBN 0-374-24817-6
>
> FIRST EDITION, 1973
>
> Printed in the United States of America
> Published simultaneously in Canada by Doubleday Canada Ltd., Toronto
> DESIGNED BY HERB JOHNSON

[1-7]¹⁶ [8]⁸ [9]¹⁶

[i-viii] ix-xiv [1-6] 7-18 [19-20] 21-59 [60-62] 63-97 [98-100] 101-174 [175-176] 177-199 [200-202] 203-212 [213-214] 215-224 [225-226] 227 [228] 229-254 [255-258]

Contents: p. i: 'RECOVERY'. p. ii: 'The Lord is known by the judgment | which he executeth: the wicked is | snared in the work of his own hands. | Higgaion. Selah. | PSALMS 9:16'. p. iii: title page. p. iv: copyright page. p. v: "To the Suffering Healers | Oh! I haue suffered | With those that I saw suffer | MIRANDA, IN SHAKESPEARE'S | SECOND REDEMPTIVE WORK, I.ii.5 | 'My doctrine is not mine' | JOHN 7¹⁶". p. vi: blank. p. vii: 'NOTE | [eight-line comment] | J.B.' p. viii: blank. pp. ix-xiv: 'John Berryman | BY SAUL BELLOW'. p. 1: table of contents. p. 2: blank. p. 3: 'Higgaion | [headpiece]'. p. 4: blank. p. 5: 'I | FIRST DAY | Sufficient Vnto the day | is the euil thereof. | MATTHEW 6³⁴'. p. 6: blank. pp. 7-18: text. p. 19: 'II | THE FIRST STEP (I-IV) | Here are the steps we took, which we suggested | as a program of recovery: | 1. We admitted we were powerless over alcohol— | that our lives had become unmanageable. | ALCOHOLICS ANONYMOUS (1939, 1955)'. p. 20: blank. pp. 21-59: text. p. 60: blank. p. 61: 'III | CONTRACT ONE | Change your life.' p. 62: blank. pp. 63-97: text. p. 98: blank. p. 99: 'IV | THE LAST TWO | FIRST STEPS | The eternal gates terrific porter lifted the northern bar. | Thel enter'd in & saw the secrets of the land unknown.' p. 100: blank. pp. 101-174: text. p. 175: 'V | CONTRACT TWO'. p. 176: blank. pp. 177-199: text. p. 200: blank. p. 201: 'VI | SELF-CONFRONTED'. p. 202: blank. pp. 203-212: text. p. 213: 'VII | DRY-DRUNK'. p. 214: blank. pp. 215-224: text. p. 225: 'VIII | THE JEWISH KICK AND | THE FIFTH STEP | [bracket] UNWRITTEN [bracket]'. p. 226: blank. p. 227: 'Selah | [headpiece] | [bracket] UNWRITTEN [bracket]'. p. 228: blank, p. 229: 'Author's Notes | He was an inveterate *note-taker, | note-maker, self-analyser. | For once the vice would serve a purpose. |* JOHN BERRYMAN, | ON A FOLDER MARKED "NOVEL NOTES" | [twenty-line note on the manuscript for *Recovery*, signed "– THE PUBLISHERS", all within brackets]'. pp. 230–242: text of author's notes. pp. 243–252: 'The Imaginary Jew'. pp. 253–254: 'The Twelve Steps'. pp. 255–258: blank.

Typography and paper: 36 ll. (occasionally 35), 6⁷/₁₆″ (6¹¹/₁₆″) × 3¹³/₁₆″. Text in 11-pt. Linotype Janson with 2-pt. leading; sections of text headed "From Severance's Journal" in 10-pt. Garamond Bold No. 3 with 4-pt. leading. "Foreword," "Author's Notes," "The Imaginary Jew," and "The Twelve Steps" in 10-pt. Linotype Janson with 2-pt. leading. Running heads: rectos, section titles in italics (for example, '*First Day*'); versos, 'RECOVERY'. Divisions within sections I–IV are numbered consecutively from 1 to 18, with numbers in italics above a headpiece (for example, '*1* | [headpiece]'); divisions within sections V–VII are indicated by the use of a headpiece. Further divisions within the main text are indicated by three asterisks (* * *); further divisions within "From Severance's Journal" are indicated by six asterisks (** ** **). Yellowish white (Centroid 92) wove paper.

Binding: Unsized calico-cloth (302), deep reddish orange (Centroid 36). Front cover: plain. Spine: '[reading vertically from top to bottom] [goldstamped] *RECOVERY John Berryman* | [reading horizontally] FARRAR | STRAUS | GIROUX'. Back cover: plain. All edges cut; top edge dyed black (267). Brilliant greenish yellow (98) wove endpapers.

Dust jacket: Wove paper, outside glossy, 8³/₈″ × 19⁵/₈″. Front cover: '[black (Centroid 267) background] [vivid reddish orange (34)] John Berryman | [strong yellow (84) outlined in dark olive green (126)] RECOVERY | [vivid reddish orange] A NOVEL | [drawing of a bentwood spindle-back chair in white (263) with light gray (264) shadowing]'. Spine: '[black background] [reading vertically from top to bottom] [vivid reddish orange] John Berryman [strong yellow outlined in dark olive green] RECOVERY | [reading horizontally] [vivid reddish orange] Farrar | Straus | Giroux'. Back cover: '[white background] [vivid reddish orange] JOHN BERRYMAN | [four black and white photographs of JB arranged in two lines] [upper left] [photograph] | [black] | 1940 | [upper right] *Photo by Rohn Engh* | [photograph] | 1962 | [lower left] *Photo by Ted Spencer* | [photograph] | 1967 | [lower right] *Photo by Tom Berthiaume* | [photograph] | 1971'. Front flap: '[white background] $6.95 | JOHN BERRYMAN |

A 24.1.a† *Recovery*   149

[vivid reddish orange] RECOVERY | [black] Foreword by SAUL BELLOW | [three-paragraph unsigned note on publication, reading in part ". . . Mr. Berryman began writing it | in 1970, signed a contract for it with | his publisher in the summer of 1971, | and had completed all but the final | section of the first draft when he died | in January 1972. . . .", fourteen lines, and the beginning of a descriptive comment on the contents, ten lines] | *(continued on back flap)*'. Back flap: '[white background] *(continued from front flap)* | [conclusion of descriptive comment, twenty lines] | *Jacket design by Janet Halverson* | [vivid reddish orange] FARRAR, STRAUS AND GIROUX | 19 UNION SQUARE WEST | NEW YORK 10003 | [black] ISBN 0-374-24817-6'.

Text: Only "The Imaginary Jew" had been previously published (see C 251). The publisher's note on p. 229 reads in part, "The text of *Recovery* printed in the preceding pages is basically that of the typescript John Berryman left, on his death in January 1972, with handwritten additions and corrections. . . . But except for several fragments he explicitly labeled *'end of book,'* no manuscript for the concluding sections, 'The Jewish Kick' and 'Selah,' has been found." "The Twelve Steps" is from Alcoholics Anonymous.

Publication: Unknown number of copies. Published May 25, 1973. $6.95.

Printing: Printed and bound by Vail-Ballou Press, Inc., Binghampton, N.Y.

Copyright: Registered under A 438492 in the name of the estate of JB.

Locations: DLC (deposit-stamp May 30, 1973); ECS (dj); Lockwood (dj); NBuU.

A 24.1.a†
Proof copy

$8^{3}/_{16}'' \times 5^{1}/_{8}''$

132 leaves (perfect binding)

[i–x] [1–7] 8–18 [19–20] 21–59 [60–63] 64–97 [98–101] 102–162 [163] 164–174 [175–177] 178–199 [200–203] 204–212 [213–215] 216–224 [225–228] 229–252 [253–254]

Contents: p. i: 'RECOVERY'. p. ii: '*by John Berryman* | [eleven titles]'. p. iii: title page. p. iv: copyright page. p. v: dedication. p. vi: blank. p. vii: epigraph. p. viii: blank. p. ix: '*NOTE*'. p. x:

blank. pp. 1-228: same as in first printing. pp. 229-240: 'Author's Notes'. pp. 241-250: 'The Imaginary Jew'. pp. 251-252: 'The Twelve Steps'. pp. 253-254: blank.

Typography and paper: Same typography as in the first printing. White (Centroid 263) wove paper

Binding: Perfect binding. Light bluish green (Centroid 163) wove paper wrappers. Front cover: '[reading diagonally] UNCORRECTED PAGE PROOF | [reading horizontally] [first letters, *J* and *B*, swash] *JOHN BERRYMAN* | *RECOVERY* | [device] | FARRAR, STRAUS AND GIROUX | *New York*'. Spine: plain. Back cover: plain. Inside fron cover: plain. Inside back cover: '[stamped] CRANE DUPLICATING SERVICE, INC. | P. O. BOX 487 | BARNSTABLE, MASS. 02630'. All edges cut. Cover cut flush.

Location: ECS.

Note: Page numbers for pp. 229-252 are written in, with p. 229 being misnumbered as 129.

A 24.1.b
First English reprint [1973]

Recovery

JOHN BERRYMAN

FABER AND FABER
3 Queen Square
London

A 24.1.b: $7^{11}/_{16}'' \times 5''$

> First published in Great Britain in 1973
> by Faber and Faber Limited
> 3 Queen Square London WC1
> Printed in Great Britain by
> Whitstable Litho, Straker Brothers Ltd., Whitstable
> All rights reserved
>
> ISBN 0 571 10292 1
>
> by the same author
>
> DELUSIONS ETC.
> LOVE AND FAME
> BERRYMAN'S SONNETS
> 77 DREAM SONGS
> HOMAGE TO MISTRESS BRADSTREET
> HIS TOY, HIS DREAM, HIS REST: 308 DREAM SONGS
> SELECTED POEMS, 1938-1968
>
> Copyright © 1973 by the Estate of John Berryman
> 'The Imaginary Jew' copyright © 1945 by John Berryman,
> copyright renewed 1973 by Kate Berryman
> Foreword copyright © 1973 by Saul Bellow

[1–17]^8

[i–viii] ix–xiv [1–6] 7–18 [19–20] 21–59 [60–62] 63–97 [98–100] 101–174 [175–176] 177–199 [200–202] 203–212 [213–214] 215–224 [225–228] 229–254 [255–258]

Contents: p. i: 'RECOVERY'. p. ii: 'The Lord is known by the judgment | which he executeth: the wicked is | snared in the work of his own hands. | Higgaion. Selah. | Psalms 9:16'. p. iii: title page. p. iv: copyright page. p. v: dedication. p. vi: blank. p. vii: 'NOTE | [eight-line comment, signed "J.B." on the eighth line]'. p. viii: blank. pp. ix–xiv: foreword. p. 1: table of contents. p. 2: blank. p. 3: '*Higgaion*'. p. 4: blank. p. 5: 'I | First Day | *Sufficient Vnto the day | is the euil thereof.* | MATTHEW 6^{34}'. p. 6: blank. pp. 7–18: text. p. 19: 'II | The First Step | (I–IV) | *Here are the steps we took, which we suggested | as a program of recovery: | 1. We admitted we were powerless over alcohol— | that our lives had become unmanageable.* | ALCOHOLICS ANONYMOUS (1939, 1955)'. p. 20: blank. pp. 21–59: text. p. 60: blank. p. 61: 'III | Contract One | *Change your life.*' p. 62: blank. pp. 63–97: text. p. 98: blank. p. 99: 'IV | The Last Two First Steps | *The eternal gates terrific porter lifted the northern bar. | Thel enter'd in & saw the secrets of the land unknown.*' p. 100: blank. pp. 101–174: text. p. 175: 'V | Contract Two'. p. 176: blank. pp. 177–199: text. p. 200: blank. p. 201:

A 24.1.b Recovery 153

'VI | Self-Confronted'. p. 202: blank. pp. 203-212: text. p. 213: 'VII | Dry-Drunk'. p. 214: blank. pp. 215-224: text. p. 225: 'VIII | The Jewish Kick and | The Fifth Step | [bracket] UNWRITTEN [bracket]'. p. 226: blank. p. 227: *'Selah* | [bracket] UNWRITTEN [bracket]'. p. 228: blank. pp. 229-242: author's notes. pp. 243-252: *'The Imaginary Jew'*. pp. 253-254: *'The Twelve Steps'*. pp. 255-258: blank.

Typography and paper: 6⅛" (6⅜") × 3⅜". Text in typeface size equivalent to 10-pt. with 2-pt. leading; sections headed "From Severance's Journal" in 9-pt. with 4-pt. leading. "Foreword," "Author's Notes," "The Imaginary Jew," and "The Twelve Steps" in typeface size equivalent to 9-pt. with 2-pt. leading. Divisions within sections I-IV are numbered consecutively from 1 to 18, with numbers in roman and without headpieces. Headpieces and asterisks are not used for divisions of sections. White (Centroid 263) wove paper.

Binding: Unsized calico-cloth (302), black (Centroid 267). Front cover: plain. Spine: '[reading vertically from top to bottom] [goldstamped] RECOVERY John Berryman | [reading horizontally] FABER'. Back cover: plain. All edges cut. White wove endpapers of different stock than text paper.

Dust jacket: Wove paper, outside glossy, 7⅞" × 19". Front cover: '[black (Centroid 267) background] [vivid reddish orange (34)] John Berryman | [brilliant greenish yellow (98) outlined in vivid reddish orange] RECOVERY | [vivid reddish orange] A NOVEL | [drawing of a bentwood spindle-back chair in white (263) with light gray (264) shadowing of a grainy appearance and with vivid reddish orange tips on the chair legs]'. Spine: '[black background] [reading vertically from top to bottom] [between white thick vertical rules at both sides of spine] [vivid reddish orange] John Berryman [brilliant greenish yellow outlined in vivid reddish orange] RECOVERY | [reading horizontally] [vivid reddish orange] Faber'. Back cover: vivid reddish orange, plain. Front flap: '[white background] RECOVERY | JOHN BERRYMAN | [three-paragraph unsigned note, comprising a nine-line statement on publication, a thirteen-line descriptive comment on contents, and a four-line note on the "Foreword"] | *Jacket design by Janet Halverson* | £2.50 | *net'*. Back flap: '[four-line quotation from a comment by A. Alvarez and eight-line quotation from a comment by Lyman Andrews] | [four-line advertisement for catalogue]'.

Publication: 3,000 copies. Published November 1973. £2.50.

Printing: Printed by offset by Whitestable Litho, Whitstable, Kent, and bound by Leighton-Straker Bookbinding Company Ltd., London.

Location: ECS.

Note: In a letter of February 11, 1974, Jane Carter of Faber and Faber wrote that 3,000 copies are bound in paper wrappers but not yet published.

B. First-Appearance Contributions to Books

Titles in which material by Berryman constitutes first publication or first book appearance, arranged chronologically by date of publication. There is a supplemental BB section listing borderline items.

B 1 COLUMBIA POETRY 1935
1935

COLUMBIA POETRY | 1935 | WITH AN INTRODUCTION BY | WILLIAM T. BREWSTER | [seal] | NEW YORK · MORNINGSIDE HEIGHTS | COLUMBIA UNIVERSITY PRESS | 1935

Selected by Joseph Auslander, Irwin Edman, Roderick Marshall, Elizabeth Reynard, and Mark Van Doren.

Published December 19, 1935, at $1.00 (printed wrappers).

"Time Does Not Engulf," p. 13; "Sonnet" ("I thought that for the enemies at length"), pp. 13-14; "Note on E. A. Robinson," p. 14; "Ars Poetica," pp. 14-18.

First publication of "Time Does Not Engulf" and "Sonnet." First book appearance of "Ars Poetica" and "Note on E. A. Robinson." See C 2, C 7.

B 2 COLUMBIA POETRY 1936
1936

COLUMBIA POETRY | 1936 | WITH AN INTRODUCTION BY | WILLIAM ROSE BENÉT | [seal] | NEW YORK · MORNINGSIDE HEIGHTS | COLUMBIA UNIVERSITY PRESS | 1936

Selected by Allan Abbott, Joseph Auslander, Herbert Brucker, George H. Genzmer, Minor W. Latham, John H. H. Lyon, Henry W. Simon, William Y. Tindall, and Mark Van Doren.

Published December 1, 1936, at $1.00 (printed wrappers).

"To an Artist Beginning Her Work," p. 11; "Notation," pp. 11-12; "Elegy: Hart Crane," pp. 12-14.

First publication of "To an Artist Beginning Her Work." First book appearance of "Elegy: Hart Crane" and "Notation." See C 8, C 11.

B 3 NEW DIRECTIONS IN PROSE AND POETRY
1938

NEW DIRECTIONS | IN PROSE & POETRY | 1938 | [device] | NEW DIRECTIONS | NORFOLK - CONN

Edited by James Laughlin.

Published October 5, 1938, at $2.50 (printed paper-covered boards).

"Three Poems": "The Return," pp. [19]-[20]; "The Translation," pp. [20]-[21]; "Caravan," p. [22].
    First publication of all. "The Return." In *20P;* as "The Possessed" in *TD* and *ShP.* "Caravan." In *20P, TD,* and *ShP.*

B 4 NEW DIRECTIONS IN PROSE AND POETRY 1939
1939

NEW DIRECTIONS | IN PROSE & POETRY | 1939 | [device] | NEW DIRECTIONS · NORFOLK · CONN.

Edited by James Laughlin.

Published November 1, 1939, at $3.00 (printed paper-covered boards).

"Six Poems": "Ceremony and Vision," pp. 123-124; "On a Portrait in Dublin," pp. 124-125; "The Second Cactus," p. 125; "Prague," pp. 125-126; "The Curse," pp. 126-127; "Parting as Descent," p. 127.
    First publication of all. "Ceremony and Vision" and "The Curse." In *20P.* "Parting as Descent." In *20P, TD, HomageAOP,* and *ShP.*

B 5 NEW POEMS 1940
1941

[six rules] | NEW POEMS: | 1940 | An Anthology of British and American Verse | Edited by Oscar Williams [ornament] A Living Age Book | The Yardstick Press [ornament] New York [ornament] 1941 | [six rules]

Published April 17, 1941, at $2.50.

First-Appearance Contributions to Books 159

On copyright page: 'FIRST PRINTING'.

"The Spinning Heart," pp. 63-64; "The Moon and the Night and the Men," pp. 65-66; "Conversation," pp. 66-67; "Desires of Men and Women," p. 68.

First publication of "The Moon and the Night and the Men." In *Poems, TD, HomageAOP, ShP,* and *SelP.* See also B 9, D 33. First book appearance of "The Spinning Heart." In *TD, HomageAOP, ShP,* and *SelP.* See also C 32. Reprinting of "Desires of Men and Women" and "Conversation." See B 9, C 26, C 27.

B 6 NEW DIRECTIONS IN PROSE AND
POETRY 1941
1941

NEW DIRECTIONS | IN PROSE & POETRY | 1941 | [within ornamental frame] [device] | [below frame] NEW DIRECTIONS · NORFOLK · CONN.

Edited by James Laughlin.

Published December 1, 1941, at $3.50.

"Five Political Poems": "River Rouge, 1933" [later titled "River Rouge, 1932"], p. 465; "Thanksgiving: Detroit," p. 466; "The Dangerous Year," pp. 466-468; "1 September 1939," pp. 468-469; "Communist," p. 469.

First publication of all. In *Poems.* "1 September 1939." Also in *TD, HomageAOP,* and *ShP.*

B 7 NEW POEMS 1943
1943

NEW POEMS | 1943 An Anthology of | British and American Verse | *Edited by* OSCAR WILLIAMS | [rule] | HOWELL, SOSKIN, PUBLISHERS

Published August 17, 1943, at $2.75.

"Boston Common," pp. 46-52; "The Statue," pp 52-54; "The Disciple," pp. 54-55.

First publication of "Boston Common." In *TD, HomageAOP,* and *ShP.* Reprinting of "The Statue" and "The Disciple." See C 23, C 25.

B 8 NEW POEMS 1944
1944

[*N* and *P* in script, greater height than other capitals] NEW POEMS *1944* | AN ANTHOLOGY OF AMERICAN AND | BRITISH VERSE, WITH A SELECTION | OF POEMS FROM THE ARMED FORCES | Edited by OSCAR WILLIAMS [three ornaments] | *New York* | HOWELL, SOSKIN, PUBLISHERS

Published August 15, 1944, at $3.00.

"The Animal Trainer I" [later titled "The Animal Trainer 1"], pp. 42–43; "The Animal Trainer II" [later titled "The Animal Trainer 2"], pp. 43–44; "Winter Landscape," p. 45.

First publication of "The Animal Trainer I" and "The Animal Trainer II." In *TD*, *HomageAOP,* and *ShP.* Reprinting of "Winter Landscape." See C 31.

B 9 THE WAR POETS
1945

The War Poets | *An Anthology of the War Poetry* | *of the 20th Century* | *Edited with an Introduction by* | Oscar Williams | The John Day Company · New York

Published June 19, 1945, at $5.00.

Essay, "On War and Poetry," pp. 29–30; "The Moon and the Night and the Men" and "Conversation," pp. 326–328.

First publication of "On War and Poetry." See D 44. Reprinting of "Conversation" and "The Moon and the Night and the Men." See C 27, D 33.

B 10 NEW DIRECTIONS 9
1946

NEW | DIRECTIONS | [within single rules frame] 9 | [below frame] *published* | *by* | *new directions* | *at* | *norfolk connecticut*

Edited by James Laughlin.

Published June 12, 1946, at $3.75.

Fiction, "The Lovers," pp. 299–306. First book appearance. See C 249.

First-Appearance Contributions to Books 161

B 11 O. HENRY PRIZE STORIES OF 1946
1946

O. HENRY MEMORIAL AWARD | *PRIZE STORIES* | OF | *1946* | [ornamental rule] | SELECTED AND EDITED BY | HERSCHEL BRICKELL | ASSISTED BY | MURIEL FULLER | [ornamental rule] | [device] | DOUBLEDAY & COMPANY, INC. | GARDEN CITY 1946 NEW YORK

Published August 22, 1946, at $2.50.

On copyright page: 'FIRST EDITION'.

Fiction, "The Imaginary Jew," pp. 65–73. First book appearance. In *Recovery*. See also C 251.

B 12 THE KENYON CRITICS
1951

[tapered rule] | The Kenyon Critics | STUDIES IN MODERN LITERATURE FROM | THE Kenyon Review EDITED BY | *John Crowe Ransom* | [rule] | [device] | *The World Publishing Company* | CLEVELAND AND NEW YORK | [tapered rule]

Published February 23, 1951, at $4.00.

On copyright page: 'First Edition'.

Book review, "The Loud Hill of Wales," pp. 255–259. First book appearance. See C 246.

B 13 ERICH KAHLER
1951

ERICH | KAHLER | [ornamental rule] | NEW YORK 1951

Edited and in part translated by Eleanor L. Wolff and Herbert Steiner.

Published November 5, 1951.

On copyright page: '350 COPIES PRINTED IN METUCHEN, NEW JERSEY, | BY VAN VECHTEN PRESS, INC.'

"The Mysteries," pp. 15–16. First publication. In *Thought* and *ShP*.

Location: DLC.

B 14 THE MONK
    1952

the Monk | Matthew G. Lewis | Original text, | variant readings, | and 'A Note on the Text' | *LOUIS F. PECK* | Introduction | *JOHN BERRYMAN* | NEW YORK : GROVE PRESS

Published April 1, 1952, at $4.75.

"Introduction," pp. 11–28. First publication.

B 15 HIGHLIGHTS OF MODERN LITERATURE
     1954

Highlights of | MODERN LITERATURE | *A Permanent Collection of Memorable Essays from* | [gothic] The New York Times Book Review | *Edited by Francis Brown* | [device] | [roman] A MENTOR BOOK | Published by THE NEW AMERICAN LIBRARY

Published March 3, 1954, at $0.35.

On copyright page: 'FIRST PRINTING, MARCH, 1954'.

Book review, "Through Dreiser's Imagination the Tides of Real Life Billowed," pp. 118–123. First book appearance. See C 264.

Location: ECS.

B 16 THE MINNEAPOLIS SYMPHONY
     ORCHESTRA
     1959

The Minneapolis Symphony Orchestra | *Fifty-Sixth Season, 1958–59* | ANTAL DORATI, *Musical Director* | GERARD SAMUEL, *Associate Conductor* | [rule] | CONTENTS | [list of contents, nine lines] | [rule] | *Published by The Minnesota Orchestral Association* | 110 Cyrus Northrop Memorial Auditorium | University of Minnesota, Minneapolis 14, Minnesota | BORIS SOKOLOFF, *Manager*

Book of programs, bound in 1959.

Program title page: Fifty-Sixth Season — 1958–59 | [rule] | THE MINNEAPOLIS SYMPHONY ORCHESTRA | ANTAL DORATI, *Musical Director* | FIFTEENTH SUBSCRIPTION

First-Appearance Contributions to Books

CONCERT | *Friday, February 6, 1959, at 8:30 p. m.* | Soloists: MAUREEN FORRESTER, *Contralto* | NORMAN TREIGLE, *Bass-Baritone* | JOHN LANGSTAFF, *Narrator* | UNIVERSITY OF MINNESOTA CHORUS, WALTER COLLINS, *Director* | [rule] | "The Way of the Cross" | CANTATA DRAMATICA | *by* | ANTAL DORATI | Text by Paul Claudel | English Translation by John Berryman | [list of the fourteen divisions of the text, with the parts of the ensemble participating in each division] | [rule] | [acknowledgments and announcements, ten lines]'.

English translation of "The Way of the Cross," a dramatic cantata, from the French text of Paul Claudel, pp. 437, 439, 441, 443, 445, 447, 448-451, 453. First publication.

The music was set to the French text by Antal Dorati, but the translation by JB was sung at the performance of February 6, 1959.

Location: DLC.

B 17 THE UNFORTUNATE TRAVELLER
1960

THOMAS NASHE | THE | UNFORTUNATE | TRAVELLER | OR | *The Life of Jack Wilton* | NEWLY EDITED, WITH AN INTRODUCTION, BY | JOHN BERRYMAN | WITH SIX ORIGINAL ILLUSTRATIONS BY | MICHAEL AYRTON | [device] | CAPRICORN BOOKS | G. P. *Putnam's Sons New York, N.Y*

Published April 15, 1960, at $1.15 (printed wrappers) and $2.50 (cloth).

"A Note on the Text," pp. 5-6; "Introduction," pp. 7-28. First publication.

Note: In "A Note on the Text," JB wrote: "The present normalized text has been constructed from the materials in R. B. McKerrow's great edition of Nashe, 1904-10 (vol. ii, notes in vols. iv and – the 1957 reprint by F. P. Wilson – v, 32-42). Dr. McKerrow unwisely adopted as copy text, however, the second edition, which clearly was looked at and touched by Nashe but introduces many printing-house sophistications; I have reverted to the original reading much more frequently than McKerrow did – sometimes with very little confidence. . . . Paragraphing and pointing I have controlled, as indeed McKerrow himself did the latter ('to alter it without scruple,' i, xiii). It has been a great pleasure to accept certain conjectural emendations of Mc-

Kerrow, Sir Walter Greg, and E. S. de Beer; I have made (I think) no suggestions of my own. Despite the uncertainties inevitable in this sort of transmission, it is hoped that the present text of Nashe's novel may be verbally the most faithful to his final intention that has yet appeared."

B 18 STEPHEN CRANE
1962

STEPHEN | CRANE | [tapered rule] | JOHN BERRYMAN | [tapered rule] | Meridian Books | THE WORLD PUBLISHING COMPANY | Cleveland and New York

Published February 1962, at $1.65 (printed wrappers).

On copyright page: 'First Meridian printing February 1962 | MCP 262'.

"Preface to the Meridian Edition," pp. ix–xii; "Additional Bibliography (1962)," pp. 331–332. First publication. See A 6.1.c.

B 19 POET'S CHOICE
1962

POET'S | CHOICE | [ornamental rule] | EDITED BY | Paul Engle and Joseph Langland | [device] | THE DIAL PRESS NEW YORK 1962

Published October 9, 1962, at $6.95.

"The Dispossessed," pp. 134–135; untitled comment on "The Dispossessed," pp. 135–136.
 First publication of comment. Reprinting of "The Dispossessed." See C 47.

B 20 NEW WORLD WRITING 21
1963

21 | NEW | WORLD | WRITING | [device] | J. B. LIPPINCOTT COMPANY | *Philadelphia & New York*

Edited by Stewart Richardson and Corlies M. Smith.

Dated 1962 on copyright page but published January 10, 1963, at $0.95 (printed wrappers) and $3.50 (cloth).

On copyright page: 'FIRST EDITION'.

First-Appearance Contributions to Books

Untitled article in "The Poet and His Critics: III: A Symposium on Robert Lowell's 'Skunk Hour,'" edited by Anthony Ostroff, pp. 148–155. First publication. Later titled "Despondency and Madness." See D 47.

B 21 OF POETRY AND POWER
1964

[two-page title] [left page] OF POETRY [right page] AND POWER | [left] POEMS OCCASIONED [right] BY THE PRESIDENCY | [left] AND BY THE DEATH [right] OF JOHN F. KENNEDY | [left] *Foreword by Arthur Schlesinger, Jr.* [right] EDITED WITH AN INTRODUCTION | *by Erwin A. Glikes and Paul Schwaber* | BASIC BOOKS, INC. | PUBLISHERS [slash] NEW YORK

Published November 6, 1964, at $5.95.

"Formal Elegy," pp. 44–47. First publication. In *ShP*.

B 22 THE AMERICAN NOVEL
1965

THE | AMERICAN | NOVEL | FROM JAMES FENIMORE COOPER | TO WILLIAM FAULKNER | *Edited by WALLACE STEGNER* | BASIC BOOKS, INC., PUBLISHERS | *New York London*

Published July 30, 1965, at $4.95.

Article, "Stephen Crane: *The Red Badge of Courage*," pp. 86–96.[1] First publication. See D 46.

---

1. In the "Preface," Wallace Stegner states that the articles included in *The American Novel* were designed "for oral presentation over the Voice of America." In a letter of January 26, 1974, Mr. Stegner wrote: "John Berryman *did* record his essay on *The Red Badge of Courage* for broadcast abroad. I chose him to do the essay because I had known him when we were instructors at Harvard together and because I admired his *Stephen Crane*. I was trying to find the top authority on the several American novelists represented in the series, and it seemed to me John was the man. As I recall, that series was ordered by the Voice of America in 1963. . . . The format was the same for all of us: We wrote the essays, I raised such small editorial questions as seemed appropriate and then approved the essays; and the authors went to the nearest available recording studio and recorded their own readings of their own essays, which were then broadcast God knows where over God knows how long a period." Further information about the broadcast of JB's article has not been determined; no recordings of it has been located.

B 23 ONE HUNDRED YEARS OF THE NATION
1965

[four florets] | *One Hundred Years of* | THE NATION | A CENTENNIAL ANTHOLOGY | Edited by HENRY M. CHRISTMAN | ABRAHAM FELDMAN, Poetry Editor | Introduction by CAREY McWILLIAMS | THE MACMILLAN COMPANY, NEW YORK | COLLIER-MACMILLAN LIMITED, LONDON

Published August 2, 1965, at $7.95.

On copyright page: 'FIRST PRINTING'.

"Three Dream Songs": "General Fatigue," p. 377; "Henry's Pencils," pp. 377–378; "Donnybrook," p. 378.

First book appearance of all. "General Fatigue" collected as Dream Song 93. In *Toy* and *TheDS*. See also C 129. "Henry's Pencils." See C 130. "Donnybrook" collected as Dream Song 97. In *Toy* and *TheDS*. See also C 131.

B 24 THE TITAN
1965

The TITAN | [rule] | THEODORE DREISER | With an Afterword by | John Berryman | A SIGNET [device] CLASSIC | PUBLISHED BY THE NEW AMERICAN LIBRARY, | NEW YORK AND TORONTO

Published October 20, 1965, at $0.95 (printed wrappers).

On copyright page: 'First Printing, October, 1965'.

"Afterword," pp. 503–511. First publication.

B 25 MASTER POEMS OF THE ENGLISH LANGUAGE
1966

MASTER | POEMS | OF THE ENGLISH LANGUAGE | [tapered rule] | *Over one hundred poems* | *together with Introductions* | *by leading poets and critics* | *of the English-speaking world* | EDITED BY | Oscar Williams | [device] | TRIDENT PRESS | *New York 1966.*

Published January 17, 1966, at $10.00.

First-Appearance Contributions to Books 167

Commentary, "Hardy: 'The Darkling Thrush,'" pp. 788-790; commentary, "Ransom: 'Captain Carpenter,'" pp. 985-987. First publication.

B 26 POETS ON POETRY
1966

POETS | ON | POETRY | *Edited by* HOWARD NEMEROV | BASIC BOOKS, INC., PUBLISHERS | *New York London*

Published January 21, 1966, at $4.95.

Essay, "Changes," pp. 94-103. First book appearance. See C 276.

B 27 RANDALL JARRELL
1967

[first letter swash] *Randall Jarrell* | [tapered rule] | 1914-1965 | EDITED BY | Robert Lowell, Peter Taylor, | & Robert Penn Warren | [device] | *Farrar, Straus & Giroux* | NEW YORK

Published August 28, 1967, at $6.50.

On copyright page: 'First printing, 1967'.

Book review, "On Poetry and the Age," pp. 10-13; essay, "Randall Jarrell," pp. 14-17; "Op. posth. no. 13," pp. 18-19.
    First publication of "Randall Jarrell." First book appearance of "On Poetry and the Age." See C 266. First book appearance of "Op. posth. no. 13." In *Toy, TheDS,* and *SelP.* See also C 147.

B 28 UNIVERSITY ON THE HEIGHTS
1969

[ornament] University [ornament] | on the Heights | [rule] | EDITED BY WESLEY FIRST | Doubleday & Company, Inc., Garden City, New York

Published April 4, 1969, at $4.95.

On copyright page: 'First Edition'.

Essay, "Three and a Half Years at Columbia," pp. 51-60. First publication.

B 29 THIS IS MY BEST
1970

America's 85 Greatest Living Authors Present | THIS IS MY BEST | IN THE THIRD QUARTER OF THE CENTURY | [rule] | Edited by Whit Burnett | 1970 | DOUBLEDAY & COMPANY, INC., GARDEN CITY, NEW YORK

Published September 18, 1970, at $10.95.

On copyright page: 'FIRST EDITION'.

Part of a letter to Whit Burnett, p. [492]; Dream Songs 1, 29, 77, 89, 382, 384, 385, pp. 493-497.

First publication of letter. Reprinting of Dream Songs. See C 71, C 81, C 75, C 146, D 26, C 178, C 137.

B 30 CRITICS ON EZRA POUND
1972

CRITICS ON | EZRA POUND | [rule] | *Readings in Literary Criticism* | Edited by E. San Juan, Jr. | [rule] | [device, height of next two lines] University of Miami Press | *Coral Gables, Florida*

Published June 15, 1972, at $3.95 (printed paper-covered boards).

Article, "The Poetry of Ezra Pound," pp. 38-43. First book appearance of part of an article that first appeared in *Partisan Review*, XVI (April 1949), 377-394. See C 262. The selection in *Critics* comprises the matter on pp. 384-391.

BB. Supplement
Borderline Items

BB 1 TWENTIETH CENTURY AUTHORS
1955

TWENTIETH CENTURY | AUTHORS | FIRST SUPPLEMENT | A Biographical Dictionary of Modern Literature | *Edited by* | STANLEY J. KUNITZ | *Assistant Editor* | VINETA COLBY | [device] | NEW YORK | THE H. W. WILSON COMPANY | NINETEEN HUNDRED FIFTY-FIVE

Published October 13, 1955.

"Berryman, John," pp. 83-84. Probably based on letter.

BB 2 DIRECTORY OF AMERICAN SCHOLARS
1957

DIRECTORY *of* | AMERICAN SCHOLARS | A BIOGRAPHICAL DIRECTORY | *Edited by* Jaques Cattell | *Editor of "American Men of Science"* | THIRD EDITION | *Published 1957* | [rule] | R. R. BOWKER COMPANY | NEW YORK, N.Y.

Published June 12, 1957.

"Berryman, John," p. 59. Probably based on questionnaire. First appearance. Revised and updated in later volumes.

BB 3 WHO'S WHO IN AMERICA
1958

WHO'S WHO | IN AMERICA | A BIOGRAPHICAL DICTIONARY OF | NOTABLE LIVING MEN AND WOMEN | REVISED AND REISSUED BIENNIALLY | Volume 30 | (1958-1959) | Sixtieth Anniversary Edition | *(Compilation begun 1898- Published continuously since 1899)* | MARQUIS - WHO'S

WHO | INCORPORATED – A NON-PROFIT FOUNDATION | (The A. N. Marquis Company – Founded 1897) | *Marquis Publications Building* | CHICAGO-11 USA

Published January 31, 1958.

"Berryman, John," p. 228. Probably based on questionnaire. First appearance. Revised and updated in later volumes.

BB 4 NATIONAL POETRY FESTIVAL
1964

National | Poetry Festival | HELD IN THE LIBRARY OF CONGRESS | OCTOBER 22-24, 1962 | *PROCEEDINGS* | [seal] | GENERAL REFERENCE AND BIBLIOGRAPHY DIVISION | REFERENCE DEPARTMENT | LIBRARY OF CONGRESS | WASHINGTON : 1964

Published July 1964.

Previously unpublished comments, pp. 43, 183–184, 186. Also includes reprintings of Dream Songs 4, 22, 16, 29, 75, and 27, pp. 183–187. See C 91, C 99, C 87, C 81, C 73, C 86.

Note: JB's comments were transcribed from recordings of the National Poetry Festival program. They have been included with the borderline items since, undoubtedly, JB's intention was that they be spoken rather than written and since, presumably, he did not have the opportunity to revise or correct the comments as they appear in print.

BB 5 JOHN BERRYMAN
1969

[at left edge, first line reading vertically from bottom to top] UNIVERSITY OF MINNESOTA | [reading horizontally] PAMPHLETS ON AMERICAN WRITERS · NUMBER 85 | [device] *John Berryman* | BY WILLIAM J. MARTZ | UNIVERSITY OF MINNESOTA PRESS · MINNEAPOLIS

Published December 3, 1969.

Biographical information on pp. 5–8 et passim based on interview.

Supplement: Borderline Items

BB 6 WHO'S WHO 1972
1972

WHO'S WHO | 1972 | AN | ANNUAL BIOGRAPHICAL DICTIONARY | ONE HUNDRED AND TWENTY-FOURTH | YEAR OF ISSUE | ADAM AND CHARLES BLACK | LONDON

Published April 13, 1972.

"Berryman, John," pp. 256–257. Based on letter or questionnaire received prior to November 1971. First appearance.

American issue: New York: St. Martin's Press, 1972.

C. Contributions to Periodicals

Materials by Berryman first published in periodicals, arranged chronologically by date of publication within two subdivisions, *Poetry* and *Prose*. Reprintings are regularly noted.

Note: The following reviews by JB were located while the bibliography was in page proof. They all appear in *The New York Times Book Review* and are listed here in an abbreviated form. The numbering designations indicate their positions in the chronological listing under *Prose*. These items are not listed in the appendices and index.

C 249a
"Mr. Moult and the Poets," January 14, 1945, p. 16.

Review of *The Best Poems of 1943,* ed. Thomas Moult.

C 249b
"New Books of Verse," March 18, 1945, p. 10.

Review of *Poems* by Jon Beck Shank and *Thirty Poems* by Thomas Merton.

C 267a
"Days of Crisis in the Great Experiment," January 9, 1955, pp. 4-5.

Review of *The New Men* by C. P. Snow.

C 272a
"Epics from Outer Space," July 21, 1963, pp. 4-5.

Review of *Aniara* by Harry Martinson, trans. Hugh MacDiarmid and Elspeth Harley Schubert, and *The Anathemata* by David Jones.

C 273a
"Neither Here nor There," May 31, 1964, pp. 3, 14.

Review of *A Piece of Lettuce* by George P. Elliot.

POETRY

C 1
"Essential," *The Columbia Review*, XVI (March 1935), 19.

C 2
"Ars Poetica," *The Columbia Review*, XVI (April 1935), 18-19.

Reprinted: Columbia Poetry 1935, ed. Joseph Auslander et al. New York: Columbia University Press, 1935.

See B 1.

C 3
"Blake," *The Columbia Review*, XVI (April 1935), 19.

C 4
Lead Out the Weary Dancers," *The Columbia Review*, XVI (April 1935), 23.

C 5
"Apostrophe," *The Columbia Review*, XVI (April 1935), 23.

C 6
"Ivory," *The Columbia Review*, XVI (May 1935), 18.

C 7
"Note on E. A. Robinson," *The Nation*, CXLI (July 10, 1935), 38.

Reprinted: (1) *Columbia Poetry 1935*, ed. Joseph Auslander et al. New York: Columbia University Press, 1935. (2) *Literary Digest*, CXXI (February 1936), 30.

See B 1.

C 8
"Elegy: Hart Crane," *The Columbia Review*, XVII (November 1935), 20-21.

Reprinted: Columbia Poetry 1936, ed. Allan Abbott et al. New York: Columbia University Press, 1936.

See B 2.

C 9
"Thanksgiving," *The Columbia Review*, XVII (November 1935), 22.

C 10
"Words to a Young Man," *The Columbia Review*, XVII (December 1935), 10.

C 11
"Notation," *The Columbia Review*, XVII (April 1936), 3.

Reprinted: Columbia Poetry 1936, ed. Allan Abbott et al. New York: Columbia University Press, 1936.

See B 2.

C 12
"The Witness," *The Columbia Review*, XVII (April 1936), 4.

C 13
"The Ancestor," *The Columbia Review*, XVII (April 1936), 5-7.

C 14
"Trophy," *The Columbia Review*, XVII (April 1936), 7.

C 15
"Night and the City," *The Southern Review*, IV (Summer 1938), 168-170.

In *20P*.

C 16
"Note for a Historian," *The Southern Review*, IV (Summer 1938), 170.

C 17
"The Apparition," *The Southern Review*, IV (Summer 1938), 171.

In *20P*.

C 18
"Toward Statement," *The Southern Review*, IV (Summer 1938), 172.

Contributions to Periodicals

C 19
"The Trial," *Twentieth Century Verse*, nos. 12-13 (September-October 1938), 99.

In *20P*.

C 20
"Letter to His Brother," *The Kenyon Review*, I (Summer 1939), 257-258.

In *20P, TD, HomageAOP*, and *ShP*.

C 21
"Nineteen Thirty-Eight," *The Kenyon Review*, I (Summer 1939), 258-259.

In *20P*.

C 22
"World-Telegram," *The New Republic*, IC (June 28, 1939), 225.

In *20P, TD, HomageAOP*, and *ShP*.

C 23
"The Statue," *Partisan Review*, VI (Summer 1939), 16-17.

In *20P, Poems, TD, HomageAOP*, and *ShP*.

Reprinted: (1) *New Poems 1943*, ed. Oscar Williams. New York: Howell, Soskin, 1943. (2) *A Little Treasury of Modern Poetry*, ed. Oscar Williams. New York: Charles Scribner's Sons, 1946. (3) *The Partisan Review*, ed. William Phillips and Philip Rahv. New York: Dial Press, 1946. (4) *The Partisan Review Anthology*, ed. William Phillips and Philip Rahv. New York: Holt, Rinehart and Winston, 1961. (5) *The New Poetry*, ed. A. Alvarez. Harmondsworth, Middlesex: Penguin Books, 1966.

C 24
"On the London Train," *Partisan Review*, VI (Summer 1939), 18.

In *20P, TD*, and *ShP*.

C 25
"The Disciple," *The Nation*, CIL (December 30, 1939), 736.

In *20P, TD, HomageAOP*, and *ShP*.

Reprinted: New Poems 1943, ed. Oscar Williams. New York: Howell, Soskin, 1943.

C 26
"Desires of Men and Women," *The Southern Review*, V (Spring 1940), 771.

In *20P, TD, HomageAOP, ShP*, and *SelP*.

Reprinted: (1) *Living Age*, CCCLIX (October 1940), 180-181. (2) *New Poems 1940*, ed. Oscar Williams. New York: Yardstick Press, 1941. (3) *A Little Treasury of Modern Poetry*, ed. Oscar Williams. New York: Charles Scribner's Sons, 1946.

C 27
"Conversation," *The Southern Review*, V (Spring 1940), 772-773.

In *20P, TD*, and *ShP*.

Reprinted: (1) *Living Age*, CCCLIX (October 1940), 181. (2) *New Poems 1940*, ed. Oscar Williams. New York: Yardstick Press, 1941. (3) *The War Poets*, ed. Oscar Williams. New York: John Day Co., 1945. (4) *A Little Treasury of Modern Poetry*, ed. Oscar Williams. New York: Charles Scribner's Sons, 1946. (5) *The Little Treasury of American Poetry*, ed. Oscar Williams. New York: Charles Scribner's Sons, 1948. (6) *The New Pocket Anthology of American Verse*, ed. Oscar Williams. New York: World Publishing Co., 1955. (7) *The Experience of Literature*, ed. Lionel Trilling. Garden City, N.Y.: Doubleday and Co., 1967.

C 28
"Homage to Film," *The Southern Review*, V (Spring 1940), 773.

C 29
"Song from *Cleopatra*" [later titled "Song from 'Cleopatra'"], *The Southern Review*, V (Spring 1940), 774.

In *20P*.

C 30
"Meditation," *The Southern Review*, V (Spring 1940), 775-777.

In *20P*.

C 31
"Winter Landscape," *The New Republic*, CIII (July 8, 1940), 52.

In 20P, TD, HomageAOP, ShP, and SelP.

Reprinted: (1) New Poems 1944, ed. Oscar Williams. New York: Howell, Soskin, 1944. (2) A Little Treasury of Great Poetry, ed. Oscar Williams. New York: Charles Scribner's Sons, 1947. (3) A Little Treasury of American Poetry, ed. Oscar Williams. New York: Charles Scribner's Sons, 1948. (4) Modern American Poetry, ed. Louis Untermeyer. New York: Harcourt, Brace and Co., 1950. (5) The Creative Reader, ed. R. W. Stallman and R. E. Watters. New York: Ronald Press Co., 1954. (6) Poetry for Pleasure. Garden City, N.Y.: Doubleday and Co., 1960. (7) The Modern Poets, ed. John Malcolm Brinnin and Bill Read. New York: McGraw-Hill Book Co., 1963. (8) American Poetry, ed. Gay Wilson Allen, Walter B. Rideout, and James K. Robinson. New York: Harper and Row, 1965. (9) Contemporary Poetry in America, ed. Miller Williams. New York: Random House, 1968. (10) Beach Glass and Other Poems, ed. Paul Molloy. New York: Four Winds Press, 1970. (11) A Little Treasury of Modern Poetry, ed. Oscar Williams. New York: Charles Scribner's Sons, 1970. (12) Twentieth Century Poetry, ed. John Malcolm Brinnin and Bill Read. New York: McGraw-Hill Book Co., 1970. (13) The Norton Introduction to Literature: Poetry, ed. J. Paul Hunter. New York: W. W. Norton Co., 1973.

C 32
"The Spinning Heart," Accent, I (Winter 1940), 98–99.

In TD, HomageAOP, ShP, and SelP.

Reprinted: (1) New Poems 1940, ed. Oscar Williams. New York: Yardstick Press, 1941. (2) Accent Anthology, ed. Kerker Quinn and Charles Shattuck. New York: Harcourt, Brace and Co., 1946. (3) A Little Treasury of Modern Poetry, ed. Oscar Williams. New York: Charles Scribner's Sons, 1946.

See B 5.

C 33
"At Chinese Checkers," The Kenyon Review, III (Spring 1941), 191–195.

In Poems, TD, and ShP.

C 34
"The White Feather" [later titled "White Feather"], The Nation, CLIV (May 16, 1942), 574.

In TD and ShP.

C 35
"Cloud and Flame," *Chimera*, I (Winter 1943), 2.

In *TD*, *HomageAOP*, and *ShP*.

Reprinted: American Poetry, ed. Gay Wilson Allen, Walter B. Rideout, and James K. Robinson. New York: Harper and Row, 1965.

C 36
"Farewell to Miles," *The Sewanee Review*, LI (Summer 1943), 396.

In *TD* and *ShP*.

C 37
"Ancestor," *The Sewanee Review*, LI (Summer 1943), 397.

In *TD*, *HomageAOP*, and *ShP*.

C 38
"Travelling South," *Chimera*, III (Summer 1945), 2.

In *TD* and *ShP*.

C 39
"The Song of the Demented Priest," *Partisan Review*, XIII (Summer 1946), 347.

In *TD*, *HomageAOP*, *ShP*, and *SelP*.

Reprinted: Modern Poetry, ed. Kimon Friar and John Malcolm Brinnin. New York: Appleton-Century-Crofts, 1951.

C 40
"The Song of the Young Hawaiian," *Partisan Review*, XIII (Summer 1946), 347-348.

In *TD*, *HomageAOP*, and *ShP*.

C 41
"Young Woman's Song," *Partisan Review*, XIII (Summer 1946), 348.

In *TD*, *HomageAOP*, and *ShP*.

C 42
"Canto Amor," *The Sewanee Review*, LV (Winter 1947), 68-70.

In *TD*, *HomageAOP*, *ShP*, and *SelP*.

Reprinted: (1) *Modern American Poetry*, ed. Louis Untermeyer. New York: Harcourt, Brace and Co., 1950. (2) *Modern Poetry*, ed. Kimon Friar and John Malcolm Brinnin. New York: Appleton-Century-Crofts, 1951. (3) *The New Pocket Anthology of American Verse*, ed. Oscar Williams. New York: World Publishing Co., 1955. (4) *Modern Verse in English, 1900–1950*, ed. David Cecil and Allen Tate. New York: Macmillan Co., 1958. (5) *The Contemporary American Poets*, ed. Mark Strand. Cleveland: World Publishing Co., 1969. (6) *The Voice That Is Great Within Us*, ed. Hayden Carruth. New York: Bantam Books, 1970. (7) *Poetry and Its Conventions*, ed. Frederick R. Lapides and John T. Shawcross. New York: Free Press, 1972.

C 43
"New Year's Eve," *Partisan Review*, XV (April 1948), 456–458.

In *TD, HomageAOP, ShP,* and *SelP*.

Reprinted: (1) *The New Partisan Reader*, ed. William Phillips and Philip Rahv. New York: Harcourt, Brace and Co., 1953. (2) *The New Poetry*, ed. A. Alvarez. Harmondsworth, Middlesex: Penguin Books, 1966. (3) *The New Modern Poetry*, ed. M. L. Rosenthal. New York: Macmillan Co., 1967. (4) *A Little Treasury of Modern Poetry*, ed. Oscar Williams. New York: Charles Scribner's Sons, 1970.

C 44
"Narcissus Moving," *Partisan Review*, XV (April 1948), 458–459.

In *TD, HomageAOP,* and *ShP*.

C 45
"A Winter-Piece to a Friend Away," *The Kenyon Review*, X (Spring 1948), 240–241.

In *TD, HomageAOP,* and *ShP*.

C 46
"Rock-Study with Wanderer," *The Kenyon Review*, X (Spring 1948), 242–244.

In *TD, HomageAOP,* and *ShP*.

C 47
"The Dispossessed," *Poetry*, LXXII (April 1948), 1–2.

In *TD, HomageAOP, ShP,* and *SelP*.

Reprinted: (1) *Poet's Choice,* ed. Paul Engle and Joseph Langland. New York: Dial Press, 1962. (2) *American Poetry,* ed. Gay Wilson Allen, Walter B. Rideout, and James K. Robinson. New York: Harper and Row, 1965. (3) *The Voice That Is Great Within Us,* ed. Hayden Carruth. New York: Bantam Books, 1970.

C 48
"World's Fair," *Poetry,* LXXII (April 1948), 3.

In *TD* and *ShP.*

C 49
"Surviving Love," *Poetry,* LXXII (April 1948), 4.

In *TD, HomageAOP,* and *ShP.*

C 50
"The Traveler" [later titled "The Traveller"], *Poetry,* LXXII (April 1948), 5.

In *TD, HomageAOP, ShP,* and *SelP.*

Reprinted: (1) *A College Book of Verse,* ed. C. F. Main. Belmont, Calif.: Wadsworth Publishing Co., 1970. (2) *The Voice That Is Great Within Us,* ed. Hayden Carruth. New York: Bantam Books, 1970.

C 51
"Fare Well," *Poetry,* LXXII (April 1948), 6.

In *TD, HomageAOP,* and *ShP.*

Reprinted: *Poetry,* CXXI (October 1972), 2.

C 52
"The Long Home," *Partisan Review,* XV (May 1948), 545–547.

In *TD, HomageAOP,* and *ShP.*

C 53
"Whether There Is Sorrow in the Demons," *The Commonweal,* XLVIII (May 7, 1948), 72.

In *TD, HomageAOP, ShP,* and *SelP.*

Reprinted: (1) *The New Poetry,* ed. A. Alvarez. Harmondsworth, Middlesex: Penguin Books, 1966. (2) *A Little Treasury of Modern Poetry,* ed. Oscar Williams. New York: Charles Scribner's Sons, 1970.

Contributions to Periodicals

C 54
"Venice" [later titled "Venice, 182–"], *American Letters*, I (December 1948), 9.

In *Thought, HomageAOP, ShP,* and *SelP*.

Reprinted: Contemporary Poetry in America, ed. Miller Williams. New York: Random House, 1968.

C 55
"The Cage," *Poetry*, LXXV (January 1950), 187-188.

C 56
"Elegy, for Alun Lewis," *Poetry*, LXXV (January 1950), 189.

C 57
"Innocent," *Poetry*, LXXV (January 1950), 190.

C 58
"The Wholly Fail," *Poetry*, LXXV (January 1950), 191.

C 59
"From *The Black Book:* not him" [later titled "from The Black Book (i)"], *Poetry*, LXXV (January 1950), 192.

In *Thought, ShP,* and *SelP*.

Reprinted: The Voice That Is Great Within Us, ed. Hayden Carruth. New York: Bantam Books, 1970.

C 60
"From *The Black Book:* 2" [later titled "from The Black Book (ii)"], *Poetry*, LXXV (January 1950), 193-194.

In *Thought* and *ShP*.

Reprinted: The Voice That Is Great Within Us, ed. Hayden Carruth. New York: Bantam Books, 1970.

C 61
"From *The Black Book:* the will," *Poetry*, LXXV (January 1950), 194-195.

C 62
"From *The Black Book:* waiting," *Poetry*, LXXV (January 1950), 195-196.

C 63
"Scots Poem," *Poetry*, LXXIX (October 1951), 25.

In *Thought, HomageAOP,* and *ShP*.

C 64
"Sonnet 25" [also titled "Sonnet XXV"], *Poetry*, LXXXI (October 1952), 11.

In *Thought, HomageAOP, BS, ShP,* and *SelP*.

Reprinted: The Norton Anthology of Modern Poetry, ed. Richard Ellmann and Robert O'Clair. New York: W. W. Norton Co., 1973.

C 65
"Homage to Mistress Bradstreet," *Partisan Review*, XX (September–October 1953), 489–503.

In *Homage, HomageAOP,* and *SelP*.

Reprinted: (1) selection, *Reading Modern Poetry*, ed. Paul Engle and Warren Carrier. Chicago: Scott, Foresman and Co., 1955. (2) selection, *The Criterion Book of Modern American Poetry*, ed. W. H. Auden. New York: Criterion Books, 1956. (3) selection, *Modern Verse in English, 1900–1950*, ed. David Cecil and Allen Tate. New York: Macmillan Co., 1958. (4) selection, *American Poetry*, ed. Karl Shapiro. New York: Thomas Y. Crowell Co., 1960. (5) *Twentieth Century American Poetry*, ed. Conrad Aiken. New York: Modern Library, 1963. (6) selection, *The Faber Book of Modern Verse*, ed. Michael Roberts. London: Faber and Faber. 1965. (7) selection, *The New Poetry*, ed. A. Alvarez. Harmondsworth, Middlesex: Penguin Books, 1966. (8) selection, *The Norton Anthology of Modern Poetry*, ed. Richard Ellmann and Robert O'Clair. New York: W. W. Norton Co., 1973.

C 66
"Of Isaac Rosenfeld," *Partisan Review*, XXIII (Fall 1956), 494.

C 67
"Not To Live," *The Virginia Quarterly Review*, XXXIII (Autumn 1957), 507.

In *Thought, HomageAOP, ShP,* and *SelP*.

Reprinted: Poems from The Virginia Quarterly Review. Charolettesville: University of Virginia Press, 1969.

C 68
"American Lights, Seen Off From Abroad" [later titled "American Lights, Seen From Off Abroad"], *Partisan Review*, XXV (Spring 1958), 226–228.

In *Thought* and *ShP*.

C 69
"Note to Wang Wei," *The New Yorker*, XXXIV (August 2, 1958), 59.

In *Thought, HomageAOP, ShP*, and *SelP*.

Reprinted: (1) *The New Yorker Book of Poems*. New York: Viking Press, 1969. (2) *The Marvellous Light*, ed. Helen Plotz. New York: Crowell, 1970.

C 70
"A Sympathy, A Welcome," *The New Yorker*, XXXIV (August 16, 1958), 22.

In *Thought, HomageAOP, ShP,* and *SelP*.

Reprinted: *The New Yorker Book of Poems*. New York: Viking Press, 1969.

C 71
Dream Song [1], *The Times Literary Supplement*, November 6, 1959, p. xviii.

In *77DS, TheDS*, and *SelP*.

Reprinted: (1) *The Noble Savage*, no. 1 (March 1960), 118.[1] (2) *This Is My Best*, ed. Whit Burnett. Garden City, N.Y.: Doubleday and Co., 1970. (3) *Contemporary American Poetry*, ed. A. Poulin, Jr. Boston: Houghton Mifflin Co., 1971. (4) *Today's Poets*, ed. Chad Walsh. New York: Charles Scribner's Sons, 1972.

C 72
Dream Song [5], *The Times Literary Supplement*, November 6, 1959, p. xviii.

---

1. JB is listed as a contributing editor in all five issues of *The Noble Savage* (no. 1, March 1960; no. 2, October 1960; no. 3, May 1961; no. 4, October 1961; no. 5, October 1962). In a letter of January 24, 1974, Saul Bellow, who was one of the editors, wrote that JB had no formal duties and supplied no unsigned work to the journal.

In 77DS, TheDS, and SelP.

Reprinted: *The Noble Savage*, no. 1 (March 1960), 119-120.

C 73
Dream Song [75], *The Times Literary Supplement*, November 6, 1959, p. xviii.

In 77DS, TheDS, and SelP.

Reprinted: (1) *The Noble Savage*, no. 1 (March 1960), 120. (2) *National Poetry Festival*. Washington, D.C.: Library of Congress, 1964. (3) *Naked Poetry*, ed. Stephen Berg and Robert Mezey. Indianapolis: Bobbs-Merrill Co., 1969. (4) *Possibilities of Poetry*, ed. Richard Kostelanetz. New York: Dell Publishing Co., 1970. (5) *The Norton Anthology of Modern Poetry*, ed. Richard Ellmann and Robert O'Clair. New York: W. W. Norton Co., 1973.

C 74
Dream Song [67], *The Times Literary Supplement*, November 6, 1959, p. xviii.

In 77DS, TheDS, and SelP.

Reprinted: (1) *The Noble Savage*, no. 1 (March 1960), 124. (2) *Naked Poetry*, ed. Stephen Berg and Robert Mezey. Indianapolis: Bobbs-Merrill Co., 1969.

C 75
Dream Song [77], *The Times Literary Supplement*, November 6, 1959, p. xviii.

In 77DS, TheDS, and SelP.

Reprinted: (1) *The Noble Savage*, no. 1 (March 1960), 124-125. (2) *Naked Poetry*, ed. Stephen Berg and Robert Mezey. Indianapolis: Bobbs-Merrill Co., 1969. (3) *This Is My Best*, ed. Whit Burnett. Garden City, N.Y.: Doubleday and Co., 1970. (4) *Twentieth Century Poetry*, ed. John Malcolm Brinnin and Bill Read. New York: McGraw-Hill Book Co., 1970. (5) *Poems: An Anthology*, ed. Burton Raffel. New York: New American Library, 1971.

C 76
Dream Song ["The jolly old man is a silly old dumb,"], *The Noble Savage*, no. 1 (March 1960), 119.

Contributions to Periodicals

C 77
"Room 333" [later untitled, Dream Song 54], *The Noble Savage*, no. 1 (March 1960), 120-121.

In 77DS, *TheDS*, and *SelP*.

C 78
"Sabbath" [Dream Song 12], *The Noble Savage*, no. 1 (March 1960), 121.

In 77DS and *TheDS*.

C 79
Dream Song [46], *The Noble Savage*, no. 1 (March 1960), 121-122.

In 77DS, *TheDS*, and *SelP*.

Reprinted: (1) *Naked Poetry*, ed. Stephen Berg and Robert Mezey. Indianapolis: Bobbs-Merrill Co., 1969. (2) *Contemporary American Poetry*, ed. A. Poulin, Jr. Boston: Houghton Mifflin Co., 1971. (3) *The New Consciousness*, ed. Albert J. La Valley. Cambridge, Mass.: Winthrop Publishers, 1972.

C 80
Dream Song [53], *The Noble Savage*, no. 1 (March 1960), 122.

In 77DS, *TheDS*, and *SelP*.

Reprinted: (1) *100 Postwar Poems*, ed. M. L. Rosenthal. New York: Macmillan Co., 1968. (2) *The Literature of America*, vol. II, ed. Irving Howe, Mark Schorer, and Larzer Ziff. New York: McGraw-Hill Book Co., 1971.

C 81
Dream Song [29], *The Noble Savage*, no. 1 (March 1960), 123.

In 77DS, *TheDS*, and *SelP*.

Reprinted: (1) *National Poetry Festival*. Washington, D.C.: Library of Congress, 1964. (2) *The Minnesota Daily*, November 9, 1967, p. 9. (3) *The New Modern Poetry*, ed. M. L. Rosenthal. New York: Macmillan Co., 1967. (4) *The Minneapolis Tribune*, May 12, 1968, p. 1E. (5) *100 Postwar Poems*, ed. M. L. Rosenthal. New York: Macmillan Co., 1968. (6) *Possibilities of Poetry*, ed. Richard Kostelanetz. New York: Dell Publishing Co., 1970. (7) *This Is My Best*, ed. Whit Burnett. Garden City, N.Y.: Doubleday and Co., 1970. (8) *Contemporary American Poetry*, ed. A. Poulin, Jr. Boston: Houghton Mifflin Co., 1971. (9) *The Literature of America,* vol. II, ed. Irving Howe, Mark Schorer, and Larzer Ziff. New York: McGraw-Hill Book Co., 1971. (10) *Poems: An Anthology,* ed. Burton Raffel. New York: New American Library, 1971. (11) *The New Pocket Anthology of American Verse,* ed. Oscar Williams. New York: Washington Square Press, 1972.

C 82
Dream Song [17], *The Noble Savage,* no. 1 (March 1960), 123–124.

In *77DS* and *TheDS.*

C 83
"Secret of the Wisdom" [later Dream Song 20: "The Secret of the Wisdom"], *The Observer,* June 3, 1962, p. 25.

In *77DS* and *TheDS.*

Reprinted: Poetry Northwest, III (Winter 1962–1963), 26.

C 84
"Columbus Day" [later untitled, Dream Song 216], *Encounter,* XIX (October 1962), 56.

In *Toy* and *TheDS.*

Reprinted: (1) *Poetry Northwest,* III (Winter 1962–1963), 24–25. (2) *Possibilities of Poetry,* ed. Richard Kostelanetz. New York: Dell Publishing Co., 1970.

C 85
Dream Song [8], *Encounter,* XIX (October 1962), 56.

In *77DS* and *TheDS.*

Reprinted: (1) *Poetry Northwest,* III (Winter 1962–1963), 25. (2) *Contemporary American Poetry,* ed. A. Poulin, Jr. Boston: Houghton Mifflin Co., 1971.

C 86
Dream Song [27], *Poetry,* CI (October 1962), 7.

In *77DS, TheDS,* and *SelP.*

Reprinted: National Poetry Festival. Washington, D.C.: Library of Congress, 1964.

C 87
Dream Song [16], *Poetry*, CI (October 1962), 7-8.

In 77*DS*, *TheDS*, and *SelP*.

Reprinted: (1) *National Poetry Festival*, Washington, D.C.: Library of Congress, 1964. (2) *The Faber Book of Modern Verse*, ed. Michael Roberts. London: Faber and Faber, 1965. (3) *American Poetry*, ed. Donald Hall. London: Faber and Faber, 1969. (4) *The Norton Anthology of Modern Poetry*, ed. Richard Ellmann and Robert O'Clair. New York: W. W. Norton Co., 1973.

C 88
Dream Song [36], *Poetry*, CI (October 1962), 8-9.

In 77*DS*, *TheDS*, and *SelP*.

C 89
Dream Song [71], *Poetry*, CI (October 1962), 9.

In 77*DS*, *TheDS*, and *SelP*.

Reprinted: *The Faber Book of Modern Verse*, ed. Michael Roberts. London: Faber and Faber, 1965.

C 90
"A Dream Song" [later untitled, Dream Song 51], *The New Republic*, CXLVII (November 17, 1962), 16.

In 77*DS*, *TheDS*, and *SelP*.

C 91
"Another Dream Song" [later untitled, Dream Song 4], *The New Republic*, CXLVIII (January 19, 1963), 20.

In 77*DS*, *TheDS*, and *SelP*.

Reprinted: (1) *National Poetry Festival*. Washington, D.C.: Library of Congress, 1964. (2) *Possibilities of Poetry*, ed. Richard Kostelanetz. New York: Dell Publishing Co., 1970. (3) *Contemporary American Poetry*, ed. A. Poulin, Jr. Boston: Houghton Mifflin Co., 1971. (4) *The New Consciousness*, ed. Albert J. La Valley. Cambridge, Mass.: Winthrop Publishers, 1972. (5) *Today's Poets*, ed. Chad Walsh. New York: Charles Scribner's Sons, 1972.

C 92
"'The Prisoner of Shark Island' with Paul Muni" [Dream Song 7], *Partisan Review*, XXIX (Fall 1962), 539.

In 77DS and *TheDS*.

C 93
"Silent Song" [Dream Song 52], *Partisan Review*, XXIX (Fall 1962), 540.

In 77DS, *TheDS*, and *SelP*.

C 94
"A Dream Song" [later untitled, Dream Song 41], *The Minnesota Review*, III (Winter 1963), 141.

In 77DS and *TheDS*.

C 95
"A Dream Song" [later untitled, Dream Song 14], *Harper's Magazine*, CCXXVI (March 1963), 36.

In 77DS, *TheDS*, and *SelP*.

Reprinted: (1) *An Introduction to Poetry*, ed. X. J. Kennedy. Boston: Little, Brown and Co., 1966. (2) *The Complete Reader*, ed. Richard S. Beal and Jacob Korg. Englewood Cliffs, N.J.: Prentice-Hall, 1967. (3) *The Experience of Literature*, ed. Lionel Trilling. Garden City, N.Y.: Doubleday and Co., 1967. (4) *Naked Poetry*, ed. Stephen Berg and Robert Mezey. Indianapolis: Bobbs-Merrill Co., 1969. (5) *A Little Treasury of Modern Poetry*, ed. Oscar Williams. New York: Charles Scribner's Sons, 1970. (6) *Twentieth Century Poetry*, ed. John Malcolm Brinnin and Bill Read. New York: McGraw-Hill Book Co., 1970. (7) *Contemporary American Poetry*, ed. A. Poulin, Jr. Boston: Houghton Mifflin Co., 1971. (8) *Earth, Air, Fire & Water*, ed. Frances M. McCullough. New York: Coward, McCann and Geoghegan, 1971. (9) *The New Consciousness*, ed. Albert J. La Valley. Cambridge, Mass.: Winthrop Publishers, 1972. (10) *50 Modern American Poets, 1920–1970*, ed. Louis Untermeyer. New York: David McKay Co., 1973. (11) *The Norton Anthology of Modern Poetry*, ed. Richard Ellmann and Robert O'Clair. New York: W. W. Norton Co., 1973.

C 96
Dream Song [64], *Ramparts*, II (May 1963), 7.

In 77DS and *TheDS*.

Contributions to Periodicals

C 97
"A Capital at Wells" [Dream Song 6], *Ramparts*, II (May 1963), 7.

In *77DS*, *TheDS*, and *SelP*.

C 98
Dream Song [105], *Ramparts*, II (May 1963), 8.

In *Toy* and *TheDS*.

C 99
"Of 1826" [Dream Song 22], *Ramparts*, II (May 1963), 8.

In *77DS*, *TheDS* and *SelP*.

Reprinted: National Poetry Festival. Washington, D.C.: Library of Congress, 1964.

C 100
"A Stimulant for an Old Beast" [Dream Song 3], *Ramparts*, II (May 1963), 9.

In *77DS* and *TheDS*.

C 101
Dream Song [69], *Ramparts*, II (May 1963), 9.

In *77DS*, *TheDS*, and *SelP*.

C 102
Dream Song ["Baby Teddy, baby did-he, drop him too a pat"], *Ramparts*, II (May 1963), 10.

C 103
Dream Song [68], *Ramparts*, II (May 1963), 11.

In *77DS* and *TheDS*.

C 104
Dream Song [98], *Ramparts*, II (May 1963), 11.

In *Toy* and *TheDS*.

C 105
Dream Song [34], *Ramparts*, II (May 1963), 12.

In *77DS*, *TheDS*, and *SelP*.

C 106
Dream Song ["Statesmanlike (on a Queer prowl, after dark)"], *Ramparts*, II (May 1963), 12.

C 107
Dream Song [13], *Ramparts*, II (May 1963), 13.

In 77DS and *TheDS*.

Reprinted: (1) *Contemporary American Poetry*, ed. A. Poulin, Jr. Boston: Houghton Mifflin Co., 1971. (2) *100 American Poems*, ed. Selden Rodman. New York: New American Library, 1972.

C 108
Dream Song [9], *Ramparts*, II (May 1963), 14.

In 77DS and *TheDS*.

Reprinted: Contemporary American Poetry, ed. A. Poulin, Jr. Boston: Houghton Mifflin Co., 1971.

C 109
Dream Song [58], *Ramparts*, II (May 1963), 14.

In 77DS and *TheDS*.

C 110
Dream Song [74], *Ramparts*, II (May 1963), 15.

In 77DS, *TheDS*, and *SelP*.

Reprinted: Naked Poetry, ed. Stephen Berg and Robert Mezey. Indianapolis: Bobbs-Merrill Co., 1969.

C 111
Dream Song [40], *The Yale Review*, LII (Summer 1963), 558.

In 77DS, *TheDS*, and *SelP*.

Reprinted: The Contemporary American Poets, ed. Mark Strand. Cleveland: World Publishing Co., 1969.

C 112
Dream Song [55], *The Yale Review*, LII (Summer 1963), 559.

In 77DS, *TheDS*, and *SelP*.

Reprinted: Contemporary American Poetry, ed. A. Poulin, Jr. Boston: Houghton Mifflin Co., 1971.

C 113
"A Strut for Roethke" [Dream Song 18], *The Times Literary Supplement,* August 23, 1963, p. 642.

In 77DS and *TheDS.*

Reprinted: (1) *The New York Review of Books,* I (October 17, 1963), 22. (2) *The Experience of Literature,* ed. Lionel Trilling. Garden City, N.Y.: Doubleday and Co., 1967. (3) *Possibilities of Poetry,* ed. Richard Kostelanetz. New York: Dell Publishing Co., 1970.

C 114
Dream Song [37: "Three around the Old Gentleman"], *The New York Review of Books,* I (August 29, 1963), 7.

In 77DS, *TheDS,* and *SelP.*

Reprinted: *American Poetry,* ed. Gay Wilson Allen, Walter B. Rideout, and James K. Robinson. New York: Harper and Row, 1965.

C 115
Dream Song [38], *The New York Review of Books,* I (August 29, 1963), 7.

In 77DS and *TheDS.*

Reprinted: *American Poetry,* ed. Gay Wilson Allen, Walter B. Rideout, and James K. Robinson. New York: Harper and Row, 1965.

C 116
Dream Song [39], *The New York Review of Books,* I (August 29, 1963), 7.

In 77DS and *TheDS.*

Reprinted: *American Poetry,* ed. Gay Wilson Allen, Walter B. Rideout, and James K. Robinson. New York: Harper and Row, 1965.

C 117
Dream Song [50], *Poetry,* CIII (October–November 1963), 1.

In 77DS and *TheDS.*

Reprinted: (1) *The Faber Book of Modern Verse,* ed. Michael Roberts. London: Faber and Faber, 1965. (2) *American Poetry,* ed. Donald Hall. London: Faber and Faber, 1969.

C 118
"Snow Line" [Dream Song 28], *Poetry*, CIII (October–November 1963), 2.

In *77DS* and *TheDS*.

Reprinted: (1) *Naked Poetry*, ed. Stephen Berg and Robert Mezey. Indianapolis: Bobbs-Merrill Co., 1969. (2) *Possibilities of Poetry*, ed. Richard Kostelanetz. New York: Dell Publishing Co., 1970.

C 119
Dream Song [31], *Poetry*, CIII (October–November 1963), 3.

In *77DS*, *TheDS*, and *SelP*.

C 120
Dream Song [21], *Poetry*, CIII (October–November 1963), 4.

In *77DS* and *TheDS*.

C 121
Dream Song [44], *Poetry*, CIII (October–November 1963), 5.

In *77DS* and *TheDS*.

Reprinted: *Naked Poetry*, ed. Stephen Berg and Robert Mezey. Indianapolis: Bobbs-Merrill Co., 1969.

C 122
Dream Song [66], *Poetry*, CIII (October–November 1963), 6.

In *77DS*, *TheDS*, and *SelP*.

Reprinted: *Today's Poets*, ed. Chad Walsh. New York: Charles Scribner's Sons, 1972.

C 123
Dream Song [56], *Poetry*, CIII (October–November 1963), 7.

In *77DS* and *TheDS*.

Reprinted: *The Observer*, December 22, 1963, p. 16.

C 124
Dream Song [48], *Poetry*, CIII (October–November 1963), 8.

In *77DS*, *TheDS*, and *SelP*.

Reprinted: *The Observer*, December 22, 1963, p. 16.

C 125
Dream Song [45], *Poetry*, CIII (October–November 1963), 9.

In 77DS, *TheDS*, and *SelP*.

Reprinted: Contemporary American Poetry, ed. A. Poulin, Jr. Boston: Houghton Mifflin Co., 1971.

C 126
Dream Song [57], *The Kenyon Review*, XXVI (Winter 1964), 209.

In 77DS and *TheDS*.

C 127
Dream Song [217], *The Kenyon Review*, XXVI (Winter 1964), 209–210.

In *Toy* and *TheDS*.

C 128
Dream Song [11], *The Kenyon Review*, XXVI (Winter 1964), 210.

In 77DS and *TheDS*.

C 129
"General Fatigue" [later untitled, Dream Song 93], *The Nation*, CXCVIII (May 25, 1964), 539.

In *Toy* and *TheDS*.

Reprinted: One Hundred Years of The Nation, ed. Henry M. Christman. New York: Macmillan Co., 1965.

See B 23.

C 130
"Henry's Pencils," *The Nation*, CXCVIII (May 25, 1964), 539.

Reprinted: One Hundred Years of The Nation, ed. Henry M. Christman. New York: Macmillan Co., 1965.

See B 23.

C 131
"Donnybrook" [later untitled, Dream Song 97], *The Nation*, CXCVIII (May 25, 1964), 539.

In *Toy* and *TheDS*.

Reprinted: One Hundred Years of The Nation, ed. Henry M. Christman. New York: Macmillan Co., 1965.

See B 23.

C 132
"Dream Song" [later untitled, Dream Song 95], *The Nation,* CC (January 25, 1965), 87.

In *Toy* and *TheDS.*

C 133
"Idyl II," *The Minneapolis Tribune,* June 27, 1965, p. 1E.

Reprinted: Agenda, IV (Summer 1966), 3.

C 134
"Eighty" [Dream Song 224], *The Times Literary Supplement,* November 25, 1965, p. 1069.

In *Toy* and *TheDS.*

C 135
"The Translator—I" [Dream Song 180], *The Times Literary Supplement,* November 25, 1965, p. 1069.

In *Toy* and *TheDS.*

C 136
"The Translator—II" [Dream Song 181], *The Times Literary Supplement,* November 25, 1965, p. 1069.

In *Toy* and *TheDS.*

C 137
"The Last Dream Song: 161" [later untitled, Dream Song 385], *The Times Literary Supplement,* November 25, 1965, p. 1069.

In *Two Dream Songs* (1965) under the same title and in *Toy, TheDS,* and *SelP* untitled.

Reprinted: (1) *This Is My Best,* ed. Whit Burnett. Garden City, N.Y.: Doubleday and Co., 1970. (2) *Contemporary American Poetry,* ed. A Poulin, Jr. Boston: Houghton Mifflin Co., 1971. (3) *The New Consciousness,* ed. Albert J. La Valley. Cambridge, Mass.: Winthrop Publishers, 1972.

C 138
"The Old Poor" [Dream Song 168], *Ivory Tower*, XIV (October 3, 1966), 17.

In *Toy*, *TheDS*, and *SelP*.

C 139
"Op. posth. no. 1" [Dream Song 78], *The Times Literary Supplement*, December 1, 1966, p. 1129.

In *Toy*, *TheDS*, and *SelP*.

C 140
"Op. posth. no. 2" [Dream Song 79], *The Times Literary Supplement*, December 1, 1966, p. 1129.

In *Toy* and *TheDS*.

C 141
"Op. posth. no. 7" [Dream Song 84], *The Times Literary Supplement*, December 1, 1966, p. 1129.

In *Toy*, *TheDS*, and *SelP*.

C 142
"Op. posth. no. 8" [Dream Song 85], *The Times Literary Supplement*, December 1, 1966, p. 1129.

In *Toy* and *TheDS*.

C 143
"Op. posth. no. 9" [Dream Song 86], *The Times Literary Supplement*, December 1, 1966, p. 1129.

In *Toy*, *TheDS*, and *SelP*.

C 144
"Op. posth. no. 10" [Dream Song 87], *The Times Literary Supplement*, December 1, 1966, p. 1129.

In *Toy*, *TheDS*, and *SelP*.

C 145
"Op. posth. no. 11" [Dream Song 88], *The Times Literary Supplement*, December 1, 1966, p. 1129.

In *Toy*, *TheDS*, and *SelP*.

C 146
"Op. posth. no. 12" [Dream Song 89], *The Times Literary Supplement*, December 1, 1966, p. 1129.

In *Toy, TheDS,* and *SelP*.

Reprinted: This Is My Best, ed. Whit Burnett. Garden City, N.Y.: Doubleday and Co., 1970.

C 147
"Op. posth. no. 13" [Dream Song 90], *The Times Literary Supplement*, December 1, 1966, p. 1129.

In *Toy, TheDS,* and *SelP*.

Reprinted: Randall Jarrell, ed. Robert Lowell, Peter Taylor, and Robert Penn Warren. New York: Farrar, Straus and Giroux, 1967.

See B 27.

C 148
"Opus posthumous, number 3" [later Dream Song 80: "Op. posth. no. 3"], *The New York Review of Books,* VII (December 15, 1966), 15.

In *Toy* and *TheDS*.

C 149
"Opus posthumous, number 4" [later Dream Song 81: "Op. posth. no. 4"], *The New York Review of Books,* VII (December 15, 1966), 15.

In *Toy* and *TheDS*.

C 150
"Opus posthumous, number 5" [later Dream Song 82: "Op. posth. no. 5"], *The New York Review of Books,* VII (December 15, 1966), 15.

In *Toy* and *TheDS*.

C 151
"Opus posthumous, number 6" [later Dream Song 83: "Op. posth. no. 6"], *The New York Review of Books,* VII (December 15, 1966), 15.

In *Toy* and *TheDS*.

C 152
Sonnet [23], *Mademoiselle*, LXIV (April 1967), 154.

In *BS*.

C 153
Sonnet [71], *Mademoiselle*, LXIV (April 1967), 154.

In *BS* and *SelP*.

C 154
Sonnet [103], *Mademoiselle*, LXIV (April 1967), 154.

In *BS*.

C 155
Dream Song [265], *The Atlantic*, CCXXI (February 1968), 68.

In *Toy* and *TheDS*.

C 156
Dream Song [187], *The Atlantic*, CCXXI (February 1968), 68.

In *Toy* and *TheDS*.

C 157
Dream Song [258], *The Atlantic*, CCXXI (February 1968), 69.

In *Toy* and *TheDS*.

C 158
Dream Song [161], *The Atlantic*, CCXXI (February 1968), 69.

In *Toy* and *TheDS*.

C 159
Dream Song [204], *Harper's Magazine*, CCXXXVI (February 1968), 57.

In *Toy* and *TheDS*.

C 160
Dream Song [210], *Harper's Magazine*, CCXXXVI (February 1968), 57.

In *Toy* and *TheDS*.

C 161
Dream Song [209], *Harper's Magazine*, CCXXXVI (February 1968), 57.

In *Toy* and *TheDS*.

C 162
"Cantatrice" [Dream Song 233], *New American Review*, no. 3 (April 1968), 105.

In *Toy*, *TheDS*, and *SelP*.

C 163
"So Long? Stevens" [Dream Song 219], *New American Review*, no. 3 (April 1968), 105-106.

In *Toy* and *TheDS*.

C 164
"Christmas, 1963" [later untitled, Dream Song 200], *New American Review*, no. 3 (April 1968), 106.

In *Toy* and *TheDS*.

C 165
Dream Song [194], *Mundus Artium*, I (Spring 1968), 15.

In *Toy* and *TheDS*.

C 166
Dream Song ["Now that my one are out, I indulge my rage,"], *Mundus Artium*, I (Spring 1968), 15-16.

C 167
Dream Song [199], *Mundus Artium*, I (Spring 1968), 16.

In *Toy* and *TheDS*.

C 168
Dream Song [147], *The Virginia Quarterly Review*, XLIV (Summer 1968), 399.

In *Toy*, *TheDS*, and *SelP*.

C 169
"Glimmerings" [Dream Song 148], *The Virginia Quarterly Review*, XLIV (Summer 1968), 399-400.

In *Toy* and *TheDS*.

C 170
Dream Song [150], *The Virginia Quarterly Review*, XLIV (Summer 1968), 400.

In *Toy* and *TheDS*.

C 171
Dream Song [151], *The Virginia Quarterly Review*, XLIV (Summer 1968), 401.

In *Toy* and *TheDS*.

C 172
Dream Song [152], *The Virginia Quarterly Review*, XLIV (Summer 1968), 401-402.

In *Toy* and *TheDS*.

C 173
Dream Song [153], *The Virginia Quarterly Review*, XLIV (Summer 1968), 402.

In *Toy*, *TheDS*, and *SelP*.

C 174
Dream Song [154], *The Virginia Quarterly Review*, XLIV (Summer 1968), 402-403.

In *Toy*, *TheDS*, and *SelP*.

C 175
Dream Song [155], *The Virginia Quarterly Review*, XLIV (Summer 1968), 403-404.

In *Toy*, *TheDS*, and *SelP*.

C 176
Dream Song [156], *The Virginia Quarterly Review*, XLIV (Summer 1968), 404.

In *Toy*, *TheDS*, and *SelP*.

C 177
Dream Song [157], *The Virginia Quarterly Review*, XLIV (Summer 1968), 404-405.

In *Toy* and *TheDS*.

C 178
Dream Song [384], *The Virginia Quarterly Review*, XLIV (Summer 1968), 405.

In *Toy, TheDS*, and *SelP*.

Reprinted: (1) *This Is My Best*, ed. Whit Burnett. Garden City, N.Y.: Doubleday and Co., 1970. (2) *Contemporary American Poetry*, ed. A. Poulin, Jr. Boston: Houghton Mifflin Co., 1971.

C 179
"Henry's Mail" [Dream Song 167], *Audience*, pilot issue (Spring 1968), 69.

In *Toy* and *TheDS*.

C 180
Dream Song [171], *Audience*, pilot issue (Spring 1968), 69.

In *Toy, TheDS*, and *SelP*.

C 181
Dream Song [191], *Audience*, pilot issue (Spring 1968), 71.

In *Toy* and *TheDS*.

C 182
Dream Song [264], *Audience*, pilot issue (Spring 1968), 71.

In *Toy* and *TheDS*.

C 183
Dream Song [172], *Audience*, pilot issue (Spring 1968), 73.

In *Toy, TheDS*, and *SelP*.

Reprinted: Contemporary American Poetry, ed. A. Poulin, Jr. Boston: Houghton Mifflin Co., 1971.

C 184
Dream Song [298], *Audience*, pilot issue (Spring 1968), 73.

In *Toy* and *TheDS*.

C 185
Dream Song [170], *TriQuarterly*, no. 12 (Spring 1968), [179].

In *Toy* and *TheDS*.

Reprinted: Contemporary American Poetry, ed. A. Poulin, Jr. Boston: Houghton Mifflin Co., 1971.

C 186
Dream Song [201], *TriQuarterly*, no. 12 (Spring 1968), [181].

In *Toy*, *TheDS*, and *SelP*.

C 187
Dream Song [165], *TriQuarterly*, no. 12 (Spring 1968), [183].

In *Toy* and *TheDS*.

C 188
Dream Song [186], *TriQuarterly*, no. 12 (Spring 1968), [185].

In *Toy*, *TheDS*, and *SelP*.

C 189
"Henry's Understanding," *The Harvard Advocate*, CIII (Spring 1969), 12.

In *DE*.

Reprinted: The Norton Anthology of Modern Poetry, ed. Richard Ellmann and Robert O'Clair. New York: W. W. Norton Co., 1973.

C 190
"Henry by Night," *The Harvard Advocate*, CIII (Spring 1969), 13.

In *DE*.

C 191
"Apollo 8," *The Harvard Advocate*, CIII (Spring 1969), 13.

Reprinted: Antaeus, no. 8 (Winter 1973), 20.

C 192
"Her and It" [later titled "Her & It"], *The Times Literary Supplement*, July 16, 1970, p. 770.

In *L&F*.

C 193
"The Heroes," *The Times Literary Supplement*, July 16, 1970, p. 770.

In *L&F*.

C 194
"The Other Cambridge," *The Times Literary Supplement,* July 16, 1970, p. 770.

In *L&F*.

C 195
"Meeting," *The Times Literary Supplement,* July 16, 1970, p. 770.

In *L&F*.

C 196
"Tea," *The Times Literary Supplement,* July 16, 1970, p. 770.

In *L&F*.

C 197
"Heaven," *The Times Literary Supplement,* July 16, 1970, p. 770.

In *L&F*.

C 198
"Antithesis" [later titled "Antitheses"], *The New Republic,* CLXIII (July 25, 1970), 17.

In *L&F*.

C 199
"The Minnesota 8 and the Letter-Writers," *The Minneapolis Tribune,* July 21, 1970, p. 8.

In *L&F* (1970).

C 200
"Death Ballad," *The New Yorker,* XLVI (July 25, 1970), 28.

In *L&F*.

C 201
"Revival," *Shenandoah,* XXI (Summer 1970), 3.

See A 20.1.a†.

C 202
"Monkhood," *Shenandoah,* XXI (Summer 1970), 4–5.

In *L&F*.

C 203
"Friendless," *Shenandoah*, XXI (Summer 1970), 5.

In *L&F*.

C 204
"Drunks," *Shenandoah*, XXI (Summer 1970), 6.

In *L&F*.

C 205
"From Five Addresses to the Lord" [later titled "Eleven Addresses to the Lord: 11"], *The Commonweal*, XCII (September 18, 1970), 461.

In *L&F*.

Reprinted: (1) *The Commonweal*, XCV (February 25, 1972), 490. (2) *The Commonweal*, XCVIII (November 16, 1973), 196.

C 206
"To B—— E——," *Stand*, XI (Fall 1970), 58.

In *L&F* (1970).

C 207
"The Search," *Stand*, XI (Fall 1970), 59.

In *L&F*.

C 208
"Five Addresses to the Lord [1]" [later titled "Eleven Addresses to the Lord: 1"], *Saturday Review*, LIII (September 26, 1970), 23.

In *L&F*.

Reprinted: (1) *Intellectual Digest*, III (December 1972), 63-64. (2) *Today's Poets*, ed. Chad Walsh. New York: Charles Scribner's Sons, 1972.

C 209
"Five Addresses to the Lord [2]" [later titled "Eleven Addresses to the Lord: 2"], *Saturday Review*, LIII (September 26, 1970), 23.

In *L&F*.

C 210
"Five Addresses to the Lord [3]" [later titled "Eleven Addresses to the Lord: 3"], *Saturday Review,* LIII (September 26, 1970), 23.

In *L&F.*

Reprinted: Intellectual Digest, III (December 1972), 64.

C 211
"Five Addresses to the Lord [4]" [later titled "Eleven Addresses to the Lord: 4"], *Saturday Review,* LIII (September 26, 1970), 23.

In *L&F.*

Reprinted: Intellectual Digest, III (December 1972), 64.

C 212
"Five Addresses to the Lord [5]" [later titled "Eleven Addresses to the Lord: 5"], *Saturday Review,* LIII (September 26, 1970), 23.

In *L&F.*

Reprinted: Intellectual Digest, III (December 1972), 64.

C 213
"A Prayer for the Self," *Harper's Magazine,* CCXLI (October 1970), 94.

In *L&F.*

Reprinted: Intellectual Digest, III (December 1972), 64.

C 214
"To a Woman," *The New York Review of Books,* XV (October 8, 1970), 6.

In *L&F.*

C 215
"The American Hero," *The New York Review of Books,* XV (October 8, 1970), 6.

C 216
"Down & Back," *The American Scholar,* XXXIX (Autumn 1970), 614–615.

In *L&F.*

C 217
"The Hell Poem," *The Atlantic*, CCXXVI (November 1970), 96.

In *L&F*.

C 218
"Olympus," *The Atlantic*, CCXXVI (November 1970), 97.

In *L&F*.

C 219
"The Soviet Union," *The Nation*, CCXI (October 26, 1970), 409.

In *L&F* (1970).

C 220
"First Night at Sea," *Antaeus*, no. 1 (Summer 1970), 90.

In *L&F*.

C 221
"Transit," *Antaeus*, no. 1 (Summer 1970), 91.

In *L&F*.

C 222
"Nowhere," *Antaeus*, no. 1 (Summer 1970), 92-93.

In *L&F*.

C 223
"Alas," *Academy*, VI (Winter 1971), [6].

C 224
"Navajo Putting the Record Straight" [later titled "Navajo Setting the Record Straight"], *Academy*, VI (Winter 1971), [7].

In *DE*.

C 225
"Washington in Love," *Esquire*, LXXV (April 1971), 172.

In *DE*.

Reprinted: Intellectual Digest, II (April 1972), [94].

C 226
"Tampa Stomp," *Esquire*, LXXV (April 1971), 181.

In *DE*.

C 227
"Ecce Homo," *The New Yorker,* XLVII (April 10, 1971), 38.

In *DE.*

C 228
"The Form," *Esquire,* LXXV (May 1971), 18.

In *DE.*

C 229
"Henry North," *Café Solo,* no. 3 (Spring 1971), 5.

C 230
"King David Dances," *The New Yorker,* XLVII (February 19, 1972), 42.

In *DE.*

C 231
"Gislebertus' Eve," *Intellectual Digest,* II (April 1972), [94]-[95].

In *DE.*

C 232
"Vespers," *Intellectual Digest,* II (April 1972), [95].

In *DE.*

C 233
"Lines to Mr Frost," *Intellectual Digest,* II (April 1972), [95].

In *DE.*

C 234
"Minnesota Thanksgiving," *Intellectual Digest,* II (April 1972), [95].

In *DE.*

C 235
"Beethoven Triumphant," *The New York Review of Books,* XVIII (April 6, 1972), 4, 6.

In *DE.*

PROSE[2]

C 236
Review of *A Winter Diary and Other Poems* by Mark Van Doren, *The Columbia Review*, XVI (April 1935), 41-43.

C 237
Review of *No Traveller Returns* by Joseph Auslander, *The Columbia Review*, XVI (May 1935), 29-30.

C 238
"Satire and Poetry," *The Columbia Review*, XVII (November 1935), 25-26.

Review of *The Dog Beneath the Skin* by W. H. Auden and Christopher Isherwood.

C 239
"Types of Pedantry," *The Nation*, CXLI (November 27, 1935), 630.

Review of *Smith: A Sylvan Interlude* by Branch Cabell, *Festival at Meron* by Harry Sackler, and *Seventy Times Seven* by Carl Christian Jensen.

C 240
"E. A. Robinson, and Others," *The Columbia Review*, XVII (December 1935), 19-22.

Review of *King Jasper* by E. A. Robinson, *Solstice, and Other Poems* by Robinson Jeffers, *Invisible Landscapes* by Edgar Lee Masters, *Selected Poems* by A.E. [George William Russell], *The Seven Sins* by Audrey Wurdemann, *This Island Called Pharos* by Archibald Fleming, and *Theory of Flight* by Muriel Rukeyser.

C 241
"The Ritual of W. B. Yeats," *The Columbia Review*, XVII (May-June 1936), 26-32.

Article.

---

2. In a letter of April 17, 1974, Roberta Willing, Librarian at South Kent School, wrote that during JB's career at the school he was an associate editor of *The Pigtail*, the student newspaper, for the years 1930-1931 and 1931-1932; however, no editorial or feature credits are given for those years. Many people intimately involved with the newspaper during that period have since died, thus making it difficult to determine JB's contributions to the publication.

C 242
"A Topical Novel," *The Nation*, CXLIII (August 29, 1936), 251.

Review of *Green Gates* by R. C. Sherriff.

C 243
"A Philosophical Poet," *New York Herald Tribune Books*, December 11, 1938, p. 21.

Review of *The Collected Poems of Laura Riding*.

C 244
"Native Verse," *New York Herald Tribune Books*, January 8, 1939, p. 12.

Review of *Lee in the Mountains, and Other Poems* by Donald Davidson.

C 245
"'Poetolatry,'" *New York Herald Tribune Books*, October 1, 1939, p. 18.

Review of *The Personal Heresy: A Controversy* by E. M. W. Tillyard and C. S. Lewis.

C 246
"The Loud Hill of Wales," *The Kenyon Review*, II (Autumn 1940), 481–485.

Reprinted: The Kenyon Critics, ed. John Crowe Ransom. New York: World Publishing Co., 1951.

Review of *The World I Breathe* by Dylan Thomas. See B 12.

C 247
"More Directions," *The Kenyon Review*, III (Summer 1941), 386–388.

Review of *New Directions in Prose and Poetry 1940*, ed. James Laughlin.

C 248
"Shakespeare's Text," *The Nation*, CLVII (August 21, 1943), 218–219.

Review of *The Editorial Problem in Shakespeare* by W. W. Greg.

C 249

"The Lovers," *The Kenyon Review*, VII (Winter 1945), 1-11.

Reprinted: (1) *New Directions 9*, ed. James Laughlin. Norfolk, Conn.: New Directions, 1946. (2) *The Best American Short Stories of 1946*, ed. Martha Foley. Boston: Houghton Mifflin Co., 1946. (3) *The Poet's Story*, ed. Howard Moss. New York: Macmillan Co., 1973.

Fiction. See B 10.

C 250

"Henry James," *The Sewanee Review*, LIII (Spring 1945), 291-297.

Review of *Stories of Writers and Artists* by Henry James, ed. F. O. Matthiessen; *The Great Short Novels of Henry James*, ed. Philip Rahv; and *Henry James: The Major Phase* by F. O. Matthiessen.

C 251

"The Imaginary Jew," *The Kenyon Review*, VII (Autumn 1945), 529-539.[3]

Reprinted: (1) *O. Henry Memorial Award Prize Stories of 1946*, ed. Herschel Brickell. Garden City, N.Y.: Doubleday and Co., 1946. (2) *Anchor in the Sea*, ed. Allan Swallow. New York: Swallow Press and William Morrow Co., 1947. (3) *Horizon*, XVI (October 1947), 124-132. (4) *Spearhead*, ed. James Laughlin. New York: New Directions, 1947. (5) *A Little Treasury of American Prose*, ed. George Mayberry. New York: Charles Scribner's Sons, 1949. (6) *The Golden Horizon*, ed. Cyril Connolly. New York: University Books, 1950. (7) *Stories of Modern America*, ed. Herbert Gold and David L. Stevenson. New York:

---

3. In addition to "The Lovers" and "The Imaginary Jew," five other stories by John Berryman reprinted in anthologies are noted in *Short Story Index* (New York: H. W. Wilson Co., 1949-1968): "Special Flight," "Space Rating," "Berom," "The Trouble with Telestar," and "Something to Say." These five stories were not written by the author of *The Dream Songs*, however, but by another John Berryman (b. 1916) who is the author of over sixty science fiction stories published in *Analog* (originally *Astounding Science Fiction*) between 1939 and 1966. Fourteen of these stories (including the five mentioned) appeared under his own name and the remainder under pseudonyms. Since both authors had begun publishing at nearly the same time, indexers probably assumed that all the stories had been written by the same person and listed them as such.

St. Martin's Press, 1961. (8) *The Modern Age: Literature,* ed. Leonard Lief and James F. Light. New York: Holt, Rinehart and Winston, 1969. (9) *Stories of the American Experience,* ed. Leonard Kriegel and Abraham H. Lass. New York: New American Library, 1973.

Fiction. In *Recovery.* See also B 11.

C 252
"F. Scott Fitzgerald," *The Kenyon Review,* VIII (Winter 1946), 103-112.

Article.

C 253
"A Scholarly History," *The Nation,* CLXIII (December 21, 1946), 733-734.

Review of *A Critical Study of English Poetry* by Herbert J. Grierson and J. C. Smith.

C 254
"Lowell, Thomas, &c.," *Partisan Review,* XIV (January-February 1947), 73-85.

Review of *Lord Weary's Castle* by Robert Lowell, *The Selected Writings of Dylan Thomas, Young Cherry Trees Secured Against Hares* by Andre Breton, *Secret Country* by Jorge Carrera Andrade, *The Flowering of the Rod* by H.D. [Hilda Doolittle], *The Earth-Bound* by Janet Lewis, *Selected Poems* by Kenneth Patchen, and *Transfigured Night* by Byron Vazakas.

C 255
"Metaphysical or So," *The Nation,* CLXIV (June 28, 1947), 775-776.

Review of *The Well-Wrought Urn* by Cleanth Brooks.

C 256
"Young Poets Dead," *The Sewanee Review,* LV (Summer 1947), 504-514.

Review of *Poems* by Samuel Greenberg and *The Collected Poems of Sidney Keyes.*

C 257
"Nightingale of the Mire," *New York Herald Tribune Books*, October 12, 1947, p. 3.

Review of *Tristan Corbiére Poems*, trans. Walter McElroy.

C 258
"Waiting for the End, Boys," *Partisan Review*, XV (February 1948), 254-263, 265-267.

Review of *Heavenly City, Earthly City* by Robert Duncan, *The Prodigal Never Returns* by Hugh Chisholm, *Poems* by William Jay Smith, *The Sun My Monument* by Laurie Lee, *Other Skies* by John Ciardi, *The Image and the Law* by Howard Nemerov, *Cry Cadence* by Howard Griffin, *The Amazing Year* by Selden Rodman, *The Ego and the Centaur* by Jean Garrigue, and *A Map of Verona and Other Poems* by Henry Reed.

C 259
"Provincial," *Partisan Review*, XV (March 1948), 379-381.

Review of *The Last of the Provincials* by Maxwell Geismar.

C 260
"A Peine Ma Piste," *Partisan Review*, XV (July 1948), 826-828.

Review of *T. S. Eliot: A Selected Critique*, ed. Leonard Unger.

C 261
Answers to "The State of American Writing, 1948: Seven Questions," *Partisan Review*, XV (August 1948), 856-860.

C 262
"The Poetry of Ezra Pound," *Partisan Review*, XVI (April 1949), 377-394.[4]

Article. See B 30.

---

4. In an unpublished letter of February 14, 1949, to Louis Untermeyer, JB wrote that he had edited Ezra Pound's *Selected Poems*, which would be published by New Directions, and that the introduction for the book would first be printed in *Partisan Review* in March. In a letter of January 5, 1973, Griselda Ohannessian of New Directions wrote that Berryman had been commissioned to write an introduction for Pound's *Selected Poems* but his work had not been used.

C 263
Letter to the Editors of *The Saturday Review of Literature, The Nation,* CLXIX (December 17, 1949), 598–599.[5]

C 264
"Through Dreiser's Imagination the Tides of Real Life Billowed," *The New York Times Book Review,* March 4, 1951, pp. 7, 29.

Reprinted: (1) *Highlights of Modern Literature,* ed. Francis Brown. New York: New American Library, 1954. (2) *The Stature of Theodore Dreiser,* ed. Alfred Kazin and Charles Shapiro. Bloomington: Indiana University Press, 1955.

Review of *Theodore Dreiser* by F. O. Matthiessen. See B 15.

C 265
"Shakespeare at Thirty," *The Hudson Review,* VI (Summer 1953), [175]–203.[6]

Article.

C 266
"Manner and Matter," *The New Republic,* CXXIX (November 2, 1953), 27–28.

Reprinted: "On Poetry and the Age," *Randall Jarrell,* ed. Robert Lowell, Peter Taylor, and Robert Penn Warren. New York: Farrar, Straus and Giroux, 1967.

Review of *Poetry and the Age* by Randall Jarrell. See B 27.

---

5. This letter is a response to Robert Hillyer's position in the controversy over the awarding of the first Bollingen Prize to Ezra Pound for his *The Pisan Cantos.* Although authorship of the letter is not certain, it was JB who circulated it for signatures, and he was one of the eighty-four writers who signed. JB submitted the letter to *Saturday Review* for publication since Hillyer's essays were printed in that journal. On December 2, 1949, Harrison Smith wrote to JB, maintaining that the document he had submitted was not a letter but a petition and, consequently, agreeing to publish it only if a reply by Hillyer also appeared. The letter was then published in *The Nation* with a covering statement by Margaret Marshall.

6. According to the notes on contributors for this issue of *The Hudson Review,* shorter versions of this article were presented as a Hodder Lecture at Princeton in 1951 and as an Elliston Lecture at the University of Cincinnati in 1952.

C 267
"Speaking of Books," *The New York Times Book Review*, December 6, 1953, p. 2.

Review of *The Adventures of Augie March* by Saul Bellow.

C 268
"The Long Way to MacDiarmid," *Poetry*, LXXXVIII (April 1956), 52-61.

Review of *The Metal and the Flower* by P. K. Page, *Poets of Today* by Harry Duncan, *Samurai and Serpent Poems* by Murray Noss, *Another Animal* by May Swenson, *Birds in the Mulberry* by George Abbe, *A Character Invented* by LeRoy Smith, *Events and Signals* by F. R. Scott, *Leaves Without a Tree* by G. S. Fraser, and *Selected Poems of Hugh MacDiarmid*.

C 269
"The Case of Ring Lardner," *Commentary*, XXII (November 1956), 416-423.

Article.

C 270
"From the Middle to the Senior Generations," *The American Scholar*, XXVIII (Summer 1959), 384, 386, 388, 390.

Review of *Words for the Wind* by Theodore Roethke, *Poems of a Jew* by Karl Shapiro, *95 Poems* by E. E. Cummings, and *Paterson (Book Five)* by William Carlos Williams.

C 271
"Thursday Out," *The Noble Savage*, no. 3 (May 1961), 186-194.

Memoir.

C 272
"Spender: The Poet as Critic," *The New Republic*, CXLVIII (June 29, 1963), 19-20.

Review of *The Making of a Poem* by Stephen Spender.

C 273
"Auden's Prose," *The New York Review of Books*, I (August 29, 1963), 19.

Review of *The Dyer's Hand* by W. H. Auden.

C 274
Letter to the Editor, *The Minnesota Daily*, April 25, 1965, p. 5.

C 275
"A Tribute [to Ezra Pound]," *Agenda*, IV (October–November 1965), 27-28.

Essay.

C 276
"One Answer to a Question," *Shenandoah*, XVII (Autumn 1965), 67-76.

Reprinted: "Changes," *Poets on Poetry*, ed. Howard Nemerov. New York: Basic Books, 1966.

Essay. See B 26.

C 277
Letter to the Editor, *The Nation*, CCXI (November 30, 1970), 546.

C 278
"Our Sins Are More Than We Can Bear," *The Twin Cities Express*, I (September 26, 1973), 19.[7]

Short story.

C 279
"Surveillance," *The Ohio Review*, XV (Winter 1974), 45.

Poem.

Note: This entry was added in proof, and chronologically comes after C 235 in the subdivision *Poetry*.

---

7. In a letter of May 18, 1974, Jonathan Sisson, Literary Editor of *The Twin Cities Express*, wrote that, according to Kate Berryman, the story was written over twenty years ago (as nearly as she could determine) and the return address on the manuscript is 120 Prospect Avenue, Princeton, N.J.

D. Collected Materials Reprinted in Anthologies

Materials first published in the books listed in Sections A and B that have been reprinted in anthologies, arranged alphabetically within two subdivisions, *Poetry* and *Prose*. In a few cases reprintings in periodicals are noted.

POETRY

D 1
"Another New Year's Eve." In *Two Poems* (1970).

Reprinted: "Year's End, 1970," *The New York Times*, January 1, 1971, p. 22.

D 2
"The Ball Poem," In *Two Poems* (1942), *TD*, *HomageAOP*, *ShP*, and *SelP*.

Reprinted: (1) *Modern American Poetry*, ed. Louis Untermeyer. New York: Harcourt, Brace and Co., 1950. (2) *The New Poetry*, ed. A. Alvarez. Harmondsworth, Middlesex: Penguin Books, 1966. (3) *53 American Poets of Today*, ed. Ruth Witt-Diamant and Rikutaro Fukuda. Tokyo: Kenkyusha, 1968. (4) *Poetry: A Thematic Approach*, ed. Sam H. Henderson and James Ward Lee. Belmont, Calif.: Wadsworth Publishing Co., 1968. (5) *The Contemporary American Poets*, ed. Mark Strand. Cleveland: World Publishing Co., 1969. (6) *Possibilities of Poetry*, ed. Richard Kostelanetz. New York: Dell Publishing Co., 1970. (7) *The Norton Anthology of Modern Poetry*, ed. Richard Ellmann and Robert O'Clair. New York: W. W. Norton Co., 1973. (8) *Sound and Sense: An Introduction to Poetry*, ed. Laurence Perrine. New York: Harcourt, Brace and Jovanovich, 1973.

D 3
"Crisis." In *L&F*.

Reprinted: *Today's Poets*, ed. Chad Walsh. New York: Charles Scribner's Sons, 1972.

D 4
"Dante's Tomb." In *L&F*.

Reprinted: *The New York Review of Books*, XVI (February 25, 1971), 4.

D 5
Dream Song 15. In *77DS* and *TheDS*.

Reprinted: Naked Poetry, ed. Stephen Berg and Robert Mezey. Indianapolis: Bobbs-Merrill Co., 1969.

D 6
Dream Song 26. In *77DS*, *TheDS*, and *SelP*.

Reprinted: Naked Poetry, ed. Stephen Berg and Robert Mezey. Indianapolis: Bobbs-Merrill Co., 1969.

D 7
Dream Song 47: "April Fool's Day, or St Mary of Egypt." In *77DS*, *TheDS*, and *SelP*.

Reprinted: Naked Poetry, ed. Stephen Berg and Robert Mezey. Indianapolis: Bobbs-Merrill Co., 1969.

D 8
Dream Song 61. In *77DS* and *TheDS*.

Reprinted: (1) *The Contemporary American Poets*, ed. Mark Strand. Cleveland: World Publishing Co., 1969. (2) *Poems: An Anthology*, ed. Burton Raffel. New York: New American Library, 1971.

D 9
Dream Song 62. In *77DS* and *TheDS*.

Reprinted: Twentieth Century Poetry, ed. John Malcolm Brinnin and Bill Read. New York: McGraw-Hill Book Co., 1970.

D 10
Dream Song 76: "Henry's Confession." In *77DS*, *TheDS*, and *SelP*.

Reprinted: (1) *Naked Poetry*, ed. Stephen Berg and Robert Mezey. Indianapolis: Bobbs-Merrill Co., 1969. (2) *Twentieth Century Poetry*, ed. John Malcolm Brinnin and Bill Read. New York: McGraw-Hill Book Co., 1970. (3) *The New Pocket Anthology of American Verse*, ed. Oscar Williams. New York: Washington Square Press, 1972. (4) *The Pocket Book of Modern Verse*, ed. Oscar Williams. New York: Washington Square Press, 1972. (5) *Today's Poets*, ed. Chad Walsh New York: Charles Scribner's Sons, 1972. (6) *The Norton Anthology of Modern Poetry*, ed. Richard Ellmann and Robert O'Clair. New York:

Collected Materials Reprinted in Anthologies

W. W. Norton Co., 1973. (7) *Shake the Kaleidoscope*, ed. Milton Klonsky. New York: Pocket Books, 1973.

D 11
Dream Song 91: "Op. posth. no. 14." In *Toy*, *TheDS*, and *SelP*.

Reprinted: Contemporary American Poetry, ed. A. Poulin, Jr. Boston: Houghton Mifflin Co., 1971.

D 12
Dream Song 149. In *Toy* and *TheDS*.

Reprinted: The Norton Anthology of Modern Poetry, ed. Richard Ellmann and Robert O'Clair. New York: W. W. Norton Co., 1973.

D 13
Dream Song 185. In *Toy* and *TheDS*.

Reprinted: Shake the Kaleidoscope, ed. Milton Klonsky. New York: Pocket Books, 1973.

D 14
Dream Song 230. In *Toy* and *TheDS*.

Reprinted: Contemporary American Poets, ed. A. Poulin, Jr. Boston: Houghton Mifflin Co., 1971.

D 15
Dream Song 263. In *Toy* and *TheDS*.

Reprinted: Shake the Kaleidoscope, ed. Milton Klonsky. New York: Pocket Books, 1973.

D 16
Dream Song 266. In *Toy* and *TheDS*.

Reprinted: Contemporary American Poetry, ed. A. Poulin, Jr. Boston: Houghton Mifflin Co., 1971.

D 17
Dream Song 312. In *Poetry Season 1967*, *Toy*, *TheDS*, and *SelP*.

Reprinted: The Norton Anthology of Modern Poetry, ed. Richard Ellmann and Robert O'Clair. New York: W. W. Norton Co., 1973.

D 18
Dream Song 315. In *Toy*, *TheDS*, and *SelP*.

Reprinted: Loves, Etc., ed. Marguerite Harris. Garden City, N.Y.: Doubleday and Co., 1973.

D 19
Dream Song 319. In *Toy* and *TheDS*.

Reprinted: The Pocket Book of Modern Verse, ed. Oscar Williams. New York: Washington Square Press, 1972.

D 20
Dream Song 344: "Herbert Park, Dublin." In *Toy* and *TheDS*.

Reprinted: Shake the Kaleidoscope, ed. Milton Klonsky. New York: Pocket Books, 1973.

D 21
Dream Song 351. In *Toy* and *TheDS*.

Reprinted: Today's Poets, ed. Chad Walsh. New York: Charles Scribner's Sons, 1972.

D 22
Dream Song 353. In *Toy* and *TheDS*.

Reprinted: Contemporary American Poetry, ed. A. Poulin, Jr. Boston: Houghton Mifflin Co., 1971.

D 23
Dream Song 371: "Henry's Guilt." In *Toy*, *TheDS*, and *SelP*.

Reprinted: Today's Poets, ed. Chad Walsh. New York: Charles Scribner's Sons, 1972.

D 24
Dream Song 375: "His Helplessness." In *Toy* and *TheDS*.

Reprinted: The Pocket Book of Modern Verse, ed. Oscar Williams. New York: Washington Square Press, 1972.

D 25
Dream Song 380: "From the French Hospital in New York, 901." In *Toy*, *TheDS*, and *SelP*.

Reprinted: Contemporary American Poetry, ed. A. Poulin, Jr. Boston: Houghton Mifflin Co., 1971.

D 26
Dream Song 382. In *Toy*, *TheDS*, and *SelP*.

Collected Materials Reprinted in Anthologies 223

Reprinted: (1) *This Is My Best,* ed. Whit Burnett. Garden City, N.Y.: Doubleday and Co., 1970. (2) *Contemporary American Poetry,* ed. A. Poulin, Jr. Boston: Houghton Mifflin Co., 1971. (3) *Shake the Kaleidoscope,* ed. Milton Klonsky. New York: Pocket Books, 1973.

D 27
"Formal Elegy." In *ShP.* See B 21.

Reprinted: (1) *Of Poetry and Power,* ed. Erwin A. Glikes and Paul Schwaber. New York: Basic Books, 1964. (2) *The New York Times Magazine,* November 4, 1973, pp. 40–41.

D 28
"from The Black Book (iii)." In *Thought* and *ShP.*

Reprinted: *The Voice That Is Great Within Us,* ed. Hayden Carruth. New York: Bantam Books, 1970.

D 29
"The Handshake, The Entrance." In *Two Dream Songs* (1969) and *DE.*

Reprinted: *Intellectual Digest,* II (April 1972), [95].

D 30
"Have a Genuine American Horror-&-Mist on the Rocks." In *L&F.*

Reprinted: *Intellectual Digest,* III (December 1972), 63.

D 31
"He Resigns." In *DE.*

Reprinted: *Loves, Etc.,* ed. Marguerite Harris. Garden City, N.Y.: Doubleday and Co., 1973.

D 32
"In Memoriam (1914–1953)." In *Two Poems* (1970) and *DE.*

Reprinted: *Intellectual Digest,* II (April 1972), [94].

D 33
"The Moon and the Night and the Men." In *Poems, TD, HomageAOP, ShP,* and *SelP.* See B 5.

Reprinted: (1) *New Poems 1940,* ed. Oscar Williams. New York: Yardstick Press, 1941. (2) *The New Treasury of War*

Poetry, ed. George Herbert Clarke. Boston: Houghton Mifflin Co., 1943. (3) *The War Poets*, ed. Oscar Williams. New York: John Day Co., 1945. (4) *The New Poetry*, ed. A. Alvarez. Harmondsworth, Middlesex: Penguin Books, 1966. (5) *53 American Poets of Today*, ed. Ruth Witt-Diamant and Rikutaro Fukuda. Tokyo: Kenkyusha, 1968. (6) *The Contemporary American Poets*, ed. Mark Strand. Cleveland: World Publishing Co., 1969. (7) *The Survival Years*, ed. Jack Salzman. New York: Western Publishing Co., 1969. (8) *The Voice That Is Great Within Us*, ed. Hayden Carruth. New York: Bantam Books, 1970.

D 34
"Of Suicide." In *L&F*.

Reprinted: The Norton Anthology of Modern Poetry, ed. Richard Ellmann and Robert O'Clair. New York: W. W. Norton Co., 1973.

D 35
"1 September 1939." In *Poems, TD, HomageAOP*, and *ShP*. See B 6.

Reprinted: (1) *New Directions in Prose and Poetry 1941*, ed. James Laughlin. Norfolk, Conn.: New Directions, 1941. (2) *The New Treasury of War Poetry*, ed. George Herbert Clarke. Boston: Houghton Mifflin Co., 1943. (3) *The Norton Introduction to Literature: Poetry*, ed. J. Paul Hunter. New York: W. W. Norton Co., 1973.

D 36
"Parting as Descent." In *20P, TD, HomageAOP*, and *ShP*. See B 4.

Reprinted: (1) *New Directions in Prose and Poetry 1939*, ed. James Laughlin. Norfolk, Conn.: New Directions, 1939. (2) *The Little Treasury of American Poetry*, ed. Oscar Williams. New York: Charles Scribner's Sons, 1948. (3) *Modern American Poetry*, ed. Louis Untermeyer. New York: Harcourt, Brace and Co., 1950. (4) *Contemporary Poetry in America*, ed. Miller Williams. New York: Random House, 1968.

D 37
"A Poem for Bhain." In *Poems, TD*, and *ShP*.

Reprinted: Contemporary Poetry in America, ed. Miller Williams. New York: Random House, 1968.

Collected Materials Reprinted in Anthologies 225

D 38
"The Poet's Final Instructions." In *Thought* and *ShP.*

Reprinted: The Voice That Is Great Within Us, ed. Hayden Carruth. New York: Bantam Books, 1970.

D 39
"A Professor's Song." In *TD* and *ShP.*

Reprinted: The Norton Anthology of Modern Poetry, ed. Richard Ellmann and Robert O'Clair. New York: W. W. Norton Co., 1973.

D 40
"The Song of the Tortured Girl." In *TD, HomageAOP, ShP,* and *SelP.*

Reprinted: (1) *The New Poetry,* ed. A. Alvarez. Harmondsworth, Middlesex: Penguin Books, 1966. (2) *The Contemporary American Poets,* ed. Mark Strand. Cleveland: World Publishing Co., 1969.

D 41
Sonnet 13. In *BS.*

Reprinted: Episodes in Five Poetic Traditions, ed. R. G. Barnes. San Francisco: Chandler Publishing Co., 1972.

D 42
Sonnet 15. In *BS.*

Reprinted: Episodes in Five Poetic Traditions, ed. R. G. Barnes. San Francisco: Chandler Publishing Co., 1972.

D 43
Sonnet 60. In *BS.*

Reprinted: (1) *Episodes in Five Poetic Traditions,* ed. R. G. Barnes. San Francisco: Chandler Publishing Co., 1972. (2) *50 Modern American Poets, 1920–1970,* ed. Louis Untermeyer. New York: David McKay Co., 1973.

PROSE

D 44
"On War and Poetry." In *The War Poets.* See B 9.

Reprinted: A *Little Treasury of Modern Poetry,* ed. Oscar Williams. New York: Charles Scribner's Sons, 1952.

D 45
Stephen Crane. See A 6.

Reprinted: (1) Selection (pp. 54-55, 76-80, 126-127), "The Significance of Crane's English Reception," *The Red Badge of Courage,* ed. Sculley Bradley, Richmond C. Beatty, and E. Hudson Long. New York: W. W. Norton and Co., 1962. (2) "Crane's Art," *Modern American Fiction,* ed. A. Walton Litz. New York: Oxford University Press, 1963. (3) "Crane's Art," *Stephen Crane,* ed. Maurice Bassan. Englewood Cliffs, N.J.: Prentice-Hall, 1967. (4) Selection (pp. 263-269), "John Berryman on Stephen Crane," *Stephen Crane's Career,* ed. Thomas A. Gullason. New York: New York University Press, 1972.

D 46
"Stephen Crane: *The Red Badge of Courage.*" In *The American Novel.* See B 22.

Reprinted: *Stephen Crane's Career,* ed. Thomas A. Gullason. New York: New York University Press, 1972.

D 47
Untitled article in "The Poet and His Critics: III: A Symposium on Robert Lowell's 'Skunk Hour.'" In *New World Writing 21.* See B 20.

Reprinted: (1) "Despondency and Madness," *The Contemporary Poet as Artist and Critic,* ed. Anthony Ostroff. Boston: Little, Brown and Co., 1964. (2) "Despondency and Madness," *Robert Lowell,* ed. Thomas Parkinson. Englewood Cliffs, N.J.: Prentice-Hall, 1968.

E. Interviews

Interviews with Berryman and articles based on interviews, arranged chronologically.

E 1
Stedman, Jane. "Poet, Editor, Teacher—Looks Forward to Own Book," *The Detroit Collegian*, October 23, 1939, p. 2.

E 2
Strudwick, Dorothy. "Homage to Mr. Berryman," *The Minnesota Daily*, November 5, 1956, pp. 6, 16.

E 3
Meras, Phyllis. "John Berryman on Today's Literature," *Providence Sunday Journal*, May 26, 1963, p. 20W.

E 4
"Pulitzer Prize Once a 'Nothing' to Him; Now Berryman's Happy to Accept," *The Minneapolis Star*, May 4, 1965, p. 18D.

E 5
"'U' Professor Awarded Pulitzer Poetry Prize," *The Minneapolis Tribune*, May 4, 1965, p. 1.

E 6
Lundegaard, Bob. "Song of a Poet: John Berryman," *The Minneapolis Sunday Tribune*, June 27, 1965, pp. 1-2E.

E 7
Sisson, Jonathan. "My Whiskers Fly: An Interview with John Berryman," *Ivory Tower*, XIV (October 3, 1966), 14-18, 34-35.

E 8
Howard, Jane. "Whisky and Ink, Whisky and Ink," *Life*, LXIII (July 21, 1967), 67-68, 70, 73-76.

E 9
Nussbaum, Elizabeth. "Berryman and Tate: Poets Extraordinaire," *The Minnesota Daily*, November 9, 1967, pp. 7, 10.

E 10
"Berryman Gets $10,000 Award," *The Minneapolis Tribune*, November 17, 1967, p. 1.

E 11
Watson, Catherine. "Berryman Ends Poem of 13 Years," *The Minneapolis Tribune*, May 12, 1968, p. 1E.

E 12
"Poetry Once Was Nonsense to Berryman," *The Minneapolis Tribune*, January 6, 1969, p. 22.

E 13
McClelland, David et al. "An Interview with John Berryman," *The Harvard Advocate*, CIII (Spring 1969), 4-9.

E 14
Murphy, Pat, "'People Individuals with Values': Poet John Berryman Talks About Life, War, Death," *The State Journal* (Lansing, Mich.), May 11, 1969, p. 9E.

E 15
Kostelanetz, Richard. "Conversation with Berryman," *The Massachusetts Review*, XI (Spring 1970), 340-347.

E 16
Berg, Martin. "A Truly Gentle Man Tightens and Paces: An Interview with John Berryman," *The Minnesota Daily*, January 20, 1971, pp. 10, 14-15, 17.

E 17
Haas, Joseph. "Who Killed Henry Pussy-cat? I did, says John Berryman, with love & a poem, & for freedom O," *Chicago Daily News*, February 6, 1971, Panorama, pp. 4-5.

E 18
Stitt, Peter A. "The Art of Poetry XVI: John Berryman 1914-72," *The Paris Review*, XIV (Winter 1972), 176-207.

The interview was conducted at St. Mary's Hospital in Minneapolis on October 27 and 29, 1970.

E 19
Heyen, William. "John Berryman: A Memoir and an Interview," *The Ohio Review*, XV (Winter 1974), 46-65.

Interviews

The memoir (pp. 46–55) includes quotations from previously unpublished letters from JB to the author. The interview (pp. 55–65) is a transcription of an hour-long television interview at the State University of New York, College at Brockport conducted by William Heyen and Jerome Mazzaro on October 8, 1970.

F. Phonorecordings

Recordings of Berryman's poetry, arranged chronologically under two headings, *Tapes* and *Discs*. No material held in private collections is listed.

TAPES

F 1
JB reading his poetry in the Recording Laboratory, February 13, 1948. Washington, D.C.: Library of Congress, 1948. LWO 2689, reel 2.

Contains "The Song of the Demented Priest," "The Statue," "New Year's Eve," "Narcissus Moving," and "Rock-Study with Wanderer."

F 2
JB reading his poetry at his home in Princeton, N.J., 1951. Washington, D.C.: Library of Congress, 1951. LWO 1963, reel 3.

Contains "The Statue," "The Disciple," "A Point of Age," "The Traveller," "The Ball Poem," "Fare Well," "The Spinning Heart," "Parting as Descent," "Desires of Men and Women," "World-Telegram," "Ancestor," "Boston Common," "The Moon and the Night and the Men," "The Enemies of the Angels," "Canto Amor," "Young Woman's Song," "The Song of the Demented Priest," "The Song of the Young Hawaiian," "The Song of the Tortured Girl," "The Song of the Bridegroom," "Rock-Study with Wanderer," "The Long Home," "New Year's Eve," "Narcissus Moving," "The Dispossessed," and "Scots Poem."

F 3
JB reading his poetry with commentary in the Coolidge Auditorium, February 24, 1958. Washington, D.C.: Library of Congress, 1958. LWO 2609.

Contains "Rock-Study with Wanderer," "The Song of the Demented Priest," "Winter Landscape," "The Ball Poem," "The Dispossessed," "Sonnet 25," "A Sympathy, A Welcome," "Not To Live," "American Lights, Seen From Off Abroad," and a selection from *Homage to Mistress Bradstreet*.

F 4
JB reading his poetry at the National Poetry Festival, held in the Coolidge Auditorium, October 23, 1962, afternoon session. Washington, D.C.: Library of Congress, 1962. LWO 2869, reel 2.

Contains Dream Song 4; Dream Song 22: "Of 1826"; Dream Song 16; Dream Song 23: "The Lay of Ike"; Dream Song 29; Dream Song 75; and Dream Song 27.

F 5
JB reading his own poetry and selections from the works of other writers with commentary at the State University of New York at Buffalo, on January 25, 1963. Buffalo, N.Y.: S.U.N.Y. at Buffalo, 1963.

Contains "As I walked out one evening" by W. H. Auden; Lucky's speech (beginning "Given the existence as uttered for in the public works of Puncher and Wattmann . . .") in Samuel Beckett's *Waiting for Godot* (New York: Grove Press, 1954), pp. 27–29; "Visits to St. Elizabeths" by Elizabeth Bishop; and JB's "Venice, 182–," "A Sympathy, A Welcome," "Note to Wang Wei," "The Ball Poem," a selection from *Homage to Mistress Bradstreet*, Dream Song 1, Dream Song 5, Dream Song 75, Dream Song 4, Dream Song 22: "Of 1826," Dream Song 3: "A Stimulant for an Old Beast," Dream Song 53, Dream Song 23: "The Lay of Ike," Dream Song ("Baby Teddy, baby did-he, drop him too a pat"), Dream Song 29, Dream Song 21, Dream Song 27, and Dream Song 71.

Location: Lockwood.

F 6
JB reading his poetry with commentary at the State University of New York at Buffalo, on December 18, 1968. Buffalo, N.Y.: S.U.N.Y. at Buffalo, 1968.

Contains "The Ball Poem"; "Song of the Tortured Girl"; Dream Song 1; Dream Song 14; Dream Song 16; Dream Song 17; Dream Song 29; Dream Song 45; Dream Song 67; Dream Song 69; Dream Song 75; Dream Song 77; Dream Song 78: "Op. posth. no. 1"; Dream Song 86: "Op. posth. no. 9"; Dream Song 87: "Op. posth. no. 10"; Dream Song 90: "Op. posth. no. 13"; Dream Song 113: "or Amy Vladeck or Riva Freifeld"; Dream Song 224: "Eighty"; Dream Song 187; Dream Song 172; Dream Song 171; Dream Song 381; Dream Song 382; Dream Song 384; Dream Song 385.

Location: Lockwood.

Phonorecordings

F 7
JB reading his poetry with commentary at the International Poetry Forum in Pittsburgh, April 15, 1970. Pittsburgh: International Poetry Forum, 1970.

Contains Dream Song 1; Dream Song 4; Dream Song 14; Dream Song 16; Dream Song 17; Dream Song 76: "Henry's Confession"; Dream Song 17; Dream Song 382; "Her & It"; "Cadenza on Garnette"; "The Hell Poem"; "Heaven."

Location: International Poetry Forum (PPi).

DISCS

F 8
Twentieth Century Poetry in English. Herbert Read, Phelps Putnam, John Berryman, and Horace Gregory reading their own poems. PL 8 (Record P33). Washington, D.C.: Library of Congress, 1952.

Contains "Winter Landscape," "The Ball Poem," "The Lightning," and "Canto Amor."

F 9
Of Poetry and Power. Poems on the Presidency and Death of John F. Kennedy by W. H. Auden, John Berryman, Robert Frost *et al.* Read by Irene Dailey and Martin Donegan. FL 9721. New York: Folkways Records, 1965.

Contains "Formal Elegy."

F 10
The Spoken Arts Treasury of 100 Modern American Poets. Edited by Paul Kresh. Vol. XII. Randall Jarrell, John Berryman, Owen Dodson, Jean Garrigue, Ruth Stone, and Hollis Summers reading their own poems. SA 1051. New York: Spoken Arts, 1969.

Contains Dream Song 4; Dream Song 22: "Of 1826"; Dream Song 16; Dream Song 29; and Dream Song 75.

F 11
The World's Great Poets Reading at the Festival of Two Worlds, Spoleto, Italy. American Poets: John Berryman, Gregory Corso, Allen Ginsberg. SP 412M. New York: Applause Productions, 1970.

Contains Dream Song 1, Dream Song 5, Dream Song 8, Dream Song 14, Dream Song 16, Dream Song 17, and Dream Song 77.

G. Dust-Jacket Blurbs

Dust jackets of books by other authors on which quotations from comments (blurbs) by Berryman appear, arranged chronologically.

G 1

Lowell, Robert. *The Mills of the Kavanaughs*. New York: Harcourt, Brace and Co., [1951].

On copyright page: *'first edition'*.

Dust jacket: Wove glossy paper, 8³/₁₆" × 19⅛". Front cover: '[vivid greenish yellow (Centroid 97) background] [dark bluish green (165) inline and shadowing] The Mills | of the | Kavanaughs | [dark bluish green background] [white (263)] A new volume of poems | by the Pulitzer Prize-winning author of | *Lord Weary's Castle* | [vivid greenish yellow] ROBERT LOWELL'. Spine: '[reading vertically from top to bottom] [vivid greenish yellow background] [dark bluish green] The Mills of the Kavanaughs [dark greenish blue background] [vivid greenish yellow] Robert Lowell [white] HARCOURT, BRACE | AND COMPANY'. Back cover: '[white background] [photograph of Lowell in tones of green and white] | [dark bluish green] *Sam Hunter* | Robert Lowell | [five-line unsigned biographical note]'. Front flap: '[white background] [dark bluish green] $2.50 | ROBERT LOWELL | The Mills | of the Kavanaughs | [two unsigned paragraphs of a descriptive comment on contents, fifteen lines] | *Drawing on title page by* | *Francis Parker* | HARCOURT, BRACE AND COMPANY | *383 Madison Avenue, New York 17, N.Y.*' Back flap: '[white background] [dark bluish green] ROBERT LOWELL | RANDALL JARRELL: | [four-line quotation from a comment] | SELDEN RODMAN: | [four-line quotation from a comment] | JOHN BERRYMAN: | "A talent whose ceiling is invisible." | PETER VIERECK: | [four-line quotation from a comment]'.

Location: ECS.

G 2

Snodgrass, W. D. *After Experience*. New York, Evanston, and London: Harper and Row, [1968].

On copyright page: 'FIRST EDITION'.

Dust jacket: Wove paper, 8⁵⁄₁₆" × 19³⁄₁₆". Front cover: '[strong green (Centroid 141) background] [white (263)] [script] After Experience | [vivid greenish yellow (97)] *POEMS* | *BY* | *W. D. SNODGRASS* | [white] AUTHOR OF [script] Heart's Needle'. Spine: '[strong green background] [reading vertically from top to bottom] [white] [script] After Experience [vivid greenish yellow] *W. D. SNODGRASS* [white] [script] Harper & Row'. Back cover: '[white background] ADVANCE COMMENTS ABOUT *After Experience:* | "W. D. Snodgrass is one of the best poets in the country." | — JOHN BERRYMAN | [nine-line quotation from a comment by Anthony Hecht] | [black and white photograph of Snodgrass]'. Front flap: '[white background] $4.95 | AFTER | EXPERIENCE | by W. D. SNODGRASS [two unsigned paragraphs, comprising a twelve-line note on Snodgrass' reputation with quotations from comments by Donald Hall and William Meredith and a twelve-line descriptive comment on contents] | 0268'. Back flap: '[white background] [fourteen-line unsigned biographical note on Snodgrass] | *Jacket design by Riki Levinson*'.

Location: ECS.

Note: In a letter of August 13, 1973, Alice Rosengard of Harper and Row supplied the following information about JB's comment on W. D. Snodgrass's *After Experience:* David I. Segal, then Snodgrass's editor, sent galleys to JB and other noted poets. During a conversation on November 20, 1967, JB gave Mr. Segal the following comment: "W. D. Snodgrass is one of the best poets in the country and his new collection is one of his most distinguished." In a letter of November 21, 1967, Mr. Segal requested that JB change his comment since *After Experience* was only Snodgrass's second book of poetry. On a postcard of December 31, 1967, JB stated that he thought the book was Snodgrass's third collection and changed the end of the comment to read "and his new collection is handsomely welcome." But apparently the postcard did not reach Mr. Segal in time — in a letter of January 12, 1968, he wrote JB that since he hadn't received a response to his request, his solution was simply to omit the last half of the comment.

G 3
Appleton, Sarah. *The Plentitude We Cry For.* Garden City, N.Y.: Doubleday and Co., 1972.

On copyright page: 'First Edition'.

Dust-Jacket Blurbs 243

Dust jacket: White (Centroid 263) wove paper, outside glossy, 8 7/16" × 20". Front cover: '[within single-rules frame with rounded corners] [first four lines swash] *The Plentitude We Cry For* | [moderate yellowish brown (77)] *A* | *Poem by* | *Sarah Appleton* | [drawings of horned nut, branch, flowers on a stem, and leaf of the horse chestnut, in strong yellow green (117), deep yellowish brown (78), moderate yellowish brown, white, black, and light gray (264)] | [moderate yellowish brown] "I know of no work quite like it, for the unfolding | organic [black] feminine [moderate yellowish brown] attentive realization of a natural | object, both direct and associative. Rilke entered | on things in a similar way but not at this length." | John Berryman'. Spine: '[reading vertically from top to bottom] [within single-rules frame with rounded corners] [first seven words swash] *The Plentitude We Cry For* [moderate yellowish brown] *Sarah Appleton* [black] *Doubleday*'. Back cover: '[ten-line quotation from a comment by Denise Levertov, two-line quotation from a comment by George Oppen, six-line quotation from a comment by Jane Cooper, six-line quotation from a comment by Anne Stevenson] | [moderate yellowish brown] [swash] *The Plentitude We Cry For*'. Front flap: 'T.P.W.C.F. | $5.95 | [first four lines swash] *The Plentitude We Cry For* | *A* | *Poem by* | *Sarah Appleton* | [beginning of unsigned three-paragraph descriptive comment on contents, twenty-four lines] | *(continued on back flap)*'. Back flap: '*(continued from front flap)* | [conclusion of comment, four lines] | [fourteen-line unsigned biographical note on Mrs. Appleton] | JACKET DESIGN BY FRANCES J. ELFENBEIN | ISBN: 0-385-00315-3 TRADE | *Printed in the U.S.A.*'

Location: ECS.

Note: In a letter of March 28, 1974, Sarah Appleton wrote that JB made the comment on the dust jacket in a letter he wrote to her on October 21, 1971. She had sent the poem to him many months before, and after it was accepted for publication he made the comment for Doubleday at her request. Mrs. Appleton also noted that JB himself emphasized the word "feminine" and that no changes were made in the comment prior to publication.

H. Poetry Selections

Selections by Berryman of the work of other poets, arranged chronologically.

H 1

"Autumn Miscellany—Seven Poems Selected by John Berryman," *The Nation,* CIL (September 30, 1939), 350–351.

Contains "On an Old Horn" by Wallace Stevens, "Matthew Arnold" by W. H. Auden, "The Statue of Shadow" and "That Summer's End" by John Peale Bishop, "Unto the Second Generation" and "Angina Pectoris" by W. R. Moses, "Of Gramatan's Transaction" by Bhain Campbell.

H 2

"Winter Miscellany—Four Poems Selected by John Berryman," *The Nation,* CL (February 10, 1940), 200, 202.[1]

Contains "A Vision of Labor" by William Carlos Williams, "My Country" by Emma Swan, "I Remember the Block Party" by Oscar Williams, "When Does the Play Begin" by James Laughlin.

---

1. The contributor's column in this issue reads: "John Berryman's poems have appeared in various magazines. He selects the small anthologies of poems which appear at frequent intervals in *The Nation.*" No other selections by JB have been located.

Appendices / Index

Appendix 1
A Chronology of the Publication
of Works by Berryman

Prose items are indicated by asterisks. The titles of individual poems are those of the collected versions.

"Essential"	March 1935
"Ars Poetica"	April 1935
"Blake"	April 1935
"Lead Out the Weary Dancers"	April 1935
"Apostrophe"	April 1935
*Review of Mark Van Doren's *A Winter Diary and Other Poems*	April 1935
"Ivory"	May 1935
*Review of Joseph Auslander's *No Traveller Returns*	May 1935
"Note on E. A. Robinson"	July 3, 1935
"Elegy: Hart Crane"	November 1935
"Thanksgiving"	November 1935
*"Satire and Poetry"	November 1935
*"Types of Pedantry"	November 20, 1935
"Words to a Young Man"	December 1935
*"E. A. Robinson, and Others"	December 1935
"Time Does Not Engulf"	December 19, 1935
"Sonnet"	December 19, 1935
"Notation"	April 1936
"The Witness"	April 1936
"The Ancestor"	April 1936
"Trophy"	April 1936
*"The Ritual of W. B. Yeats"	June 1936
*"A Topical Novel"	August 26, 1936
"To an Artist Beginning Her Work"	December 1, 1936
"Night and the City"	June 27, 1938
"Note for a Historian"	June 27, 1938
"The Apparition"	June 27, 1938
"Toward Statement"	June 27, 1938
"The Trial"	October 1938

"The Return"   October 5, 1938
"The Translation"   October 5, 1938
"Caravan"   October 5, 1938
*"A Philosophical Poet"   December 11, 1938

*"Native Verse"   January 8, 1939
"Letter to His Brother"   June 17, 1939
"Nineteen Thirty-Eight"   June 17, 1939
"World-Telegram"   June 22, 1939
"The Statue"   July 17, 1939
"On the London Train"   July 17, 1939
*"'Poetolatry'"   October 1, 1939
"Ceremony and Vision"   November 1, 1939
"On a Portrait in Dublin"   November 1, 1939
"Second Cactus"   November 1, 1939
"Prague"   November 1, 1939
"The Curse"   November 1, 1939
"Parting as Descent"   November 1, 1939
"The Disciple"   December 27, 1939

"Desires of Men and Women"   April 18, 1940
"Conversation"   April 18, 1940
"Homage to Film"   April 18, 1940
"Song from 'Cleopatra'"   April 18, 1940
"Meditation"   April 18, 1940
"Winter Landscape"   July 3, 1940
*"The Loud Hill of Wales"   October 15, 1940
Twenty Poems   November 19, 1940

"The Spinning Heart"   January 16, 1941
"At Chinese Checkers"   March 20, 1941
"The Moon and the Night and the Men"   April 17, 1941
*"More Directions"   June 10, 1941
"River Rouge, 1932"   December 1, 1941
"Thanksgiving: Detroit"   December 1, 1941
"The Dangerous Year"   December 1, 1941
"1 September 1939"   December 1, 1941
"Communist"   December 1, 1941

"White Feather"   May 14, 1942
Poems   September 28, 1942
Two Poems   ca. December 1942

"Cloud and Flame"   February 20, 1943
"Farewell to Miles"   July 1943
"Ancestor"   July 1943

A Chronology of Publication of Works by Berryman 253

"Boston Common"	August 17, 1943
*"Shakespeare's Text"	August 19, 1943
"The Animal Trainer (1)"	August 15, 1944
"The Animal Trainer (2)"	August 15, 1944
*"The Lovers"	December 15, 1944
*"Henry James"	April 1, 1945
*"On War and Poetry"	June 19, 1945
"Travelling South"	August 16, 1945
*"The Imaginary Jew"	September 20, 1945
*"F. Scott Fitzgerald"	December 15, 1945
"The Song of the Demented Priest"	July 1, 1946
"The Song of the Young Hawaiian"	July 1, 1946
"Young Woman's Song"	July 1, 1946
*"A Scholarly History"	December 19, 1946
"Canto Amor"	January 1, 1947
*"Lowell, Thomas, &c."	January 9, 1947
*"Metaphysical or So"	June 26, 1947
*"Young Poets Dead"	July 1, 1947
*"Nightingale of the Mire"	October 12, 1947
*"Waiting for the End, Boys"	February 1, 1948
*"Provincial"	March 1, 1948
"New Year's Eve"	April 1, 1948
"Narcissus Moving"	April 1, 1948
"A Winter-Piece to a Friend Away"	April 2, 1948
"Rock-Study with Wanderer"	April 2, 1948
"The Dispossessed"	April 10, 1948
"World's Fair"	April 10, 1948
"Surviving Love"	April 10, 1948
"The Traveller"	April 10, 1948
"Fare Well"	April 10, 1948
"The Long Home"	May 1, 1948
"Whether There Is Sorrow in the Demons"	May 4, 1948
The Dispossessed	May 10, 1948
*"A Peine Ma Piste"	July 1, 1948
*Answers to "The State of American Writing, 1948: Seven Questions"	August 1, 1948
"Venice, 182–"	December 1948
*"The Poetry of Ezra Pound"	April 1, 1949
*Letter to the editors of *The Saturday Review of Literature*	December 15, 1949

"The Cage"	January 3, 1950
"Elegy, for Alun Lewis"	January 3, 1950
"Innocent"	January 3, 1950
"The Wholly Fail"	January 3, 1950
"from the Black Book (i)"	January 3, 1950
"from the Black Book (ii)"	January 3, 1950
"From *The Black Book:* the will"	January 3, 1950
"From *The Black Book:* waiting"	January 3, 1950
Stephen Crane	November 10, 1950
*"Through Dreiser's Imagination the Tides of Real Life Billowed"	March 4, 1951
"Scots Poem"	September 22, 1951
"The Mysteries"	November 5, 1951
*"Introduction" to *The Monk*	April 1, 1952
"Sonnet 25"	October 8, 1952
*"Shakespeare at Thirty"	June 23, 1953
"Homage to Mistress Bradstreet"	September 3, 1953
*"Manner and Matter"	October 29, 1953
*"Speaking of Books"	December 6, 1953
*"The Long Way to MacDiarmid"	April 16, 1956
Homage to Mistress Bradstreet	October 1, 1956
"Of Isaac Rosenfeld"	October 16, 1956
*"The Case of Ring Lardner"	November 2, 1956
"Not To Live"	October 1, 1957
"American Lights, Seen From Off Abroad"	April 15, 1958
"Note to Wang Wei"	July 31, 1958
"A Sympathy, A Welcome"	August 14, 1958
His Thought Made Pockets & The Plane Buckt	December 15, 1958
*Translation of Paul Claudel's *The Way of the Cross*	February 6, 1959
Homage to Mistress Bradstreet and Other Poems	April 24, 1959
*"From the Middle to the Senior Generations"	June 2, 1959
Dream Song 1	November 6, 1959
Dream Song 5	November 6, 1959
Dream Song 75	November 6, 1959
Dream Song 67	November 6, 1959
Dream Song 77	November 6, 1959

A Chronology of Publication of Works by Berryman 255

*The Arts of Reading	April 8, 1960
*"A Note on the Text" of The Unfortunate Traveller	April 15, 1960
*"Introduction" to The Unfortunate Traveller	April 15, 1960
Dream Song ["The jolly old man is a silly old dumb,"]	April 22, 1960
Dream Song 54	April 22, 1960
Dream Song 12: "Sabbath"	April 22, 1960
Dream Song 46	April 22, 1960
Dream Song 53	April 22, 1960
Dream Song 29	April 22, 1960
Dream Song 17	April 22, 1960
*"Thursday Out"	May 22, 1961
"Preface to the Meridian Edition" of Stephen Crane	February 1962
"Additional Bibliography (1962)" to Stephen Crane	February 1962
Dream Song 20: "The Secret of the Wisdom"	June 3, 1962
Dream Song 216	October 1962
Dream Song 8	October 1962
*Comment on "The Dispossessed"	October 9, 1962
Dream Song 27	October 12, 1962
Dream Song 16	October 12, 1962
Dream Song 36	October 12, 1962
Dream Song 71	October 12, 1962
Dream Song 51	November 9, 1962
"Despondency and Madness"	January 10, 1963
Dream Song 4	January 11, 1963
Dream Song 7: "'The Prisoner of Shark Island' with Paul Muni"	January 21, 1963
Dream Song 52: "Silent Song"	January 21, 1963
Dream Song 41	January 25, 1963
Dream Song 14	February 28, 1963
Dream Song 64	May 7, 1963
Dream Song 6: "A Capital at Wells"	May 7, 1963
Dream Song 105	May 7, 1963
Dream Song 22: "Of 1826"	May 7, 1963
Dream Song 3: "A Stimulant for an Old Beast"	May 7, 1963
Dream Song 69	May 7, 1963

Dream Song ["Baby Teddy, baby did-he, drop him too a pat"]	May 7, 1963
Dream Song 68	May 7, 1963
Dream Song 98	May 7, 1963
Dream Song 34	May 7, 1963
Dream Song ["Statesmanlike (on a Queer prowl, after dark)"]	May 7, 1963
Dream Song 13	May 7, 1963
Dream Song 9	May 7, 1963
Dream Song 58	May 7, 1963
Dream Song 74	May 7, 1963
Dream Song 40	June 1, 1963
Dream Song 55	June 1, 1963
*"Spender: The Poet as Critic"	June 22, 1963
Dream Song 18: "A Strut for Roethke"	August 23, 1963
Dream Song 37: "Three around the Old Gentleman"	August 29, 1963
Dream Song 38	August 29, 1963
Dream Song 39	August 29, 1963
*"Auden's Prose"	August 29, 1963
Dream Song 50	October 21, 1963
Dream Song 28: "Snow Line"	October 21, 1963
Dream Song 31	October 21, 1963
Dream Song 21	October 21, 1963
Dream Song 44	October 21, 1963
Dream Song 66	October 21, 1963
Dream Song 56	October 21, 1963
Dream Song 48	October 21, 1963
Dream Song 45	October 21, 1963
Dream Song 57	January 10, 1964
Dream Song 217	January 10, 1964
Dream Song 11	January 10, 1964
77 Dream Songs	April 27, 1964
Dream Song 93	May 20, 1964
"Henry's Pencils"	May 20, 1964
Dream Song 97	May 20, 1964
"Formal Elegy"	November 6, 1964
Dream Song 95	January 20, 1965
*Letter to the editor of The Minnesota Daily	April 25, 1965
"Idyl II"	June 27, 1965
*"Stephen Crane: The Red Badge of Courage"	July 30, 1965
*"Afterword" to The Titan	October 20, 1965

A Chronology of Publication of Works by Berryman   257

*"A Tribute [to Ezra Pound]"	October 30, 1965
Dream Song 224: "Eighty"	November 25, 1965
Dream Song 180: "The Translator—I"	November 25, 1965
Dream Song 181: "The Translator—II"	November 25, 1965
Dream Song 385	November 25, 1965
*"One Answer to a Question"	December 13, 1965
Two Dream Songs	ca. December 1965
*"Hardy: The Darkling Thrush"	January 17, 1966
*"Ransom: Captain Carpenter"	January 17, 1966
Dream Song 168: "The Old Poor"	October 3, 1966
Dream Song 78: "Op. posth. no. 1"	December 1, 1966
Dream Song 79: "Op. posth. no. 2"	December 1, 1966
Dream Song 84: "Op. posth. no. 7"	December 1, 1966
Dream Song 85: "Op. posth. no. 8"	December 1, 1966
Dream Song 86: "Op. posth. no. 9"	December 1, 1966
Dream Song 87: "Op. posth. no. 10"	December 1, 1966
Dream Song 88: "Op. posth. no. 11"	December 1, 1966
Dream Song 89: "Op. posth. no. 12"	December 1, 1966
Dream Song 90: "Op. posth. no. 13"	December 1, 1966
Dream Song 80: "Op. posth. no. 3"	December 8, 1966
Dream Song 81: "Op. posth. no. 4"	December 8, 1966
Dream Song 82: "Op. posth. no. 5"	December 8, 1966
Dream Song 83: "Op. posth. no. 6"	December 8, 1966
Sonnet 23	March 30, 1967
Sonnet 71	March 30, 1967
Sonnet 103	March 30, 1967
Berryman's Sonnets	April 24, 1967
Poetry Season 1967	June 19, 1967
*"Randall Jarrell"	August 28, 1967
Short Poems	December 1, 1967
Dream Song 265	January 11, 1968
Dream Song 187	January 11, 1968
Dream Song 258	January 11, 1968
Dream Song 161	January 11, 1968
Dream Song 204	January 30, 1968
Dream Song 210	January 30, 1968
Dream Song 209	January 30, 1968
Dream Song 233: "Cantatrice"	April 22, 1968
Dream Song 219: "So Long? Stevens"	April 22, 1968
Dream Song 200	April 22, 1968
Dream Song 194	May 18, 1968
Dream Song ["Now that my one are out, I indulge my rage,"]	May 18, 1968

Dream Song 199	May 18, 1968
Dream Song 147	June 26, 1968
Dream Song 148: "Glimmerings"	June 26, 1968
Dream Song 150	June 26, 1968
Dream Song 151	June 26, 1968
Dream Song 152	June 26, 1968
Dream Song 153	June 26, 1968
Dream Song 154	June 26, 1968
Dream Song 155	June 26, 1968
Dream Song 156	June 26, 1968
Dream Song 157	June 26, 1968
Dream Song 384	June 26, 1968
Dream Song 167: "Henry's Mail"	July 2, 1968
Dream Song 171	July 2, 1968
Dream Song 191	July 2, 1968
Dream Song 264	July 2, 1968
Dream Song 172	July 2, 1968
Dream Song 298	July 2, 1968
Dream Song 170	July 29, 1968
Dream Song 201	July 29, 1968
Dream Song 165	July 29, 1968
Dream Song 186	July 29, 1968
His Toy, His Dream, His Rest	October 25, 1968
*National Book Award for Poetry 1969 Acceptance Speech	March 12, 1969
*"Three and a Half Years at Columbia"	April 4, 1969
"Henry's Understanding"	April 9, 1969
"Henry by Night"	April 9, 1969
"Apollo 8"	April 9, 1969
The Dream Songs	December 5, 1969
Two Dream Songs	ca. December 1969
"Her & It"	July 16, 1970
"The Heroes"	July 16, 1970
"The Other Cambridge"	July 16, 1970
"Meeting"	July 16, 1970
"Tea"	July 16, 1970
"Heaven"	July 16, 1970
"Antitheses"	July 17, 1970
"The Minnesota 8 and the Letter-Writers"	July 21, 1970
"Death Ballad"	July 22, 1970
"Revival"	August 3, 1970
"Monkhood"	August 3, 1970
"Friendless"	August 3, 1970
"Drunks"	August 3, 1970

A Chronology of Publication of Works by Berryman

"Eleven Addresses to the Lord: 11"	September 10, 1970
"To B ‒ ‒ E ‒ ‒"	September 15, 1970
"The Search"	September 15, 1970
*Letter to Whit Burnett	September 18, 1970
"Eleven Addresses to the Lord: 1"	September 22, 1970
"Eleven Addresses to the Lord: 2"	September 22, 1970
"Eleven Addresses to the Lord: 3"	September 22, 1970
"Eleven Addresses to the Lord: 4"	September 22, 1970
"Eleven Addresses to the Lord: 5"	September 22, 1970
"A Prayer for the Self"	September 25, 1970
"To a Woman"	October 1, 1970
"The American Hero"	October 1, 1970
"Down & Back"	October 3, 1970
"The Hell Poem"	October 20, 1970
"Olympus"	October 20, 1970
"The Soviet Union"	October 21, 1970
"First Night at Sea"	November 1, 1970
"Transit"	November 1, 1970
"Nowhere"	November 1, 1970
*Letter to the editors of *The Nation*	November 25, 1970
Love & Fame	December 14, 1970
Two Poems	ca. December 1970
"Alas"	January 6, 1971
"Navajo Setting the Record Straight"	January 6, 1971
"Washington in Love"	March 11, 1971
"Tampa Stomp"	March 11, 1971
"Ecce Homo"	April 7, 1971
"The Form"	April 13, 1971
"Henry North"	September 15, 1971
*"Afterword" to *Love & Fame*	November 22, 1971
"King David Dances"	February 16, 1972
"Gislebertus' Eve"	March 21, 1972
"Vespers"	March 21, 1972
"Lines to Mr Frost"	March 21, 1972
"Minnesota Thanksgiving"	March 21, 1972
"Beethoven Triumphant"	March 30, 1972
Delusions, Etc.	April 28, 1972
Selected Poems 1938–1968	May 1, 1972
*"Scholia to Second Edition" of *Love & Fame*	November 15, 1972
**Recovery*	May 25, 1973
*"Our Sins Are More Than We Can Bear"	September 26, 1973
"Surveillance"	March 6, 1974

Appendix 2

Periodicals in Which Material by Berryman First Appeared

Academy, VI (Winter 1971). University of Minnesota.
Accent, I (Winter 1941).
Agenda, IV (October–November 1965); IV (Summer 1966).
American Letters, I (December 1948).
The American Scholar, XXVIII (Summer 1959); XXIX (Autumn 1970).
Antaeus, no. 1 (summer 1970).
The Atlantic, CCXXI (February 1968); CCXXVI (November 1970).
Audience, pilot issue (Spring 1968).
Café Solo, no. 3 (Spring 1971).
Chimera, I (Winter 1943); III (Summer 1945).
The Columbia Review, XVI (March 1935); XVI (April 1935); XVI (May 1935); XVII (November 1935); XVII (December 1935); XVII (April 1936); XVII (June 1936). Columbia University.
Commentary, XX (November 1956).
The Commonweal, XLVIII (May 7, 1948); XCII (September 18, 1970).
Encounter, XIX (October 1962).
Esquire, LXXV (April 1971); LXXV (May 1971).
Harper's Magazine, CCXXVI (March 1963); CCXXXVI (February 1968); CCXLI (October 1970).
The Harvard Advocate, CIII (Spring 1969).
The Hudson Review, VI (Summer 1953).
Intellectual Digest, II (April 1972).
Ivory Tower, XIV (October 3, 1966). University of Minnesota.
The Kenyon Review, I (Summer 1939); II (Autumn 1940); III (Spring 1941); III (Summer 1941); VII (Winter 1945); VII (Autumn 1945); VIII (Winter 1946); X (Spring 1948); XXVI (Winter 1964).
Mademoiselle, LXIV (April 1967).
The Minneapolis Tribune, June 27, 1965; July 21, 1970.
The Minnesota Daily, April 25, 1965. University of Minnesota.
The Minnesota Review, III (Winter 1963).
Mundus Artium, I (Spring 1968).

The Nation, CXLI (July 10, 1935); CXLI (November 27, 1935); CXLIII (August 29, 1936); CIL (December 30, 1939); CLIV (May 16, 1942); CLVII (August 21, 1943); CLXIII (December 21, 1946); CLXIV (June 28, 1947); CLXIX (December 17, 1949); CXCVIII (May 25, 1964); CCXI (October 26, 1970); CCXI (November 30, 1970).
New American Review, no. 3 (April 1968).
The New Republic, IC (June 28, 1939); CIII (July 8, 1940); CXXIX (November 2, 1953); CXLVII (November 17, 1962); CXLVIII (January 19, 1963); CXLVIII (June 29, 1963); CLXIII (July 25, 1970).
The New Yorker, XXXIV (August 2, 1958); XXXIV (August 16, 1958); XLVI (July 25, 1970); XLVII (April 10, 1971); XLVII (February 19, 1972).
New York Herald Tribune Books, December 11, 1938; January 8, 1939; October 1, 1939; October 12, 1947.
The New York Review of Books, I (August 29, 1963); I (October 17, 1963); VII (December 15, 1966); XV (October 8, 1970); XVIII (April 1972).
The New York Times Book Review, March 4, 1951; December 6, 1953.
The Noble Savage, no. 1 (March 1960); no. 3 (May 1961).
The Observer, June 3, 1962; December 22, 1963. London.
The Ohio Review, XV (Winter 1974).
Partisan Review, VI (Summer 1939); XIII (Summer 1946); XIV (January–February 1947); XV (February 1948); XV (March 1948); XV (April 1948); XV (May 1948); XV (July 1948); XV (August 1948); XVI (April 1949); XX (September–October 1953); XXIII (Fall 1956); XXV (Spring 1958); XXIX (Fall 1962).
Poetry, LXXII (April 1948); LXXV (January 1950); LXXIX (October 1951); LXXXI (October 1952); LXXXVIII (April 1956); CI (October 1962); CIII (October–November 1963).
Poetry Northwest, III (Winter 1962–1963).
Ramparts, II (May 1963).
Saturday Review, LIII (September 26, 1970).
The Sewanee Review, LI (Summer 1943); LIII (Spring 1945); LV (Winter 1947); LV (Summer 1947).
Shenandoah, XVII (Autumn 1956); XXI (Summer 1970).
The Southern Review, IV (Summer 1938); V (Spring 1940).
Stand, XI (Fall 1970).
The Times Literary Supplement, November 6, 1959; August 23, 1963; November 25, 1965; December 1, 1966; July 16, 1970.

TriQuarterly, XII (Spring 1968).
Twentieth Century Verse, nos. 12-13 (September–October 1938).
The Twin Cities Express, I (September 26, 1973).
The Virginia Quarterly Review, XXXIII (Autumn 1957); XLIV (Summer 1968).
The Yale Review, LII (Summer 1963).

Index

Abbe, George, C 268
Abbott, Allan, B 2
Academy, C 223, C 224, App. 2
Accent, C 32, App. 2
Accent Anthology: reprinting in, C 32
Adam and Charles Black Ltd., BB 6
"Additional Bibliography" in *Stephen Crane,* A 6.1.c, B 18
The Adventures of Augie March: review of, C 267
A.E. [George William Russell], C 240
After Experience: blurb for, G 2
"Afterword" in *L&F,* A 20.2.a
"Afterword" in *The Titan,* B 24, App. 1
Agenda, C 133, C 275, App. 2
"Alas," C 223, App. 1
"Alteration": comment and questions on, A 5
The Amazing Year: review of, C 258
American Book-Stratford Press, A 11.1.a, A 16.1.a
"The American Hero," C 215, App. 1
American Letters, C 54, App. 1
"American Lights, Seen From Off Abroad," A 8, A 15, C 68, F 3, App. 1
"American Lights, Seen Off From Abroad," C 68. *See also* "American Lights Seen From Off Abroad"
The American Men of Letters Series, A 6
The American Novel, B 22

American Poetry, ed. Donald Hall: reprintings in, C 87, C 117
American Poetry, ed. Gay Wilson Allen et al.: reprintings in, C 31, C 35, C 47, C 114–C 116
American Poetry, ed. Karl Shapiro: reprinting in, C 65
The American Scholar, C 216, C 270, App. 2
"Amos," A 22
"Ancestor," A 4, A 9, A 15, C 37, F 2, App. 1
"The Ancestor," C 13, App. 1
Anchor in the Sea: reprinting in, C 251
Andrade, Jorge Carrera, C 254
"The Animal Trainer 1" and "2," A 4, A 9, A 15, B 8, App. 1
"The Animal Trainer I" and "II," B 8. *See also* "Animal Trainer 1" and "2"
Another Animal: review of, C 268
"Another Dream Song," C 91. *See also* Dream Song 4
"Another New Year's Eve," A 21, D 1
Antaeus, C 191, C 220–C 222, App. 1
"Antitheses," A 20, C 198, App. 1
"Antithesis," C 198. *See also* "Antitheses"
"Anyway," A 20.2.a. *See also* "Away"
"A Peine Ma Piste," C 260, App. 1
Applause Productions, F 11
"Apollo 8," C 191, App. 1
"Apostrophe," C 5, App. 1

"The Apparition," A 1, C 17, App. 1
Appleton, Sarah, G 3
"April Fool's Day, or, St Mary of Egypt." *See* Dream Song 47
"Araby": questions on, A 10
"The Armada Song." *See* Dream Song 361
"Ars Poetica," B 1, C 2, App. 1
"The Art of Poetry XVI: John Berryman 1914-72," E 18
The Arts of Reading, A 10, App. 1
"At Chinese Checkers," A 2, A 4, A 15, C 33, App. 1
The Atlantic, C 155-C 158, C 217, C 218, App. 2
Auden, W. H., C 238, C 273
"Auden's Prose," C 273, App. 1
Audience, C 179-C 184, App. 2
Auslander, Joseph, B 1, B 2, C 237
"Autumn Miscellany – Seven Poems Selected by John Berryman," H 1
"Away," A 20
A. W. Bain and Company Ltd., A 11.1.b
Ayrton, Michael, B 17

Babel, Isaak, A 10
"Back," A 22
"The Ball Poem," A 3, A 4, A 9, A 15, A 23, D 2, F 2, F 3, F 5, F 6, F 8
Barnard, Mary, A 1
Basic Books, Inc., B 21, B 22, B 26
Beach Glass and Other Poems: reprinting in, C 31
"Beethoven Triumphant," A 22, C 235, App. 1
"Before the Law": questions on, A 10
"Beginning Ultimate Treatment," A 20.1.a†
Bellow, Saul, A 24.1.a, C 7/*n*, C 267
Benét, William Rose, B 2
Berg, Martin, E 16
"Berryman and Tate: Poets Extraordinaire," E 9

"Berryman Ends Poem of 13 Years," E 11
"Berryman Gets $10,000 Award," E 10
Berryman's Sonnets, A 13, C 64, C 152-C 154, D 41-D 43, App. 1
Berthiaume, Tom, A 22.1.a, A 24.1.a
The Best American Short Stories of 1946: reprinting in, C 249
"Big Buttons, Cornets: the advance." *See* Dream Song 2
Birds in the Mulberry: review of, C 268
"Blake," C 3, App. 1
"Blind." *See* Dream Song 49
Book Printers, Inc., A 18.1.a
"Boston Common," A 4, A 9, A 15, B 7, F 2, App. 1
The Bowering Press, A 20.2.a
Breton, Andre, C 254
Brewster, William T., B 1
Brickell, Herschel, B 11
Brooks, Cleanth, C 255
Brown, Francis, B 15
Brucker, Herbert, B 2
Burnett, Whit, B 29

Cabell, Branch, C 239
"Cadenza on Garnette," A 20, F 7
Café Solo, C 229, App. 2
"The Cage," C 55, App. 1
C. & J. Kitkat, Ltd., A 20.2.a
"Cantatrice." *See* Dream Song 233
"Canto Amor," A 4, A 9, A 15, A 23, C 42, F 2, F 8, App. 1
"The Captain's Song," A 4, A 9, A 15
"A Capital at Wells." *See* Dream Song 6
"Caravan," A 1, A 4, A 15, B 3, App. 1
"The Carpenter's Son." *See* Dream Song 234
Carruth, Hayden, A 2*n*, C 277
"The Case of Ring Lardner," C 269, App. 1
Cattell, Jaques, BB 2

Index

"Cattle the Meadows Spread": commentary on, A 5
"Ceremony and Vision," A 1, B 4, App. 1
"Certainty Before Lunch," A 22
"Changes," B 26, C 276, App. 1
A Character Invented: review of, C 268
Chekhov, Anton, A 10
Chicago Daily News, E 17
Chimera, C 35, C 38, App. 2
Chisholm, Hugh, C 258
Christman, Henry M., B 23
"Christmas, 1963," C 164. *See also* Dream Song 200
"Christ-Song: Carpenter's Son." *See* Dream Song 234
Ciardi, John, C 258
Claudel, Paul, B 16
"A Clean, Well-Lighted Place": commentary on, A 10
"Cloud and Flame," A 4, A 9, A 15, C 35, App. 1
Clyne, Ronald, A 15.1.a
Colby, Vinetta, BB 1
The Collected Poems of Laura Riding: review of, C 243
The Collected Poems of Sidney Keyes: review of, C 256
A College Book of Verse: reprinting in, C 50
Collier-Macmillan Limited, B 23
Columbia Poetry 1935, B 1, C 2, C 7
Columbia Poetry 1936, B 2, C 8, C 11
The Columbia Review, C 1–C 6, C 8–C 14, C 236–C 238, C 240, C 241, App. 2
Columbia University Press, B 1, B 2
"Columbus Day," C 84. *See also* Dream Song 216
"Combat Assignment." *See* Dream Song 138
Commentary, C 269, App. 2
The Commonweal, C 53, C 205, App. 2
"Communist," A 2, B 6, App. 1

The Complete Reader: reprinting in, C 95
"Compline," A 22
"Concerning Less of the Sea": commentary on, A 5
Contemporary American Poetry: reprintings in, C 71, C 79, C 81, C 85, C 91, C 95, C 107, C 108, C 112, C 125, C 137, C 178, C 183, C 185, D 11, D 14, D 16, D 22, D 25, D 26
The Contemporary American Poets: reprintings in, C 42, C 111, D 2, D 8, D 33, D 40
The Contemporary Poet as Artist and Critic: reprinting in, D 47
Contemporary Poetry in America: reprintings in, C 31, C 54, D 36, D 37
"Conversation," A 1, A 4, A 15, B 5, B 9, C 27, App. 1
"Conversation with Berryman," E 15
Corbière, Tristan, C 257
"Courier": questions on, A 10
Crane, Stephen, A 5, A 10, D 45
Crane Duplicating Service, Inc., A 16.1.a†, A 20.1.a†, A 24.1.a†
The Creative Reader: reprinting in, C 31
Crews, J. C., A 5
"Crisis," A 20, D 3
The Criterion Book of Modern American Poetry: reprinting in, C 65
A Critical Study of English Poetry: review of, C 253
A Critical Supplement to Poetry, A 5, App. 1, App. 2
Critics on Ezra Pound, B 30, C 262
Cry Cadences: review of, C 258
Cummings, E. E., C 270
"The Curse," A 1, B 4, App. 1

Dale, Nancy, A 10.1.a
"Damned," A 20

"Damn You, Jim D., You Woke
    Me Up," A 22
"The Dangerous Year," A 2, B 6,
    App. 1
"Dante's Tomb," A 20, D 4
Davidson, Donald, C 244
"Death Ballad," A 20, C 200,
    App. 1
"Defensio in Extremis," A 22
De la Mare, Walter, A 10
Delusions, Etc., A 22, C 189,
    C 190, C 224–C 228,
    C 230–C 235, D 29, D 31,
    D 32, App. 1
"Desire Is a World by Night,"
    A 4, A 9, A 15
"Desires of Men and Women,"
    A 1, A 4, A 9, A 15, A 23, B 5,
    C 26, F 2, App. 1
"Despair," A 20
"Despondency and Madness,"
    B 20, D 47, App. 1
The Detroit Collegian, E 1
"The Dialogue, aet. 51." *See*
    Dream Song 341
Dial Press, B 19
Directory of American Scholars,
    BB 2
"The Disciple," A 1, A 4, A 9, A 15,
    B 7, C 25, F 2, App. 1
"The Dispossessed," A 4, A 9,
    A 15, A 23, B 19, C 47, F 2,
    F 3, App. 1; comment on,
    B 19, App. 1
The Dispossessed, A 4, A 15, A 23,
    B 3–B 8, B 19, C 20, C 22–
    C 27, C 31–C 53, D 2, D 33,
    D 35–D 37, D 39, D 40, App. 1
The Dog Beneath the Skin: review
    of, C 238
The Dolmen Press Limited, A 14
"Donnybrook," C 131. *See also*
    Dream Song 97
D[oolittle], H[ilda], C 254
Dorati, Antal, B 16
Doubleday and Company, Inc.,
    B 11, B 28, B 29, G 3
"Down & Back," A 20, C 216,
    App. 1

"Down and Back," A 20.1.a†.
    See "Down and Back"
"Dream Song," C 132. *See also*
    Dream Song 95
Dream Song ["Baby Teddy, baby
    did-he, drop him too a pat"],
    C 102, F 5, App. 1
Dream Song ["The jolly old man
    is a silly old dumb,"], C 76,
    App. 1
Dream Song ["Now that my one
    are out, I indulge my rage,"],
    C 166, App. 1
Dream Song ["Statesmanlike
    (on a Queer prowl, after
    dark)"], C 106, App. 1
"A Dream Song," C 90, C 94,
    C 95. *See also* Dream Songs
    14, 41, 51
Dream Song 1: A 11, A 18, A 23,
    B 29, C 71, F 5–F 7, F 11,
    App. 1
Dream Song 2: A 11, A 18
Dream Song 3: A 11, A 18, C 100,
    F 5, App. 1
Dream Song 4: A 11, A 18, A 23,
    BB 4, C 91, F 4, F 5, F 7, F 10,
    App. 1
Dream Song 5: A 8, A 11, A 18,
    A 23, C 72, F 5, F 11, App. 1
Dream Song 6: A 11, A 18, A 23,
    C 97, App. 1
Dream Song 7: A 11, A 18, C 92,
    App. 1
Dream Song 8: A 11, A 18, C 85,
    F 11, App. 1
Dream Song 9: A 11, A 18, C 108,
    App. 1
Dream Song 10: A 11, A 18
Dream Song 11: A 11, A 18, C 128,
    App. 1
Dream Song 12: A 11, A 18, C 78,
    App. 1
Dream Song 13: A 11, A 18, C 107,
    App. 1
Dream Song 14: A 11, A 18, A 23,
    C 95, F 6, F 7, F 11, App. 1
Dream Song 15: A 11, A 18,
    D 5

Index

Dream Song 16: A 11, A 18, A 23, BB 4, C 87, F 4, F 6, F 7, F 10, F 11, App. 1
Dream Song 17: A 11, A 18, C 82, F 6, F 7, F 11, App. 1
Dream Song 18: A 11, A 18, C 113, App. 1
Dream Song 19: A 11, A 18
Dream Song 20: A 11, A 18, C 83, App. 1
Dream Song 21: A 11, A 18, C 120, F 5, App. 1
Dream Song 22: A 11, A 18, A 23, BB4, C 99, F 4, F 5, F 10, App. 1
Dream Song 23: A 11, A 18, F 4, F 5
Dream Songs 24, 25: A 11, A 18
Dream Song 26: A 11, A 18, A 23, D 6, App. 1
Dream Song 27: A 11, A 18, A 23, C 86, F 4, F 5, App. 1
Dream Song 28: A 11, A 18, C 118, App. 1
Dream Song 29: A 11, A 18, A 23, B 29, BB 4, C 81, F 4–F 6, F 10, App. 1
Dream Song 30: A 11, A 18
Dream Song 31: A 11, A 18, A 23, C 119, App. 1
Dream Songs 32, 33: A 11, A 18
Dream Song 34: A 11, A 18, A 23, C 105, App. 1
Dream Song 35: A 11, A 18
Dream Song 36: A 11, A 18, A 23, C 88, App. 1
Dream Song 37: A 11, A 18, A 23, C 114, App. 1
Dream Song 38: A 11, A 18, C 115, App. 1
Dream Song 39: A 11, A 18, C 116, App. 1
Dream Song 40: A 11, A 18, C 111, App. 1
Dream Song 41: A 11, A 18, C 94, App. 1
Dream Song 42: A 11, A 18, A 23
Dream Song 43: A 11, A 18
Dream Song 44: A 11, A 18, C 121, App. 1
Dream Song 45: A 11, A 18, A 23, C 125, F 6, App. 1
Dream Song 46: A 11, A 18, A 23, C 79, App. 1
Dream Song 47: A 11, A 18, A 23, D 7
Dream Song 48: A 11, A 18, A 23, C 124, App. 1
Dream Song 49: A 11, A 18, A 23
Dream Song 50: A 11, A 18, C 117, App. 1
Dream Song 51: A 11, A 18, A 23, C 90, App. 1
Dream Song 52: A 11, A 18, A 23, C 93, App. 1
Dream Song 53: A 11, A 18, A 23, C 80, F 5, App. 1
Dream Song 54: A 11, A 18, A 23, C 77, App. 1
Dream Song 55: A 11, A 18, A 23, C 112, App. 1
Dream Song 56: A 11, A 18, C 123, App. 1
Dream Song 57: A 11, A 18, C 126, App. 1
Dream Song 58: A 11, A 18, C 109, App. 1
Dream Songs 59, 60: A 11, A 18
Dream Song 61: A 11, A 18, D 8
Dream Song 62: A 11, A 18, D 9
Dream Song 63: A 11, A 18
Dream Song 64: A 11, A 18, C 96, App. 1
Dream Song 65: A 11, A 18
Dream Song 66: A 11, A 18, A 23, C 122, App. 1
Dream Song 67: A 11, A 18, A 23, C 74, F 6, App. 1
Dream Song 68: A 11, A 18, C 103, App. 1
Dream Song 69: A 11, A 18, A 23, C 101, F 6, App. 1
Dream Song 70: A 11, A 18
Dream Song 71: A 11, A 18, A 23, C 89, F 5, App. 1
Dream Songs 72, 73: A 11, A 18
Dream Song 74: A 11, A 18, A 23, C 110, App. 1

Dream Song 75: A 11, A 18, A 23,
  BB 4, C 73, F 4–F 6, F 10,
  App. 1
Dream Song 76: A 11, A 18, A 23,
  D 10, F 7
Dream Song 77: A 11, A 18, A 23,
  B 29, C 75, F 6, F 7, F 11,
  App. 1
Dream Song 78: A 16, A 18, A 23,
  C 139, F 6, App. 1
Dream Song 79: A 16, A 18, C 140,
  App. 1
Dream Song 80: A 16, A 18, C 148,
  App. 1
Dream Song 81: A 16, A 18, C 149,
  App. 1
Dream Song 82: A 16, A 18, C 150,
  App. 1
Dream Song 83: A 16, A 18, C 151,
  App. 1
Dream Song 84: A 16, A 18, A 23,
  C 141, App. 1
Dream Song 85: A 16, A 18, C 142,
  App. 1
Dream Song 86: A 16, A 18, A 23,
  C 143, F 6, App. 1
Dream Song 87: A 16, A 18, A 23,
  C 144, F 6, App. 1
Dream Song 88: A 16, A 18, A 23,
  C 145, App. 1
Dream Song 89: A 16, A 18, A 23,
  B 29, C 146, App. 1
Dream Song 90: A 16, A 18, A 23,
  C 147, F 6, App. 1. *See also* "Op.
  posth. no. 13"
Dream Song 91: A 16, A 18, A 23,
  D 11
Dream Song 92: A 16, A 18, A 23
Dream Song 93: A 16, A 18, B 23,
  C 129, App. 1
Dream Song 94: A 16, A 18
Dream Song 95: A 16, A 18, C 132,
  App. 1
Dream Song 96: A 16, A 18
Dream Song 97: A 16, A 18, B 23,
  C 131, App. 1
Dream Song 98: A 16, A 18, C 104,
  App. 1
Dream Song 99: A 16, A 18, A 23

Dream Songs 100–104: A 16, A 18
Dream Song 105: A 16, A 18, C 98,
  App. 1
Dream Songs 106, 107: A 16, A 18
Dream Song 108: A 16, A 18, A 23
Dream Songs 109–112: A 16, A 18
Dream Song 113: A 16, A 18, F 6
Dream Songs 114–117: A 16, A 18
Dream Song 118: A 16, A 18, A 23
Dream Songs 119–131: A 16, A 18
Dream Song 132: A 16, A 18, A 23
Dream Songs 133–141: A 16, A 18
Dream Song 142: A 16, A 18, A 23
Dream Songs 143, 144: A 16, A 18
Dream Songs 145, 146: A 16,
  A 18, A 23
Dream Song 147: A 16, A 18, A 23,
  C 168, App. 1
Dream Song 148: A 16, A 18,
  C 169, App. 1
Dream Song 149: A 16, A 18, D 12
Dream Song 150: A 16, A 18,
  C 170, App. 1
Dream Song 151: A 16, A 18,
  C 171, App. 1
Dream Song 152: A 16, A 18,
  C 172, App. 1
Dream Song 153: A 16, A 18, A 23,
  C 173, App. 1
Dream Song 154: A 16, A 18, A 23,
  C 174, App. 1
Dream Song 155: A 16, A 18, A 23,
  C 175, App. 1
Dream Song 156: A 16, A 18, A 23,
  C 176, App. 1
Dream Song 157: A 16, A 18,
  C 177, App. 1
Dream Songs 158–160: A 16, A 18
Dream Song 161: A 16, A 18,
  C 158, App. 1
Dream Songs 162–164: A 16, A 18
Dream Song 165: A 16, A 18,
  C 187, App. 1
Dream Song 166: A 16, A 18, A 23
Dream Song 167: A 16, A 18,
  C 179, App. 1
Dream Song 168: A 16, A 18, A 23,
  C 138, App. 1
Dream Song 169: A 16, A 18

Index

Dream Song 170: A 16, A 18, C 185, App. 1
Dream Song 171: A 16, A 18, A 23, C 180, F 6, App. 1
Dream Song 172: A 16, A 18, A 23, C 183, F 6, App. 1
Dream Song 173: A 16, A 18, A 23
Dream Songs 174-179: A 16, A 18
Dream Song 180: A 16, A 18, C 135, App. 1
Dream Song 181: A 16, A 18, C 136, App. 1
Dream Songs 182, 183: A 16, A 18
Dream Song 184: A 16, A 18, A 23
Dream Song 185: A 16, A 18, D 13
Dream Song 186: A 16, A 18, A 23, C 188, App. 1
Dream Song 187: A 16, A 18, C 156, F 6, App. 1
Dream Songs 188-190: A 16, A 18
Dream Song 191: A 16, A 18, C 181, App. 1
Dream Songs 192, 193: A 16, A 18
Dream Song 194: A 16, A 18, C 165, App. 1
Dream Song 195: A 16, A 18, A 23
Dream Songs 196-198: A 16, A 18
Dream Song 199: A 16, A 18, C 167, App. 1
Dream Song 200: A 16, A 18, C 164, App. 1
Dream Song 201: A 16, A 18, A 23, C 186, App. 1
Dream Songs 202, 203: A 16, A 18
Dream Song 204: A 16, A 18, C 159, App. 1
Dream Songs 205-208: A 16, A 18
Dream Song 209: A 16, A 18, C 161, App. 1
Dream Song 210: A 16, A 18, C 160, App. 1
Dream Songs 211-215: A 16, A 18
Dream Song 216: A 16, A 18, C 84, App. 1
Dream Song 217: A 16, A 18, C 127, App. 1
Dream Song 218: A 16, A 18
Dream Song 219: A 16, A 18, C 163, App. 1
Dream Songs 220-222: A 16, A 18
Dream Song 223: A 16, A 18, A 23
Dream Song 224: A 16, A 18, C 134, F 6, App. 1
Dream Songs 225-229: A 16, A 18
Dream Song 230: A 16, A 18, D 14
Dream Songs 231, 232: A 16, A 18
Dream Song 233: A 16, A 18, A 23, C 162, App. 1
Dream Song 234: A 12, A 16, A 18
Dream Songs 235-238: A 16, A 18
Dream Song 239: A 16, A 18, A 23
Dream Songs 240-257: A 16, A 18
Dream Song 258: A 16, A 18, C 157, App. 1
Dream Songs 259-262: A 16, A 18
Dream Song 263: A 16, A 18, D 15
Dream Song 264: A 16, A 18, C 182, App. 1
Dream Song 265: A 16, A 18, C 155, App. 1
Dream Song 266: A 16, A 18, D 16
Dream Songs 267-278: A 16, A 18
Dream Songs 279, 280: A 16, A 18, A 23
Dream Song 281: A 16, A 18
Dream Songs 282, 283: A 16, A 18, A 23
Dream Songs 284-287: A 16, A 18
Dream Songs 288, 289: A 16, A 18, A 23
Dream Songs 290-297: A 16, A 18
Dream Song 298: A 16, A 18, C 184, App. 1
Dream Songs 299, 300: A 16, A 18
Dream Songs 301, 302: A 16, A 18, A 23
Dream Songs 303, 304: A 16, A 18
Dream Song 305: A 16, A 18, A 23
Dream Songs 306-311: A 16, A 18
Dream Song 312: A 14, A 16, A 18, A 23, D 17
Dream Songs 313, 314: A 16, A 18
Dream Song 315: A 16, A 18, A 23, D 18
Dream Song 316: A 16, A 18, A 23
Dream Songs 317, 318: A 16, A 18
Dream Song 319: A 16, A 18, D 19

Dream Song 320: A 16, A 18
Dream Song 321: A 16, A 18, A 23
Dream Songs 322, 323: A 16, A 18
Dream Songs 324, 325: A 16, A 18, A 23
Dream Songs 326–331: A 16, A 18
Dream Song 332: A 16, A 18, A 23
Dream Song 333: A 16, A 18
Dream Song 334: A 16, A 18, A 23
Dream Songs 335, 336: A 16, A 18
Dream Songs 337, 338: A 16, A 18, A 23
Dream Songs 339–341: A 16, A 18
Dream Song 342: A 16, A 18, A 23
Dream Song 343: A 16, A 18
Dream Song 344: A 16, A 18, D 20
Dream Songs 345–350: A 16, A 18
Dream Song 351: A 16, A 18, D 21
Dream Song 352: A 16, A 18
Dream Song 353: A 16, A 18, D 22
Dream Songs 354–356: A 16, A 18
Dream Song 357: A 16, A 18, A 23
Dream Songs 358–360: A 16, A 18
Dream Song 361: A 16, A 18, A 23
Dream Songs 362–365: A 16, A 18
Dream Songs 366, 367: A 16, A 18, A 23
Dream Songs 368, 369: A 16, A 18
Dream Song 370: A 16, A 18, A 23
Dream Song 371: A 16, A 18, A 23, D 23
Dream Song 372: A 16, A 18, A 23
Dream Songs 373, 374: A 16, A 18
Dream Song 375: A 16, A 18, D 24
Dream Songs 376–378: A 16, A 18
Dream Song 379: A 16, A 18, A 23
Dream Song 380: A 16, A 18, A 23, D 25
Dream Song 381: A 16, A 18, F 6
Dream Song 382: A 16, A 18, A 23, B 29, D 26, F 6, F 7
Dream Song 383: A 16, A 18
Dream Song 384: A 16, A 18, A 23, B 29, C 179, F 6, App. 1
Dream Song 385: A 12, A 16, A 18, A 23, B 29, C 137, F 6, App. 1
The Dream Songs, A 18, App. 1. See also *77 Dream Songs* and *His Toy, His Dream, His Rest*
Dreiser, Theodore, B 15, B 24, C 264
"Drugs Alcohol Little Sister," A 22
"Drunks," A 20, C 204, App. 1
Duncan, Harry, C 268
Duncan, Robert, C 258
The Dyer's Hand: review of, C 273

Eaglin, Kay, A 9.1.c
"E. A. Robinson, and Others," C 240
Earth, Air, Fire & Water: reprinting in, C 95
The Earth-Bound: review of, C 254
"Ecce Homo," A 22, C 227, App. 1
The Editorial Problem in Shakespeare: review of, C 248
Edman, Irwin, B 1
The Ego and the Centaur: review of, C 258
"Eighty." See Dream Song 224
"The Elder Presences." See Dream Song 72
"Elegy, for Alun Lewis," C 56, App. 1
"An Elegy for W.C.W., the lovely man." See Dream Song 324
"Elegy: Hart Crane," B 2, C 8, App. 1
"Eleven Addresses to the Lord: A Prayer for the Self," A 20, C 213, App. 1
"Eleven Addresses to the Lord: "1," "2," "3," "4," and "5": A 20, C 208–C 212, App. 1
"Eleven Addresses to the Lord: 6" and "7": A 20
"Eleven Addresses to the Lord: 8," A 20.1.a†. See "Eleven Addresses to the Lord: A Prayer for the Self"
"Eleven Addresses to the Lord: 9" and "10": A 20
"Eleven Addresses to the Lord: 11": A 20, C 205, App. 1
E. L. Hildreth and Company, A 2*n*

Index

Eliot, T. S., A 10, C 260
Encounter, C 84, C 85, App. 2
"The Enemies of the Angels," A 4, A 9, A 15, F 2
Engh, Rohn, A 13.1.a, A 24.1.a
Engle, Paul, B 19
"Epilogue," A 2
Episodes in Five Poetic Traditions: reprintings in, D 41–D 43
Erich Kahler, B 13
Esquire, C 225, C 226, C 228, App. 2
"Essential," C 1, App. 1
Events and Signals: review of, C 268
The Experience of Literature: reprintings in, C 27, C 95, C 113
Eyre Methuen Ltd., A 6.1.a*

Faber and Faber, Ltd., A 9.1.a, A 9.1.a†, A 9.1.b, A 11.1.b, A 11.1.g, A 13.1.b, A 13.1.b†, A 16.1.c, A 16.1.c†, A 20.2.a, A 22.1.c, A 22.1.c†, A 23, A 24.1.b
The Faber Book of Modern Verse: reprintings in, C 65, C 88, C 89, C 117
"The Facts & Issues," A 22
"Fare Well," A 4, A 9, A 15, C 51, F 2, App. 1
"Farewell to Miles," A 4, A 15, C 36, App. 1
Farrar, Straus and Company, A 7.1.b, A 11.1.a
Farrar, Straus and Cudhay, A 7.1.a
Farrar, Straus and Giroux, A 7.1.c, A 7.1.d, A 9.1.c, A 9.1.d, A 9.1.e, A 9.1.f, A 11.1.c, A 11.1.d, A 11.1.f, A 11.1.h, A 13.1.a, A 13.1.c, A 13.1.d, A 13.1.e, A 13.1.f, A 13.1.g, A 15.1.a, A 16.1.a, A 16.1.a†, A 16.1.b, A 16.1.d, A 16.1.e, A 18.1.a, A 18.1.b, A 18.1.c, A 20.1.a, A 20.1.a*, A 20.1.a†, A 20.3.a, A 20.3.b, A 22.1.a, A 22.1.b, A 22.1.d, A 22.1.e, A 24.1.a, A 24.1.a†, B 27
Feldman, Abraham, B 23
Festival at Meron: review of, C 239
50 Modern American Poets, 1920–1970: reprintings in, C 95, D 43
53 American Poets of Today: reprintings in, D 2, D 33
"Finale": comment on, A 5
First, Wesley, B 28
"First Night at Sea," A 20, C 220, App. 1
"Five Addresses to the Lord," C 208–C 212. *See also* "Eleven Addresses to the Lord: 1" "2," "3," "4," and "5"
Five Young American Poets, A 1, App. 1
Fleming, Archibald, C 240
Fleming, Guy, A 16.1.a, A 22.1.a
The Flowering of the Rod: review of, C 254
Folkways Records, F 9
"The Following Gulls." *See* Dream Song 281
"For His Marriage," A 3
"The Form," A 22, C 228, App. 1
"Formal Elegy," A 15, B 21, D 27, F 9, App. 1
Fraser, G. S., C 268
"A Fratricide": questions on, A 10
Fredericks, Claude, A 8
"Freshman Blues," A 20
"Friendless," A 20, C 203, App. 1
"From Five Addresses to the Lord," C 205. *See also* "Eleven Addresses to the Lord: 11"
"from The Black Book (i)," A 8, A 15, A 23, C 59, App. 1
"from The Black Book (ii)," A 8, A 15, C 60, App. 1
"from The Black Book (iii)," A 8, A 15, D 28

"From *The Black Book:* not him,"
    C 59. *See also* "from The
    Black Book (i)"
"From *The Black Book:* the will,"
    C 61, App. 1
"From *The Black Book:* 2," C 60.
    See also "from The Black
    Book (ii)"
"From *The Black Book:* waiting,"
    C 62, App. 1
"From the French Hospital in
    New York, 901." *See* Dream
    Song 380
"From the Middle to the Senior
    Generation," C 270
"F. Scott Fitzgerald," C 252
Fuller, Muriel, B 11

Garrigue, Jean, C 258
Geismar, Maxwell, C 259
"General Fatigue," B 23, C 129.
    See also Dream Song 93
Genzmer, George H., B 2
"The Gift of the Magi": questions
    on, A 10
Giroux, Robert, A 20.1.a*n*, A 20.1.a*
"Gislebertus' Eve," A 22, C 231,
    App. 1
Glikes, Erwin A., B 21
"Glimmerings." *See* Dream Song
    148
The Golden Horizon: reprinting
    in, C 251
G. P. Putnam's Sons, B 17
*The Great Short Novels of Henry
    James:* review of, C 250
Greenberg, Samuel, C 256
Green Gates: review of, C 242
Greg, W. W., C 248
Grierson, Herbert, C 253
Griffin, Howard, C 258
"The Gripe." *See* Dream Song 358
Grove Press, Inc., B 14

Haas, Joseph, E 17
Halverson, Janet, A 24.1.a,
    A 24.1.b
"The Handshake, The Entrance,"
    A 19, A 22, D 29

"The Handshake, The Entrance:
    Henry's Prayer," A 19. *See
    also* "The Handshake, The
    Entrance"
"A Handsome Young Airman":
    comment and questions on,
    A 10
Harcourt, Brace and Co., G 1
Hardy, Thomas, B 25
"Hardy: The Darkling Thrush,"
    B 25
Harper and Row, G 2
Harper's Magazine, C 95,
    C 159–C 161, C 213, App. 2
The Harvard Advocate, C 189–
    C 191, E 13, App. 2
"Have a Genuine Horror-&-Mist
    on the Rocks," A 20.1.a,
    A 20.1.a*, A 20.2.a, A 20.3.a,
    D 30
Hawthorn House, A 2
H.D., C 254
"Heaven," A 20, C 197, F 7,
    App. 1
Heavenly City, Earthly City:
    review of, C 258
"*Hello*," A 22
"The Hell Poem," A 20, C 217,
    F 7, App. 1
Hemingway, Ernest, A 10
Henry, O., A 10
"Henry by Night," A 22, C 190,
    App. 1
"Henry Comforted." *See* Dream
    Song 300
"Henry James," C 250, App. 1
Henry James: The Major Phase:
    review of, C 250
"Henry North," C 229, App. 1
"Henry's Confession." *See*
    Dream Song 73
"Henry's Crisis." *See* Dream Song
    367
"Henry's Farewell–I." *See*
    Dream Song 276
"Henry's Farewell–II." *See*
    Dream Song 277
"Henry's Farewell–III." *See*
    Dream Song 278

Index

"Henry's Guilt." *See* Dream Song 371
"Henry's Mail." *See* Dream Song 167
"Henry's Meditation in the Kremlin." *See* Dream Song 59
"Henry's Programme for God." *See* Dream Song 238
"Henry's Pencils," B 23, C 130, App. 1
"Henry's Understanding," A 22, C 189, App. 1
"Her & It," A 20, C 192, F 7, App. 1
"Her and It," C 192. *See also* "Her & It"
"Herbert Park, Dublin." *See* Dream Song 344
"He Resigns," A 22, D 31
"The Heroes," A 20, C 193, App. 1
Heyen, William, E 19
Highlights of Modern Literature, B 15, C 264
Hillyer, Robert, C 263n
"His Helplessness." *See* Dream Song 375
His Thought Made Pockets & The Plane Buckt, A 8, A 15, A 23, B 13, C 54, C 59, C 60, C 63, C 64, C 67–C 70, D 28, D 38, App. 1
His Toy, His Dream, His Rest, A 16, A 16.1.a†, A 16.1.c†, A 18, A 23, B 23, B 27, B 29, C 84, C 98, C 127, C 129, C 131, C 132, C 134–C 151, C 155–C 165, C 167–C 188, D 11–D 26, App. 1
"Homage to Film," C 28, App. 1
"Homage to Mr. Berryman," E 2
"Homage to Mistress Bradstreet," A 7, A 9, A 23, C 65, F 3, F 5, App. 1
Homage to Mistress Bradstreet, A 7, A 9, A 23, C 65, App. 1
Homage to Mistress Bradstreet and Other Poems, A 9, B 4–B 8, C 20, C 22, C 23, C 25, C 26, C 31, C 32, C 35, C 37,
C 39–C 47, C 49–C 54, C 63–C 65, C 67, C 69, C 70, D 2, D 33, D 35, D 36, D 40, App. 1
"The Home Ballad," A 20
Horizon: reprinting in, C 251
Howard, Jane, E 8
"'How Do You Do, Dr Berryman, Sir,'" A 22
Howell, Soskin, Publishers, B 7, B 8
"A Huddle of Need," A 20
The Hudson Review, C 265, App. 2
H. Wolff Book Manufacturing Company, A 4, A 6.1.a, A 13.1.a, A 15.1.a, A 18.1.a, A 20.1.a, A 20.1.a*, A 22.1.a
H. W. Wilson Company, BB 1

"Idyl II," C 133, App. 1
"'I *Know*,'" A 20
"'I *Know*,'" A 20.1.a†. *See* "'I *Know*'"
The Image and the Law: review of, C 258
"Images of Elspeth," A 20
"The Imaginary Jew," A 24, B 11, C 251, App. 1
"An Imperial Message": questions on, A 10
"In & Out," A 20
"In Memoriam (1914–1953)," A 21, A 22, D 32
"In Mem: R. P. Blackmur." *See* Dream Song 173
"Innocent," C 57, App. 1
"In Odessa": commentary on, A 10
"An Instructions to Critics." *See* Dream Song 308
Intellectual Digest, C 208, C 210–C 213, C 225, C 231–C 234, D 29, D 30, D 32, App. 2
International Poetry Forum, F 7
"Interstitial Office," A 22
"An Interview with John Berryman," E 13
"Introduction" in *The Monk*, B 14, App. 1

"Introduction" in *The Unfortunate Traveller,* B 17, App. 1
An Introduction to Poetry: reprinting in, C 95
Invisible Landscapes: review of, C 240
Isherwood, Christopher, C 238
"Ivory," C 6, App. 1
Ivory Tower, A 8.1.a*, C 138, E 7, App. 2

James, Henry, C 250
James Burn and Company Ltd., A 13.1.b, A 16.1.c, A 22.1.c
Jarrell, Randall, A 1, B 27, C 266
J. B. Lippincott Company, B 20
Jeffers, Robinson, C 240
Jensen, Carl Christian, C 239
J. J. Little Ives and Company, A 1
John Berryman, BB 5
"John Berryman: A Memoir and an Interview," E 19
"John Berryman on Today's Literature," E 3
The John Day Company, B 9
John Dickens and Company, Ltd., A 13.1.b, A 16.1.c, A 22.1.c
Johnson, Herb, A 13.1.a
Joyce, James, A 10
"July 11." *See* Dream Song 275

Kafka, Franz, A 10
"Karesansui, Ryoan-ji." *See* Dream Song 73
The Kenyon Critics, B 12, C 246
The Kenyon Review, B 12, C 20, C 21, C 33, C 45, C 46, C 126–C 128, C 246, C 247, C 249, C 251, C 252, App. 2
Keyes, Sidney, C 256
"King David Dances," A 22, C 230, App. 1
"A Kingdom's Utter Rail": commentary on, A 5
King Jasper: review of, C 240
Kostelanetz, Richard, E 15
Kunitz, Stanley J., BB 1

"Kyrie Eleison." *See* Dream Song 174

Langland, Joseph, B 19
Lardner, Ring, C 269
"The Last Dream Song: 161," C 137. *See also* Dream Song 385
The Last of the Provincials: review of, C 259
Latham, Minor W., B 2
"Lauds," A 22
Laughlin, James, A 1, A 2, B 3, B 4, B 6, B 10, C 247
"The Lay of Ike." *See* Dream Song 23
"Lead Out the Weary Dancers," C 4, App. 1
Leaves Without a Tree: review of, C 268
Lee, Laurie, C 258
Lee, Marshall, A 11.1.a
Lee in the Mountains, and Other Poems: review of, C 244
Leighton-Straker Bookbinding Company Ltd., A 24.1.b
"A Letter," A 20.1
Letters from JB: to Whit Burnett, B 29, App. 1; to the editor of *The Minnesota Daily,* C 274, App. 1; to the editors of *The Nation,* C 277, App. 1; to the editors of *The Saturday Review of Literature,* C 263, App. 1
"Letter to His Brother," A 1, A 4, A 9, A 15, C 20, App. 1
Lewis, Alun, A 10
Lewis, C. S., C 245
Lewis, Janet, C 254
Lewis, Matthew G., B 14
Library of Congress, BB 4, F 1–F 4, F 8
Life, E 8
"The Lightning," A 4, A 9, A 15, A 23, F 8
Lindley, Daniel A., A 11.1.a
"Lines to Mr Frost," A 22, C 233, App. 1

Index

The Literature of America: reprintings in, C 80, C 81
The Little Treasury of American Poetry: reprintings in, C 27, D 36
A Little Treasury of American Prose: reprinting in, C 251
A Little Treasury of Great Poetry: reprinting in, C 31
A Little Treasury of Modern Poetry: reprintings in, C 23, C 26, C 27, C 31, C 32, C 43, C 53, C 95, D 44
"London," A 20
"The Long Home," A 4, A 9, A 15, C 52, F 2, App. 1
"The Long Way to MacDiarmid," C 268, App. 1
Lord Weary's Castle: review of, C 254
Literary Digest: reprinting in, C 7
Living Age: reprintings in, C 26, C 27
"The Loud Hill of Wales," B 12, C 246, App. 1
Love & Fame, A 20, C 192–C 200, C 202–C 214, C 216–C 220, C 222, D 3, D 4, D 30, D 34, App. 1
"Love & Honour to the Chinese," A 20.1.a†
"The Lovers," B 10, C 249
Loves, Etc.: reprintings in, D 18, D 31
"The Love Song of J. Alfred Prufrock": commentary on, A 10
"Lowell, Thomas, &c.," C 254, App. 1
Lundegaard, Bob, E 6
Lyon, John H. H., B 2

McClelland, David, E 13
MacDiarmid, Hugh, C 268
McElroy, Walter, C 257
The Macmillan Company, B 23
McWilliams, Carey, B 23

Mademoiselle, C 152–C 154, App. 2
The Making of a Poem: review of, C 272
"Manner and Matter," C 266, App. 1
A Map of Verona and Other Poems: review of, C 258
Marquis - Who's Who Inc., BB 3
"A Marriage Proposal": questions on, A 10
Marshall, Roderick, B 1
Martz, William J., BB 5
The Marvellous Light, C 69
The Massachusetts Review, E 15
Master Poems of the English Language, B 25
Masters, Edgar Lee, C 240
"Matins," A 22
Matthiessen, F. O., C 250, C 264
Mazzaro, Jerome, E 19
"Meditation," A 1, C 30, App. 1
"Meeting," A 20, C 195, App. 1
Meras, Phyllis, E 3
"Message," A 20
The Metal and the Flower: review of, C 268
"Metaphysical or So," C 255, App. 1
Midway Printing Company, A 5
The Mills of the Kavanaughs: blurb for, G 1
The Minneapolis Star, E 4
The Minneapolis Symphony Orchestra, B 16
The Minneapolis Tribune, C 133, C 199, E 5, E 6, E 10–E 12, App. 2
The Minnesota Daily, C 81, C 274, E 2, E 9, E 16, App. 2
"The Minnesota 8 and the Letter Writers," A 20.1, C 199, App. 1
The Minnesota Orchestral Association, B 16
The Minnesota Review, C 94, App. 2
"Minnesota Thanksgiving," A 22, C 234, App. 1

Modern American Fiction:
  reprinting in, D 45
Modern American Poetry:
  reprintings in, C 31, C 42, D 2,
  D 36
Modern Poetry: reprintings in,
  C 39, C 42
Modern Poetry Association, A 5
The Modern Poets: reprinting in,
  C 31
*Modern Verse in English,
  1900-1950*: reprintings in,
  C 42, C 65
The Monk, B 14
"Monkhood," A 20, C 202, App. 1
"The Moon and the Night and
  the Men," A 2, A 4, A 9, A 15,
  A 23, B 5, B 9, D 33, F 2,
  App. 1
Moore, Nicholas, A 5
"More Directions," C 247, App. 1
Moses, W. R., A 1
Mundus Artium, C 165-C 167,
  App. 2
Murphy, Pat, E 14
Murray Printing Company,
  A 9.1.c, A 20.3.a
"Music of Colours: The Blossom
  Scattered": commentary and
  questions on, A 5
"My Special Fate," A 20
"The Mysteries," A 8, A 15, B 13,
  App. 1
"My Whiskers Fly: An Interview
  with John Berryman,"
  A 8.1.a*, E 7

Naked Poetry: reprintings in,
  C 73-C 75, C 79, C 95, C 110,
  C 118, C 121, D 5-D 7, D 10
"Narcissus Moving," A 4, A 9,
  A 15, C 44, F 1, F 2, App. 1
Nashe, Thomas, B 17
The Nation, C 7, C 25, C 34,
  C 129-C 132, C 219, C 239,
  C 242, C 248, C 253, C 255,
  C 277, H 1, H 2, App. 2
*National Book Award for Poetry
  1969 Acceptance Speech*,
  A 17, App. 1

The National Book Committee,
  A 17
National Poetry Festival, BB 4;
  reprintings in, C 73, C 81,
  C 86, C 87, C 91, C 99
"Native Verse," C 244, App. 1
"Navajo Putting the Record
  Straight," C 224. *See also*
  "Navajo Setting the Record
  Straight"
"Navajo Setting the Record
  Straight," A 22, C 224, App. 1
Nemerov, Howard, B 26, C 258
Nevett, Key and Whiting Ltd.,
  A 9.1.a
The New American Library, B 15,
  B 24
New American Review, C 162-
  C 164, App. 2
The New Consciousness:
  reprintings in, C 79, C 91,
  C 95, C 137
New Directions, A 1, A 2, B 3,
  B 4, B 6, B 10
*New Directions in Prose and
  Poetry 1938*, B 3
*New Directions in Prose and
  Poetry 1939*, B 4, D 36
*New Directions in Prose and
  Poetry 1940*: review of, C 247
*New Directions in Prose and
  Poetry 1941*, B 6, D 35
New Directions 9: B 10, C 249
A New Directions Reader, A 2n
The New Modern Poetry:
  reprintings in, C 43, C 81
The New Partisan Reader:
  reprinting in, C 43
*The New Pocket Anthology of
  American Verse*: reprintings
  in, C 27, C 42, C 81, D 10
New Poems 1940, B 5, C 32, D 33;
  reprintings in, C 26, C 27
New Poems 1943, B 7; reprintings
  in, C 23, C 25
New Poems 1944, B 8; reprinting
  in, C 31
The New Poetry: reprintings in,
  C 23, C 43, C 53, C 65, D 2,
  D 33, D 40

Index   277

The New Republic, C 22, C 31,
  C 90, C 91, C 198, C 266,
  C 272, App. 2
"News of God." *See* Dream Song
  183
*The New Treasury of War
  Poetry:* reprintings in, D 33,
  D 35
New World Writing 21, B 20, D 47
"New Year's Eve," A 4, A 9, A 15,
  A 23, C 43, F 1, F 2, App. 1
The New Yorker, C 69, C 70,
  C 200, C 227, C 230, App. 2
The New Yorker Book of Poems:
  reprintings in, C 69, C 70
New York Herald Tribune Books,
  C 243–C 245, C 257, App. 2
The New York Review of Books,
  C 113–C 116, C 148–C 151,
  C 214, C 215, C 235, C 273,
  App. 2; reprinting in, D 4
The New York Times: reprinting
  in, D 1
*The New York Times Book
  Review,* B 15, C 264, C 267,
  App. 2. *See also p. 174*
The New York Times Magazine:
  reprinting in, D 27
"Night and the City," A 1, C 15,
  App. 1
"Nightingale of the Mire,"
  C 257, App. 1
"Nineteen Thirty-Eight," A 1,
  C 21, App. 1
95 Poems: review of, C 270
"No," A 22
The Noble Savage, C 71–C 82,
  C 271, App. 2
"Nones," A 22
The Noonday Press, A 9.1.c,
  A 11.1.h, A 13.1.d, A 20.3.a,
  A 22.1.d, A 22.1.e
*The Norton Anthology of Modern
  Poetry:* reprintings in, C 64,
  C 65, C 73, C 87, C 95, C 189,
  D 2, D 10, D 12, D 17, D 34,
  D 39
*The Norton Introduction to
  Literature: Poetry:* reprint-
  ings in, C 31, D 35

Noss, Murray, C 268
"Notation," B 2, C 11, App. 1
"Note for a Historian," C 16,
  App. 1
"Note on E. A. Robinson," B 1,
  C 7, App. 1
"A Note on Poetry," A 1
"A Note on the Text" in *The
  Unfortunate Traveller,* B 17
"Note to Wang Wei," A 8, A 9,
  A 15, A 23, C 69, F 5, App. 1
No Traveller Returns: review of,
  C 237
"Not To Live," A 8, A 9, A 15,
  A 23, C 67, F 3, App. 1
"Nowhere," A 20, C 222, App. 1
Nussbaum, Elizabeth, E 9

The Observer, C 83, C 123,
  C 124, App. 2
"Ode." *See* Dream Song 231
O'Donnell, George Marion, A 1
"Of 1826." *See* Dream Song 22
"Of Isaac Rosenfeld," C 66, App. 1
Of Poetry and Power, B 21, D 27,
  F 9
"Of Suicide," A 20, D 34
Ogg, Oscar, A 4, A 6.1.a
O. Henry Prize Stories of 1946,
  B 11, C 251
The Ohio Review, C 279, E 19,
  App. 2
"O Jo in Shock," A 20.1.a†
"Old Man Goes South Again
  Alone," A 22
"The Old Poor." *See* Dream Song
  168
"Olympus," A 20, C 218, App. 1
"On a Portrait in Dublin," B 4,
  App. 1
"One Answer to a Question,"
  C 276. *See also* "Changes"
100 Postwar Poems: reprintings
  in, C 80, C 81, C 107
*One Hundred Years of The
  Nation,* B 23, C 129–C 131
"1 September 1939," A 2, A 4,
  A 9, A 15, B 6, D 35, App. 1
"On Poetry and the Age," B 27.
  See "Manner and Matter"

"On the London Train," A 1, A 4,
A 15, C 24, App. 1
"On War and Poetry," B 9, D 44,
App. 1
"The Open Boat": commentary
on, A 10
"Op. posth. no. 1." *See* Dream
Song 78
"Op. posth. no. 2." *See* Dream
Song 79
"Op. posth. no. 3." *See* Dream
Song 80
"Op. posth. no. 4." *See* Dream
Song 81
"Op. posth. no. 5." *See* Dream
Song 82
"Op. posth. no. 6." *See* Dream
Song 83
"Op. posth. no. 7." *See* Dream
Song 84
"Op. posth. no. 8." *See* Dream
Song 85
"Op. posth. no. 9." *See* Dream
Song 86
"Op. posth. no. 10." *See* Dream
Song 87
"Op. posth. no. 11." *See* Dream
Song 88
"Op. posth. no. 12." *See* Dream
Song 89
"Op. posth. no. 13," B 27. *See also*
Dream Song 90
"Op. posth. no. 14." *See* Dream
Song 91
"or Amy Vladeck or Riva
Freifeld." *See* Dream Song
113
"The Other Cambridge," A 20,
C 194, App. 1
Other Skies: review of, C 258
"Our Sins Are More Than We Can
Bear," C 278, App. 1
"Overseas Prayer," A 22

"The Pacifist's Song," A 4, A 9,
A 15
Page, P. K., C 268
The Paris Review, E 18

"Parting as Descent," A 1, A 4,
A 9, A 15, B 4, D 36, F 2,
App. 1
Partisan Review, C 23, C 24,
C 39–C 41, C 43, C 44, C 52,
C 65, C 66, C 68, C 92, C 93,
C 254, C 258–C 262, App. 2
The Partisan Review: reprinting
in, C 23
The Partisan Review Anthology:
reprinting in, C 23
Patchen, Kenneth, C 254
Paterson (Book Five): review of,
C 270
Pawlet Pamphlets, A 8.1.a*
Peck, Louis F., B 14
"'People Individuals with
Values': Poet John Berryman
Talks About Life, War,
Death," E 14
"Pereant qui ante nos nostra
dixerunt." *See* Dream Song
225
Pericles, Prince of Tyre:
comment and questions on a
speech from, A 10
Perosa, Sergio, A 7.1.a
*The Personal Heresy: A
Controversy*: review of, C 245
Peter Pauper Press, A 7.1.a
"A Philosophical Poet," C 243,
App. 1
The Plentitude We Cry For:
blurb for, G 3
*The Pocket Book of Modern
Verse*: reprintings in, D 10,
D 19, D 24
"A Poem for Bhain," A 2, A 4,
A 15, D 37
Poems, A 2, B 5, B 6, C 23, C 33,
D 33, D 35, D 37, App. 1
Poems: An Anthology: reprintings
in, C 75, C 81, D 8
*Poems from The Virginia
Quarterly Review*: reprinting
in, C 67
Poems of a Jew: review of, C 270
Poems: review of Samuel
Greenberg's, C 256

Index

Poems: review of William Jay Smith's, C 258
"Poet, Editor, Teacher—Looks Forward to Own Book," E 1
Poet of the Month Series, A 2
"Poetolatry," C 245, App. 1
Poetry, A 5, C 47–C 51, C 55–C 64, C 86–C 89, C 117–C 125, C 268, App. 2
Poetry and Its Conventions: reprinting in, C 42
Poetry and the Age: review of, B 27, C 266
Poetry: A Thematic Approach: reprinting in, D 2
Poetry for Pleasure: reprinting in, C 31
Poetry Northwest, C 83–C 85, App. 2
"The Poetry of Ezra Pound," B 30, C 262, App. 1
"Poetry Once Was Nonsense to Berryman," E 12
Poetry Season 1967, A 14, D 17, App. 1
Poet's Choice, B 19; reprinting in, C 47
"The Poet's Final Instructions," A 8, A 15, D 38
Poets of Today: review of, C 268
Poets on Poetry, B 26, C 276
The Poet's Story: reprinting in, C 249
"A Point of Age," A 2, A 4, A 15, F 2
"The Poise of Restless Wonder," commentary on, A 5
"The Possessed," A 4, A 15, B 3
Possibilities of Poetry: reprintings in, C 73, C 81, C 84, C 91, C 113, C 118, D 2
Pound, Ezra, B 30, C 262n, C 263n, C 275
"Prague," B 4, App. 1
"A Prayer After All," A 22
"A Prayer for the Self," C 213. See also "Eleven Addresses to the Lord: A Prayer for the Self"
"The Prayer of the Middle-Aged Man," A 22
"Preface to the Meridian Edition," in *Stephen Crane,* A 6.1.c, B 18
"Prime," A 22
"'The Prisoner of Shark Island' with Paul Muni." See Dream Song 7
The Prodigal Never Returns: review of, C 258
"A Professor's Song," A 4, A 9, A 15, D 39
Providence Sunday Journal, E 3
"Provincetown, Mass.": comment and questions on, A 5
"Provincial," C 259, App. 1
"Pulitzer Prize Once a 'Nothing' to Him; Now Berryman's Happy to Accept," E 4
"Purgatory," A 20

Rahv, Philip, C 250
Ramparts, C 96–C 110, App. 2
"Randall Jarrell," B 27, App. 1
Randall Jarrell, B 27, C 147, C 266
Ransom, John Crowe, B 12, B 25
"Ransom: 'Captain Carpenter,'" B 25
Reading Modern Poetry: reprinting in, C 65
"Recovery," A 20
Recovery, A 24, B 11, C 251, App. 1
The Red Badge of Courage, D 45
Reed, Henry, C 258
"A Refusal to Mourn the Death, by Fire, of a Child in London": comment and questions on, A 10
"Regents' Professor Berryman's Crack on Race," A 20.1
"Relations," A 20
"Rembrandt Van Rijn Obiit 8 October 1669," A 19
"The Return," A 1, A 4, B 3, App. 1
"Revival," A 20.1.a†, C 201, App. 1

Reynard, Elizabeth, B 1
Richardson, Stewart, B 20
Riding, Laura, C 243
"The Ritual of W. B. Yeats," C 241
"River Rouge, 1932," A 2, B 6, App. 1
"River Rouge, 1933," B 6. See also "River Rouge, 1932"
Robert Lowell: reprinting in, D 47
Robinson, E. A., C 240
"Rock-Study with Wanderer," A 4, A 9, A 15, C 46, F 1–F 3, App. 1
Rodman, Selden, C 258
Roethke, Theodore, C 270
Romaine, Octave, A 4
"Room 333," C 77. See also Dream Song 54
"Room 231: the fourth week." See Dream Song 92
Ross, Ralph, A 10
R. R. Bowker Company, BB 2
Rukeyser, Muriel, C 240

"Sabbath." See Dream Song 12
Sackler, Harry, C 239
"Sailing to Byzantium," 'A Note' on, A 10
St. Martin's Press, BB 6
Samurai and Serpent Poems: review of, C 268
"Sanctuary," A 1
San Juan, E., Jr., B 30
Saportas, Frances Cabané Scovel, A 6.1.a
"Satire and Poetry," C 238, App. 1
Saturday Review, C 208–C 212, App. 2
The Saturday Review of Literature, C 263
Saul, Milton, A 8.1.a*
Schlesinger, Arthur, Jr., B 21
"A Scholarly History," C 253, App. 1
"Scholars at the Orchid Pavilion," A 22

"Scholia to Second Edition," A 20.3.a
Schwaber, Paul, B 21
Schwebell, Gertrude C., A 7.1.a
"Scots Poem," A 8, A 9, A 15, C 63, F 2, App. 1
Scott, F. R., C 268
"The Search," A 20, C 207, App. 1
"The Second Cactus," B 4, App. 1
Secret Country: review of, C 254
"Secret of the Wisdom," C 83. See also Dream Song 20
"The Secret of the Wisdom." See Dream Song 20
Selected Poems: review of A.E.'s, C 240
Selected Poems: review of Kenneth Patchen's, C 254
Selected Poems 1938–1968, A 23, B 5, B 27, C 26, C 31, C 32, C 39, C 42, C 43, C 47, C 50, C 53, C 54, C 59, C 64, C 65, C 67, C 69, C 70–C 75, C 77, C 79–C 81, C 86–C 91, C 93, C 95, C 97, C 99, C 101, C 105, C 110, C 112, C 114, C 119, C 122, C 124, C 125, C 137–C 139, C 141, C 143–C 147, C 162, C 168, C 173–C 176, C 178, C 180, C 183, C 186, C 188, D 2, D 6, D 7, D 10, D 11, D 17, D 18, D 23, D 25, D 26, D 33, D 40, App. 1
Selected Poems of Hugh MacDiarmid: review of, C 268
The Selected Writings of Dylan Thomas: review of, C 254
The Seven Sins: review of, C 240
77 Dream Songs, A 11, A 18, A 23, B 29, C 71–C 75, C 77–C 83, C 85–C 97, C 99–C 101, C 103–C 105, C 107–C 126, C 128, D 5–D 10, App. 1
Seventy Times Seven: review of, C 239
The Sewanee Review, C 36, C 37, C 42, C 250, C 256, App. 2
"Sext," A 22

Index

Shahn, Ben, A 7.1.a, A 9.1.c
Shakespeare, William, A 10, C 248, C 265
"Shakespeare at Thirty," C 265, App. 1
"Shakespeare's Text," C 248, App. 1
Shake the Kaleidoscope: reprintings in, D 10, D 13, D 15, D 20, D 26
Shapiro, Harvey, A 5
Shapiro, Karl, C 270
Shenandoah, C 201-C 204, C 276, App. 2
Sherriff, R. C., C 242
"Shirley & Auden," A 20
Short Poems, A 15, B 3, B 4, B 6-B 8, B 13, B 21, C 20, C 22-C 27, C 31-C 54, C 59, C 60, C 63, C 64, C 67-C 70, D 2, D 27, D 28, D 33, D 35-D 40, App. 1
"Silent Song." *See* Dream Song 52
Simon, Henry W., B 2
Sisson, Jonathan, A 8.1.a*, E 7
Skaggs, Charles, A 18.1.a, A 20.1.a*, A 20.3.a
"Slattery's, in Ballsbridge." *See* Dream Song 355
"A Small Dream." *See* Dream Song 132
Smith, Corlies M., B 20
Smith, J. C., C 253
Smith, LeRoy, C 268
Smith, Peter, A 6.1.b
Smith, William Jay, C 258
Smith: A Sylvan Interlude: review of, C 239
Snodgrass, W. D., G 2
"Snow Line." *See* Dream Song 28
"So Long? Stevens." *See* Dream Song 219
Solstice, and Other Poems: review of, C 240
"Somber Prayer," A 22
"Song": comment and questions on Alun Lewis's, A 10
"Song from 'Cleopatra,'" A 1, C 29, App. 1
"Song from *Cleopatra*," C 29. *See also* "Song from 'Cleopatra'"
"Song of a Poet," E 6
"The Song of the Bridegroom," A 4, A 9, A 15, F 2
"The Song of the Demented Priest," A 4, A 9, A 15, A 23, C 39, F 1-F 3, App. 1
"The Song of the Mad Prince": questions on, A 10
"Song of the Man Forsaken and Obsessed," A 4, A 9, A 15
"The Song of the Tortured Girl," A 4, A 9, A 15, A 23, D 40, F 2, F 5
"The Song of the Young Hawaiian," A 4, A 9, A 15, C 40, F 2, App. 1
"Sonnet," B 1, App. 1
"Sonnet": comment and questions on William Wordsworth's, A 10
Sonnets 1-8, 10-11, 14, 16-20, 24, 26-33, 35-36, 38-59, 61-64, 66-70, 72-74, 76-78, 80-96, 98-102, 104, 105, 107, 108, 111, 113-115: A 13
Sonnets 9, 12, 21, 22, 34, 37, 65, 75, 79, 97, 106, 109, 112: A 13, A 23
Sonnet 13: A 13, A 23, D 41
Sonnet 15: A 13, D 42
Sonnet 23: A 13, C 152, App. 1
Sonnet 25 (also titled "Sonnet XXV"): A 8, A 9, A 13, A 15, A 23, C 64, F 3, App. 1
Sonnet 60: A 13, D 43
Sonnet 71: A 13, A 23, C 153, App. 1
Sonnet 103: A 13, C 154, App. 1
The Southern Review, C 15-C 18, C 26-C 30, App. 2
"The Soviet Union," A 20.1, C 219, App. 1
"Speaking of Books," C 267, App. 1

Spearhead: reprinting in, C 251
Spencer, Terence, A 15.1.a, A 16.1.a, A 20.1.a*, A 24.1.a
Spender, Stephen, C 272
"Spender: The Poet as Critic," C 272, App. 1
"The Spinning Heart," A 4, A 9, A 15, A 23, B 5, C 32, F 2, App. 1
Spoken Arts, F 10
The Spoken Arts Treasury of 100 Modern American Poets, F 10
Stand, C 206, C 207, App. 2
The State Journal, E 14
"The State of American Writing, 1948: Seven Questions": answers to, C 261, App. 1
State University of New York at Buffalo, F 5, F 6
"The Statue," A 1, A 2, A 4, A 9, A 15, B 7, C 23, F 1, F 2, App. 1
The Stature of Theodore Dreiser: reprinting in, C 264
Stedman, Jane, E 1
Stegner, Wallace, B 22
Steiner, Herbert, B 13
Stephen Crane, A 6, B 18, D 45
Stephen Crane, ed. Maurice Basson: reprinting in, D 45
Stephen Crane's Career: reprintings in, D 45, D 46
"Stephen Crane: *The Red Badge of Courage,*" B 22, D 46
Stevens, Wallace, A 5
"A Stimulant for an Old Beast." *See* Dream Song 3
Stitt, Peter A., E 18
Stories of Modern America: reprinting in, C 251
Stories of Writers and Artists: review of, C 250
Strudwick, Dorothy, E 2
"A Strut for Roethke." *See* Dream Song 18
Sunburst Books, A 18.1.b
The Sun My Monument: review of, C 258
"Surveillance," C 279, App. 1

The Survival Years: reprinting in, D 33
"Surviving Love," A 4, A 9, A 15, C 49, App. 1
Swenson, May, C 268
"A Sympathy, A Welcome," A 8, A 9, A 15, A 23, C 70, F 3, F 5, App. 1

"Tampa Stomp," A 22, C 226, App. 1
Tate, Allen, A 10
Taylor, Peter, B 27
"Tea," A 20, C 196, App. 1
"Temples." *See* Dream Song 99
"Thanksgiving," C 9, App. 1
"Thanksgiving: Detroit," A 2, B 6, App. 1
"Thank You, Christine," A 20.1
Theodore Dreiser: review of, C 264
Theory of Flight: review of, C 240
"They Have," A 8, A 9, A 15
"Things of August": commentary on, A 5
This Island Called Pharos: review of, C 240
This Is My Best, B 29; reprintings in, C 71, C 75, C 81, C 137, C 146, C 178, D 26
Thomas, Dylan, A 10, C 246, C 254
Thomas Y. Crowell Company, A 10
Thompson, Edmund, A 2
"Three and a Half Years at Columbia," B 28, App. 1
"Three around the Old Gentleman." *See* Dream Song 37
"Three in Heaven I Hope." *See* Dream Song 303
"Through Dreiser's Imagination the Tides of Real Life Billowed," B 15, C 264, App. 1
"A Thurn." *See* Dream Song 126
"Thursday Out," C 271, App. 1
"Tierce," A 22
Tillyard, E. M. W., C 245

"Time Does Not Engulf," B 1, App. 1
The Times Literary Supplement, C 71–C 75, C 113, C 134–C 137, C 139–C 147, C 192–C 197, App. 2
Tindall, William Y., B 2
The Titan, B 24
"To an Artist Beginning Her Work," B 2, App. 1
"To a Woman," A 20.1.a, A 20.1.a*, A 20.2.a, A 20.3.a, C 214, App. 1
"To B—— E——," A 20.1, C 206, App. 1
Today's Poets: reprintings in, C 71, C 91, C 122, C 208, D 3, D 10, D 21, D 23
"A Topical Novel," C 242, App. 1
"Toward Statement," C 18, App. 1
The Tragedy of Macbeth: commentary on, A 10
Transfigured Night: review of, C 254
"Transit," A 20, C 221, App. 1
"The Translation," B 3, App. 1
"The Translator–I." *See* Dream Song 180
"The Translator–II." *See* Dream Song 181
"The Traveler," C 50. *See also* "The Traveller"
"The Traveller," A 4, A 9, A 15, A 23, C 50, F 2, App. 1
"Travelling South," A 4, A 15, C 38, App. 1
"The Trial," A 1, C 19, App. 1
"A Tribute," C 275, App. 1
Trident Press, B 25
TriQuarterly, C 185–C 188, App. 2
Tristan Crobière Poems: review of, C 257
"Trophy," C 14, App. 1
"A Truly Gentle Man Tightens and Paces: An Interview with John Berryman," E 16
T. S Eliot: A Selected Critique: review of, C 260

"The Twa Corbies": comment on, A 10
Twentieth Century American Poetry: reprinting in, C 65
Twentieth Century Authors: First Supplement, BB 1
Twentieth Century Poetry: reprintings in, C 31, C 75, C 95, D 9, D 10
Twentieth Century Poetry in English, F 8
Twentieth Century Verse, C 19, App. 2
"28 July." *See* Dream Song 106
Twenty Poems, A 1, B 3, B 4, C 15, C 17, C 19–C 27, C 29–C 31, D 36, App. 1
The Twin Cities Express, C 278, App. 2
Two Dream Songs (1965), A 12, C 137, App. 1
Two Dream Songs (1969), A 19, App. 1
"Two Organs," A 20
Two Poems (1942), A 3, D 2, App. 1
Two Poems (1970), A 21, D 1, D 32, App. 1
"Types of Pedantry," C 239, App. 1

The Unfortunate Traveller, B 17
Unger, Leonard, C 260
"Unity Quitbread at Eltham": commentary on, A 5
University of Miami Press, B 30
University of Minnesota Press, BB 5
University on the Heights, B 28
"Unknowable? perhaps not altogether," A 22
Untermeyer, Louis, C 262n
"'U' Professor Awarded Pulitzer Poetry Prize," E 5
"A Usual Prayer," A 22

Vail-Ballou Press, Inc., A 10.1.a, A 24.1.a
Van Doren, Mark, B 1, B 2, C 236

Van Vechten Press, Inc., B 13
Vazakas, Byron, C 254
"Venice," C 54. *See also* "Venice, 182–"
"Venice, 182–," A 8, A 9, A 15, A 23, C 54, F 5, App. 1
"Vespers," A 22, C 232, App. 1
"Vietnam." *See* Dream Song 162
"Views of Myself," A 20
The Virginia Quarterly Review, C 67, C 168–C 178, App. 2
The Voice That Is Great Within Us: reprintings in, C 42, C 47, C 50, C 59, C 60, D 28, D 33, D 38

Wagoner, David, A 5
"Waiting for the End, Boys," C 258, App. 1
"A Wake-Song." *See* Dream Song 245
"Walking, Flying – I." *See* Dream Song 251
"Walking, Flying – II." *See* Dream Song 252
"Walking, Flying – III." *See* Dream Song 253
The War Poets, B 9, D 44; reprintings in, C 27, D 33
Warren, Robert Penn, B 27
"Washington in Love," A 22, C 225, App. 1
Watkins, Vernon, A 5
Watson, Catherine, E 11
"The Way of the Cross," B 16, App. 1
The Well-Wrought Urn: review of, C 255
Werner, Arno, A 8.1.a*
"Whether There Is Sorrow in the Demons," A 4, A 9, A 15, A 23, C 53, App. 1
"Whisky and Ink, Whisky and Ink," E 8
"White Feather," A 4, A 15, C 34, App. 1
"The White Feather," C 34. *See also* "White Feather"

Whitstable Litho, A 9.1.a, A 11.1.b, A 23, A 24.1.b
"Who Killed Henry Pussy-cat? I did, says John Berryman, with love & a poem, & for freedom O," E 17
"The Wholly Fail," C 58, App. 1
Who's Who in America, BB 3
Who's Who 1972, BB 6
Williams, Oscar, B 5, B 7–B 9, B 25, C 23
Williams, William Carlos, C 270
William Sloane Associates, A 4, A 6.1.a, A 6.1.b
A Winter Diary and Other Poems: review of, C 236
"Winter Landscape," A 1, A 4, A 9, A 15, A 23, B 8, C 31, F 3, F 8, App. 1
"Winter Miscellany – Four Poems Selected by John Berryman," H 2
"A Winter-Piece to a Friend Away," A 4, A 9, A 15, C 45, App. 1
"The Witness," C 12, App. 1
Wolff, Eleanor L., B 13
Words for the Wind: review of, C 270
"Words to a Young Man," C 10, App. 1
Wordsworth, William, A 10
The World I Breathe: review of, C 246
The World Publishing Company, A 6.1.c, B 12, B 18
"World's Fair," A 4, A 15, C 48, App. 1
The World's Great Poets Reading at the Festival of Two Worlds, Spoleto, Italy, F 11
"World-Telegram," A 1, A 4, A 9, A 15, C 22, F 2, App. 1
Wurdemann, Audrey, C 240

The Yale Review, C 111, C 112, App. 2
Yardstick Press, B 5

Index

"Year's End, 1970," D 1. *See also* "Another New Year's Eve"
Yeats, W. B., A 10, C 241
Young Cherry Trees Secured Against Hares: review of, C 254

"Young Poets Dead," C 255
"Young Woman's Song," A 4, A 9, A 15, C 41, F 2, App. 1
"Your Birthday in Wisconsin You Are 140," A 22